Total Quality Management in Action

Total Quality Management in Action

Edited by

Gopal K. Kanji

Head of the Centre for Quality and Innovation
Sheffield Hallam University
Sheffield
UK

Organized by the
Centre for Quality and Innovation
Sheffield Hallam University

 CHAPMAN & HALL

London · Weinheim · New York · Tokyo · Melbourne · Madras

Published by Chapman & Hall, 2–6 Boundary Row, London SE1 8HN, UK

Chapman & Hall, 2–6 Boundary Row, London SE1 8HN, UK

Chapman & Hall GmbH, Pappelallee 3, 69469 Weinheim, Germany

Chapman & Hall USA, 115 Fifth Avenue, New York, NY 10003, USA

Chapman & Hall Japan, ITP-Japan, Kyowa Building, 3F, 2-2-1 Hirakawacho, Chiyoda-ku, Tokyo 102, Japan

Chapman & Hall Australia, 102 Dodds Street, South Melbourne, Victoria 3205, Australia

Chapman & Hall India, R. Seshadri, 32 Second Main Road, CIT East, Madras 600 035, India

First edition 1996

© 1996 Chapman & Hall
© Chapter 3 Joiner Associates Inc.
© Chapter 13 John MacDonald

Printed in Great Britain by TJ Press (Padstow) Ltd., Padstow, Cornwall

ISBN 0 412 78220 0

A catalogue record for this book is available from the British Library
Library of Congress Catalog Card Number: 96–84769

∞ Printed on permanent acid-free text paper, manufactured in accordance with ANSI/NISO Z39.48-1992 and ANSI/NISO Z39.48-1984 (Permanence of Paper).

CONTENTS

PREFACE

Following the very successful First World Congress for Total Quality Management in Sheffield last year, let me welcome you once again to the Second Quality Conference organized by the Centre for Quality and Innovation at Sheffield Hallam University. The theme for our 1996 conference is 'TQM in Action' and we have focused on the practical aspects of TQM, including the challenges, the pitfalls, the techniques, the benefits etc.

In this book, leading experts from various parts of the world have provided real opportunities to share best practice and the experiences of world class quality activities, operating in public and private sectors, manufacturing, service industry, education and local government.

As last year, we are also very proud to include the second British Deming Memorial lecture which will be presented by Dr Brian L. Joiner, on the theme of 'Leadership in the 21st. Century'.

Papers for this conference have been categorised according to different aspects of TQM. They include:

1 principle of practices of TQM
2 community and education
3 the role of Self Assessment
4 international comparisons
5 enterprise and industry
6 quality methods
7 continuous improvement process
8 quality measurement

I would very much like to thank all the conference delegates, speakers and organisations for their generous contributions without which there would be no 'TQM in Action' conference.

A very sincere welcome to you all and I wish you a fruitful and enjoyable stay in Sheffield.

PART ONE

TQM Principles and Practice

1

The European Foundation for Quality Management: latest developments

Geert de Raad
Secretary General, European Foundation for Quality Management
Avenue des Pleiades 15
Brussels, B-1200, Belgium
Tel : +32 2 775 35 11   Fax : +32 2 775 35 35

The history of the current Model

When Japan started to rebuild its economy in the late 1940s, Deming and Juran introduced their global management approach and related tools. As early as 1951 they created the Deming Prize, the first Quality Management Award, as a way to promote the concept. It was not until the 1980s that awareness of total quality as a management method increased in the US, leading to the Baldrige Award in 1987.

Because these economies were applying management philosophies and techniques which were more effective in terms of cost, cycle time, quality of products and services, European business began to lose ground. A number of European companies reacted in isolation. Then, some of them became progressively aware that to ensure the prosperity of our economy in the years and decades to come, localised and necessarily limited changes would not be enough. The economic world of today is made up of closely interdependent businesses in which the good or poor quality provided by any supplier in terms of cost, delivery or performance has a direct influence on the satisfaction of the end customer - the customer whose freedom of choice is widened by the fierce competition we experience today.

As a result, 14 leading European companies decided in 1988, encouraged by Mr Jacques Delors, at the time President of the European Commission, to create the European Foundation for Quality Management (EFQM), the objective of which is to create conditions to enhance the position of the European economy, by :
- supporting the management of European organisations in accelerating the process of making quality a decisive factor for achieving global competitive advantage
- stimulating and assisting all organisations throughout Europe to participate in improvement activities leading ultimately to excellence in customer satisfaction and overall performance.

The European Model for Total Quality Management

Being convinced that developing and promoting a method for European companies to benchmark against the best and most effective practices is a top priority led the EFQM to the development of the European Model for Total Quality Management, which encompasses all aspects of business management.

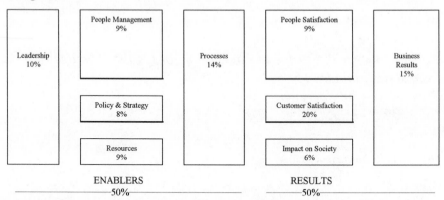

Basically the Model demonstrates that customer satisfaction, employee satisfaction and positive impact on society, are achieved through leadership driving policy and strategy, people management, resources and processes, leading ultimately to excellence in business results.

Each of these 9 elements, therefore, is a criterion that can be used to assess the organisation's progress towards TQM. The *"Results"* group of criteria indicate what the company has achieved and is achieving; the *"Enablers"* are how those results are being achieved.

The Model shows that people of various levels in different functions working together as a cross-functional team are co-responsible for the vital results and not necessarily through the traditional vertical structure split in the usual functions such as R&D, manufacturing, finance, marketing and sales, etc.

Each of the criteria of the Model is broken down into sub criteria which more clearly define the meaning of the heading; for Leadership these are for example:

1a   visible involvement in leading Total Quality
1b   a consistent Total Quality culture
1c   timely recognition and appreciation of the efforts and successes of individuals and teams
1d   support of Total Quality by provision of appropriate resources and assistance
1e   involvement with customers and suppliers
1f   the active promotion of Total Quality outside the organisation

How the Model is used

In using the Model as a basis for Self-Assessment, an organisation would measure its performance against the areas highlighted in the Model and identify strengths and areas for improvement. This can be done in a variety of ways from a simple workshop approach to a comprehensive report which reflects the current situation in the company and is assessed either internally or externally. The more thorough report approach is probably the most time consuming method of Self-Assessment; however it is also the most accurate and a highly stable base upon which to build improvements.

Continuous improvement of the Model

Every year the Model is examined and improved with the help of member organisations who share experiences and best practices with the direct aim of improving the Model on an annual basis.
Working groups, sharing events and courses to implement Self-Assessment programmes for continuous improvement are some of the activities implemented by the members of EFQM and its staff to achieve the vision to make Total Quality Management the vehicle for the achievement of business excellence in European organisations.

The Scoring System

The scoring system of the Model acknowledges the clear differences between the enablers and the results. Enablers are scored on the basis of two considerations:

Enablers

Approach

This is the method which has been used to implement improvements in the criterion area. The scale of excellence when assessing this element relies upon how much the approach is soundly based in TQ principles, which are defined as
- customer focus
- involvement and empowerment of people and teams
- prevention based
- integrated and reviewed

Ultimately the approach would score highly if it encompassed these TQ principles to a high degree and could be judged as a role model to other companies.

Deployment

This is how far the approach has been used throughout the company when compared to its full potential. The scale of excellence in this factor relies on an assessment of how many relevant areas have been included in the improvement process both in terms of numbers and functions.

An average of the two areas in terms of percentages would be generally used to score each criteria and sub criteria to ultimately reach an overall score for a company which would also highlight improvement actions which would lead to business excellence.

Results

The actual results presented under the results criteria are assessed in terms of actual relevance to what they are trying to achieve. Also the actual results presented are assessed on how good they are in terms of internal targets, competitors and best in class.

The European Quality Award

The European Quality Award was launched in 1991, with the support of the European Organization for Quality and the European Commission. The European Quality Award is presented during the annual European Quality Management Forum organised by EFQM. This Award was created to enhance the awareness of Total Quality Management issues and the benefits. There are two categories:

- The European Quality Award, for the best exponent of Total Quality Management
- European Quality Prizes, for those companies which excel in Total Quality Management as a fundamental process of continuous improvement

To apply for the European Quality Award and Prizes, organisations have to complete a Self-Assessment file based on the European Model for Total Quality Management and would complete a report of no more than 75 pages. The applications are assessed by a team of six or seven people; all graduates and quality professionals. The applications are then studied by the Award Jury, comprising senior managers and academics from various European countries. The Jury then selects a number of companies to visit in order to clarify, verify and monitor the quality practices of the applicants selected. Whether amongst the winners or not, the most valuable benefit of applying is the feedback report from the specially trained assessors allowing the measurement of the continuous improvement process and the strengths and areas for further improvements.

New Developments

In 1995 the EFQM expanded the scope of the European Quality Award to include for the first time an award for organisations in the Public Sector. This award is based on the same overall Model but specific guidance has been produced to aid interpretation for each of the following areas within the Public Sector

- Healthcare
- Education
- Local and Central Government

The first presentations of these awards will take place in 1996, and a conference has been arranged specifically for the Public Sector to mark the launch of the Award. This will be an annual event where best practices from the public and private sectors will be exchanged to improve working in this major area.

There is also work being undertaken to introduce an adapted Model for smaller companies. A revised Model has been devised and is currently being piloted throughout Europe prior to the launch in 1996 with the first awards in 1997. National organisations have been asked to co-operate and support the award in its application and development.

All of the Awards administered by the EFQM are aimed to produce role model examples of excellence for the specific sectors. To help organisations with Self-Assessment, EFQM has published brochures entitled "Self-Assessment Guidelines" based on the European Model for Total Quality Management (available in English. French, German, Italian and Spanish). They are currently available for Companies and the Public Sector.

These guidelines define each criterion and sub criterion by giving a list of areas that could be addressed within each defined area. There are also examples of how to record results and the scoring methods so that organisations can check their own progress.

The Future

The success of the Model does not mean that EFQM is standing still and in 1995 it refocused its aims and looked forward to create a vision for the future. That is :

> "to be a leading organisation recognised on a global basis, for the development, promotion and facilitation of a coherent approach to Total Quality Management as the vehicle for the achievement of business excellence in European organisations"

The vision is underpinned by the following objectives :

1.   The European Model for Business Excellence is recognised as providing the key strategic framework and criteria for managing an organisation and identifying improvement opportunities regardless of the nature of that organisation.

2.   The winning of The European Quality Award or a Prize is recognised internationally as a major achievement and the Winners are acknowledged as role models of Business Excellence.

3.   EFQM provides membership satisfaction, achieved through value for money services.

4.   The philosophy, methods, tools and techniques of Total Quality are a key element of curricula at all levels of education and training in Europe.

5.   There are coherent and constructive relationships between the EFQM and other organisations.

6.   The EFQM operates on a sound financial basis.

EFQM aims to be at the leading edge of development and is constantly reviewing current products, with the help of its members, the EU and other organisations to ensure it maintains the Model to be truly one of business excellence.

2

Creating robust product and process design

H. J. Bajaria
Multiface, Inc. 6721 Merriman Road, Garden City, Michgan 48135, USA

1. ABSTRACT

Interactions among variables in products and processes require expert human intervention to produce acceptable results. Similarly, correlated output characteristics require a delicate balance either in manufacture by production personnel or in use of the products by the users. Robustness concepts in product and process designs can deal with both of these situations effectively. In first case, robustness can minimize or eliminate human intervention. In second case, robustness can decouple the correlation between output characteristics no longer requiring a delicate balance in manufacture or use of the products.

2. INTRODUCTION

Variations in operational environment, ambient conditions, and human tendencies make products and processes susceptible to failures. To some extent product and process designers intuitively include effects of these variation when creating products and processes. However, inclusion of these considerations are highly dependent on individual engineering instinct rather than disciplines that are practiced. *Designing for robustness* is that discipline. Robustness captures the idea of minimizing failures by understanding the interactions between uncontrollable variables and controllable variables in inception stages and then designing appropriate mechanisms either in product designs or in process designs to deal with them without any human intervention. Thus, *robustness can be defined as an attribute of design that integrates the interactions between uncontrollable variables (noise variables) and controllable variables requiring no human intervention for acceptable performance.*

This definition of robustness is not broad enough to include a wide variety of applications where human interventions are expected to manufacture or to operate product properly. For example, take a case of the products where two or more negatively correlated output characteristics define the goodness of the product. That is, any attempt to improve one will degrade the other. Product and process designs try to strike a delicate balance between the two requirements. To maintain the balance requires human intervention either in user environments or in manufacturing environments. With robustness concept it is possible to decouple this negative correlation so that each output can be individually improved and human intervention is minimized. This line of reasoning could also apply to positively correlated characteristics as well. The concept of robustness can thus be broadened to include the case of correlated characteristics and is redefined as follows. *Robustness can be defined as an attribute of design that integrates the interactions between uncontrollable variables (noise variables) and controllable variables requiring no human intervention for acceptable performance with respect to a single or multiple correlated characteristics.*

3. ROBUSTNESS OPTIONS FOR PRODUCT OR PROCESS DESIGNS

There are three options available to create robust products or processes. They are: (1) Detach interaction between uncontrollable variables and controllable variables, (2) Automate interactions between uncontrollable and controllable variables, and (3) Decouple relationship between two or more output variables. These possibilities are listed in Table 1.

Table 1 - Robustness Options

	Detach Interactions between Uncontrollable variables and Controllable variables	Automate Interactions between Uncontrollable variables and Controllable variables	Decouple relationship between two or more output variables
Product Design	Category 1	Category 2	Category 3
Process Design	Category 4	Category 5	Category 6

The following examples clarify the robustness concepts in each category.

3.1 An Example In Category 1

This example is about product design. Take a case of driving an automobile on varying road conditions. The designers know that it is natural to expect rough road conditions in some segments of travel. We will refer to the *rough road condition as an uncontrollable variable*. What is driver likely to do when he/she perceives that rough road condition is approaching? Most likely the driver might slow down. The *driver's action we will refer to as controllable variable*. Thus, we can see in this example that there is a definite interaction between road condition and driver's reaction.

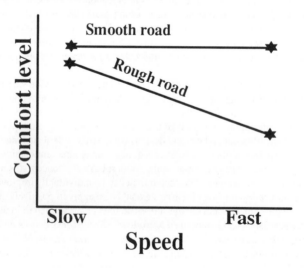

The design objective should be to understand and to control this interaction to provide a smooth ride as well as to minimize damage to the automobile. Now we can think about how to design product that will either minimize or eliminate human intervention altogether. One idea is that we can design a suspension such that it would adjust automatically and continuously to a varying degree of roughness. If such design is feasible then driver neither has to slow down nor feel any discomfort when rough road conditions are encountered. Thus, the interaction between uncontrollable and controllable variables is successfully detached. This product design will be labeled robust against rough road conditions.

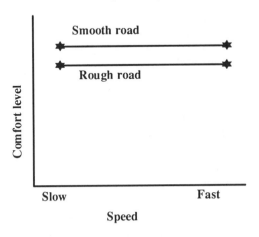

3.2 An Example In Category 2

The interaction between driver and rough road conditions in the preceding example can be approached in another way. Suppose we incorporate a sensor to sense the rough road conditions in the form of an acceleration and to provide a signal to a controller to adjust the speed in accordance with what drivers would consider to be a smooth ride.

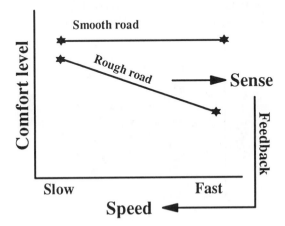

With this design concept, the resulting smoothness will be the same as that in category 1, however, the automobile speed will have to be slower to get equivalent results. Also, there will be a time lag between sensing an acceleration due to rough road conditions and corresponding reaction. The concept of robust design in category 1, on the other hand, responds instantaneously to the rough road conditions. In any case, both designs will be considered robust because they would have removed human intervention to deal with uncontrollable rough road conditions. The economics and marketing of implementing such robust design ideas need to be considered to make a final choice.

3.3 An Example In Category 3

A teeter-totter design is exemplary of robustness option in this category. Position 1 and position 2 at the teeter-totter ends are negatively correlated. That is, if position 1 person goes up, the position 2 person comes down.

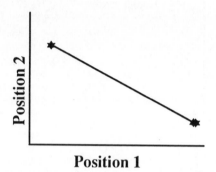

Position 1

Now, let us say that we wish to decouple correlation between two positions, so that one person can go up and down independent of other person's movement. We could design a torsional spring integral with the hinge such that one half of the teeter-totter board would be attached to one end of the spring and the other half would be attached to the other end of the spring. This concept would successfully decouple the correlation between two positions. That is, persons at each end can move up and down independently.

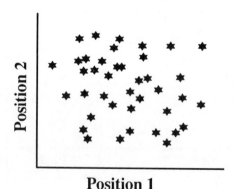

Position 1

3.4 An Example In Category 4

This case is about process design. The process designers know that the material to be machined is received with a varying degree of hardness. The hardness variation experienced is natural and is within specification limits for the product application. However, previous experience has shown that such hardness variation causes chatter in the machining process which ultimately results in an unacceptable finish. The operator's most likely reaction is to play with the machine speed and the tool feed to deal with chatter conditions. On some occasions operator's actions are helpful. On other occasions they are not. Thus, this scenario can be labeled as *not-robust process*. Here, *uncontrollable variable is material hardness* and the *controllable variables are machine speed and tool feed*. A conventional way of handling this problem is to tighten the specification limits on material hardness. However, tightening the hardness spec may not be an acceptable solution if heat treat process capability is not compatible. Another possible solution is to examine robustness design concepts.

One of the possibility is to divide material hardness variation in to two groups - relatively hard and relatively soft. There are two types of tools available - one type works better with harder materials, where as the other type works better with softer materials. A mechanism could be designed to hold both types of tools in the machine which can be called upon depending on the workpiece hardness. Suppose we design a process to automatically measure hardness of every incoming piece. Then, we can electronically send a signal for a matching tool to come into action. Thus, we could successfully eliminate the human intervention with the speed and feed.

Another solution is to discover the material having machining properties that can be machined at constant machine speed and tool feed to produce acceptable finish regardless of its hardness variation. Such a material will have to satisfy all the product functional and reliability requirements. If such material can be found, then process would be considered robust. Once again economics will play a role in selecting robustness options that are feasible and marketable.

3.5 An Example In Category 5

The preceding example can be treated in this category. We could consider automating the interactions among material hardness, speed, and feed. A designed experiment would be necessary to determine the relationships among material hardness, machine speed, and tool feed. As a result, the complete process map would be known for these three variables showing the effect of multiple settings on surface finish. We can feed hardness signals electronically to the process map to select the most appropriate values of machine speed and tool feed. In this manner, the machine will be automatically adjusted to obtain an acceptable machined surface without the chatter. Such a process design would be considered robust. Once again we note that we have removed human intervention from tackling natural hardness variation (uncontrollable variable).

3.6 An Example In Category 6

This case considers a correlated process output characteristics requiring delicate balance. A powder press is producing a pressed-metal part. There are two characteristics of importance - weight and height of the part. These characteristics are positively correlated. That is, when height is higher the weight is higher. The sequence of operation in the present process is: fill the cavity with powder, wipe the cavity surface, and hit the punch to finish the product. This process sequence results in the weight and height being correlated. The experience has shown that it is very difficult to control these characteristics within desired limits and maintain the positive relationship between them. It has been desirable to decouple the relationship between the two characteristics so that they can be independently controlled. The process sequence could be altered as follows: measure the powder volume to reflect the weight of the part proportional to powder density, fill the cavity just below the cavity surface, and hit the punch. This sequence would successfully decouple the correlation between the part weight and the part height so that they can be independently controlled.

4. ROBUSTNESS CHALLENGE

The following is a description of challenging problems which could use robust design ideas. The conceptual robust options are identified for each problem.

4.1 Problem 1

Seat belt design has two output requirements that require delicate balance. These requirements are: (1) for passenger comfort seat belt should be snug to the body without excessive force in normal driving conditions and (2) for passenger safety, seat belt should be holding passenger in place during sudden deceleration to avoid bouncing. The first requirement is stated as maximum belt force and the second requirement is stated as minimum belt force. In the present seat belt design a single spring mechanism is used to provide the belt force. It's value is slightly biased in favor of safety. The passengers many times are known to create a slight slack between the body and a belt to increase the comfort level. However, this is undesirable because in a collision situation the belt will lock in a slack position with a possibility that a passenger can slide out. Thus, the safety purpose of seat belt is defeated. This problem requires us to think how to decouple the relationship between the comfort level belt force and the safety level belt force.

This is a problem of two correlated outputs. The seat belt mechanism have to be modified to come with one value of belt force under normal driving condition and another value of belt force under sudden deceleration.

4.2 Problem 2

In a rubber molding process, rubber has been found to stick to the mold cavities. This problem has been found to be seasonal. In summer, this problem is more likely, than any other season. The humidity variation is high on the molders' list of suspects. Molders prefer to maintain molding variables constant. We have to desensitize the interaction between humidity variation and the mold variables.

This is a problem of interaction between ambient condition and molding variables. The interactions between humidity and molding variables need to be understood. Additionally, when these relationships are determined, they will have to be automated.

Another possible solution is to research humidity-friendly material so that there will be only one set of molding variables regardless of varying humidity condition.

4.3 Problem 3

A plant is using corrugated boxes to ship products. These boxes are used on the automated packaging line. Occasionally packaging lines get jammed with these boxes.

Thickness variation of incoming boxes from the suppliers is blamed. Present packaging line is designed to accept boxes in a flat-folded condition. A leaf spring is used as a stopper for the incoming box. A kicker bar comes in and opens the box so that it can be filled with the product. The reason for machine getting jammed is that a box either travels too much or not enough into the leaf spring. Both conditions of travel result in a jammed machine. The customer blames this on excessive thickness variation of the incoming boxes. We have to create an equipment design change where the interaction between the thickness variation and the spring is eliminated.

This is a problem of interaction between a property of incoming material and a process variable. The packaging machine spring mechanism will have to be modified to accept the natural variation of box thickness.

4.4 Problem 4

There are two mating parts with a fit requiring certain amount of gap. The gap cannot be too small because it will result in an interference fit. On the other hand, the gap cannot be too large, otherwise, it will result in a sloppy fit. The individual parts are toleranced to assure this gap requirement. Unfortunately, the process capabilities are not compatible with specifications. Both processes are incapable. We have to create a robust solution to this problem without having to buy new machines.

This is a problem of interaction between tolerances. A forgiving mechanism will have to be created which would be insensitive to existing process capabilities of mating components.

Another possible solution is to introduce classified fits to obtain the desired gap. From a business perspective, this is not a desirable solution.

4.5 Problem 5

A process makes corrugated board. Raw material consists of paper rolls from paper mills. The critical output characteristic is paper joint strength. Occasionally, joint strength is not met. Operators feel that this is due to varying amount of moisture in the rolls of paper they purchase. Current procedure is to adjust temperature and speed settings to compensate for varying degree of moisture. This procedure is considered clumsy because temperature and speed settings are not conveniently located for ease of adjustments. Even if these controls were accessible, operators dislike the idea that they have to play continuously with machine settings. We have to come up with a robust solution to deal with moisture variation in the incoming paper rolls.

This is a problem of interaction between a property of incoming material and clumsy adjustments. The interactions need to be understood and mechanized.

Another possible solution is to research a new paper material which always produces an acceptable joint regardless of its moisture content.

4.6 Problem 6

A food company is developing a recipe for muffins. Food chemists have come up with a procedure that requires preheating the oven to 400 °F, using ½ cup of water to be mixed with one egg, and baking it until golden brown. The recipe developing team realizes that there are many operational variables that can grossly vary in spite of the recommendations printed on the back of the box. For example, a consumer may start baking immediately after turning the oven on instead of preheating, somewhat carelessly measure ½ cup of water, and may use any size egg. We need to develop a robust recipe that will result in edible muffins against these operational variables.

This is a problem of uncontrollable operational variables. The interactions between recipe ingredients and operational variables need to be understood to come up with a mixture that can withstand the cooks' habits.

5. GENERIC ROBUSTNESS PRINCIPLES

The following generic robustness principles are derived from the preceding examples.
- Correlated output characteristics must be decoupled so that each output characteristic can be individually manipulated.
- Designs and processes must be insensitive to user habits.
- Materials must be developed that are insensitive to ambient conditions.
- Designs or processes must be made tolerance insensitive whenever process capabilities are not adequate.
- Ambient conditions must be compensated automatically.
- Machines should have mechanisms to deal with incoming material variation without human intervention.

To practice these principles, engineering creativity and effective investigative methods are required.

6. CONCLUSION

Robustness is a necessary element in creating product and process designs to counter natural variations in operational environments, ambient conditions, and human tendencies that make products and processes susceptible to failures. Without robustness, human interventions have to be highly accurate to produce acceptable performance. Such accuracies are impractical to have or to maintain in operational environments.

There are examples of robust products and processes found all around us, but they came into being due to intuition of a handful of designers. To teach robustness as a design discipline we need to explore some age old problems that beg solutions. Through these solutions, we begin to master generic robustness principles identified in this paper. To practice these principles we must follow sound investigation practices and learn serious creativity. Use of serious creativity helps us to identify control variables and investigation practices help us to determine the nature of relationships between noise variables and control variables. Once these relationships are known, an appropriate technologies can help us to mechanize the solutions.

REFERENCES

Bajaria, H. J., *Creating Robust Manufacturing Processes*, Manufacturing Engineering, p. 12, January 1996.

Bajaria, H. J. and Palady, Paul, *A Quality, Reliability Primer*, Ford Motor Company, PTO Reliability and Quality Office, 1993.

Biondi, Angelo, *The Creative Process*, D. O. K. Publishers, Buffalo, New York, 1972

Cohen, Lou, *Quality Function Deployment - How to make QFD work for you*, Addison-Wesley, Reading, Massachusetts, 1995.

DeBono, Edward, *Serious Creativity*, HarperCollins Publishers, 1992.

Harry, Mikel J., *The Vision of Six Sigma: Tools and Methods for Breakthrough*, Sigma Publishing Company, Phoenix, Arizona, 1994.

Nadler, Gerald, Hibino, Shozo, and Farrell, John, *Creative Solution Finding*, Prima Publishing, Rocklin, CA, 1994.

Pugh, Stuart, *Concept Selection - A Method That Works* , Proceedings of the International Conference on Engineering Design, Rome, pp. 479-506, March, 1981.

Sprow, Eugene E., *What Hath Taguchi Wrought?*, Manufacturing Engineering, pp. 57-60, April 1992.

Taguchi, Genichi, *Introduction to Quality Engineering - Designing Quality into Products and Processes*, Asian Productivity Organization, Quality Resources, White Plains, New York, 1986.

Taguchi, Genichi, *Taguchi on Robust Technology Development - Bringing Quality Engineering Upstream*, ASME Press, New York, New York, 1993.

3

Leadership in the 21st century

B.L. Joiner
Joiner Associates Inc.
PO Box 5445
3800 Regent St.
Madison, WI 53705, U.S.A.
PH: 608-238-8134
FAX: 608-238-2908
Email: Joinerinc@aol.com

Abstract

Effective leadership has always been needed in organizations but is needed even more in today's rapidly changing world. The formal organization structure is not sufficient by itself to deal with the pace of change; we must involve more people in taking on leadership responsibilities and helping to make change happen. Each of us can and must gain knowledge and acquire skills that will allow us to act on the Leadership Cycle of Challenging What Is, Imagining What Will Be, and Making It Happen. Above all, we must help to create an environment of openness, honesty, challenge, and support so that we can surface the real issues and deal with them..

Keywords

Leadership; management; challenge; imagine; make it happen; human side of change; Democracy

1   INTRODUCTION

Leadership has always been a key factor in an organization's performance, and never more so than in today's dynamic world. Shrinking budgets, shifting customer needs and priorities, rapidly changing technologies, globalization, increased market pressures, and restructuring are just some of the factors causing great confusion and turmoil in the workplace. Ironically, these problems are compounded further by the general failure of the various efforts taken to fix them. As revealed in a recent survey, as many as 70% of reengineering efforts failed to achieve their goals, and 60% of over 900 executives who participated in restructuring efforts reported no productivity gains (*Information Week*, 12 September 1994). And this is not limited to reengineering and restructuring. Similar figures are reported for other major change efforts.

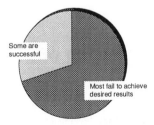

Figure 1: The great majority of change efforts, be they reengineering, TQM, divestitures, acquisitions, downsizing, or restructuring, fail to achieve the desired results.

Effective leadership is key to overcoming these obstacles to improvement and will be a deciding factor in which organizations survive in the 21st century.

Some people think great leaders are born, not made. While that is true to some extent, there are skills, methods, and attributes that anyone in any organization can and must learn and practice to become a better leader. These apply to every employee, not just to those in positions of authority. This paper discusses a simple model of effective leadership and describes some methods and techniques for translating this model into practice.

2 THE LEADERSHIP CYCLE

The leadership cycle in Figure 2 captures the essence of a leader's job. Like all cycles, there is no specific beginning or ending. You can enter at any stage; the point is to continue to rotate the cycle. The basic steps, discussed in more detail below, are to
- **Challenge what is**: open your eyes to the assumptions, beliefs, and practices that shape today's results. Do these support or prevent progress?
- **Imagine what will be**: think creatively about what the future could be. Develop a clear picture of the future that you *will* help to create.
- **Make it happen**: think about both the technical aspects and human aspects of the changes you anticipate. Who will need to change? Involve these people in making the change happen. Don't abdicate your responsibility: follow up; make corrections; provide support.

Figure 2   Leaders continually rotate through this cycle. They continually seek to understand and to challenge what is. They develop a vision of what could and will be, and they roll up their sleeves and help make it happen.

All three of these–Challenge, Imagine, Make it Happen–are needed over and over, for changes both small and large. If you don't Make It Happen, you're wasting your time, just dreaming. If you don't really Imagine What Will Be, you'll be stuck in the mud of the problems of today. If you don't understand and Challenge What Is your organization will likely be held back by hidden assumptions, stumbling from one bright idea to the next, never realizing the full potential of any of them.

All of us find some phases of this cycle more natural than others. One of our challenges is to use and continue to enhance our strengths while shoring up our weaknesses by refining our own abilities and by collaborating with others who have complementary capabilities. Another is to tie these phases together, to make this cycle a natural part of how work is done–and as a result create an organization in which all employees are working to create an organization that constantly renews itself. To make this happen, in each phase we must:

• Create an environment that allows and encourages the needed behaviors
• Develop appropriate knowledge and skills
• Take action

While there is some overlap between the environment, skills, and strategies needed for each phase, there are also distinct differences, as described below.

3   CHALLENGE WHAT IS

Of all the work required to reap the rewards of the leadership cycle, having to Challenge What Is is in many ways the most difficult. Challenging the status quo runs counter to much of human nature. We have all been taught to 'Leave well enough alone'.

In his book *Knowledge for Action*, Chris Argyris (1993) says that the human mind seems to be programmed to defend the way it thinks today, accepting the signals that say we're right in the way we think and rejecting those signals that suggest we may be wrong. For example, we choose to belong to organizations and to listen to radio or TV newscasters who reinforce the way we already think. This keeps us comfortable and helps us avoid having to do the disconcerting work of examining our thinking patterns.

Kearns and Nadler (1992) have a wonderful analogy about the 'moose on the table'. These are the issues that everyone knows about but no one openly discusses. People will talk over, under, and around the moose, but no one says 'There's a moose here that we have to deal with'. Every organization has a moose on the table though some have ignored them for so long that they've forgotten the moose is there. A newcomer soon learns that to mention the moose is to unleash a barrage of defensive abuse. All too soon a newcomer adopts the corporate myopia and joins the forces that attack other moose-sighters.

Every organization has its moose, or herd of moose. So does each of us as individuals. To make real progress, we must first be able to see the moose. We need to examine the unexamined, to discuss the undiscussable, to challenge the unchallengeable. In most cases, that's where the real leverage lies.

Why do we as individuals and as organizations resist the challenges? It seems as if the table under the moose is made of fine crystal. One mention of the moose will be enough to shatter our whole foundation–and then where will we be? Are our thought structures so delicate that they can't bear an honest exploration of the facts? In times past when the pace of change was much slower, perhaps we could afford to solidify our thinking patterns for long periods. But not today. In Argyris's view, we overprotect ourselves. We are not so delicate. We can afford to examine the moose. Doing so may open up new pathways. We may even find the moose to be a new ally. In any event, in times of rapid change, we must be willing to challenge anything. The solutions of yesterday will almost surely not be the solutions of tomorrow.

Creating the environment

How do we get beyond these biological and organizational barriers to change? One of the most important ingredients is to create an environment of openness and honesty, where bad news is welcomed along with the good. This will help us surface the truth. Without that, an organization will have secrets and, as a colleague once put it, 'an organization is as sick as its secrets'.

We also have another key responsibility when it comes to challenging what is. We must seek feedback on own behavior. We must have conversations with peers, employees, and managers, asking them what it's like to work with us. Getting honest answers takes work; in today's world, most people are going to be suspicious at first. But it works. Doing this regularly will help you find patterns in your own behavior that are contributing to your own moose on the table (Oestreich 1995).

Another part of the environment is emphasizing dialogue over debate (Senge 1994). Arguments and debates are like battles: we expect there to be a winner and a loser. Dialogue, on the other hand, is done for the purpose of mutual understanding and mutual learning. People openly share ideas and the evidence to support those ideas. They welcome new evidence and new theories. They listen without feeling defensive. Their goal is to understand what someone else is saying and to search together for deeper shared truths. To paraphrase Covey (1989), they seek to understand before seeking to be understood.

Developing knowledge and skills

A second aspect of being able to Challenge What Is is to make sure we and others have the knowledge and skills to understand what is happening. There are four particular areas where indepth knowledge is needed:

- **Customer needs and values**: Our goal is not only to understand our customers needs today but also to understand their agendas for the future. We need to understand what they are trying to achieve and what barriers they are encountering. Leadership can be much more effective when all employees understand customers and seek to contribute to customers' well-being.
- **The 'technologies' of your business**: Dr. W. Edwards Deming often said, 'there is no substitute for knowledge' (Deming 1986). To be a great orchestra requires a deep understanding of each instrument and of the music being played. A chemical company, for example, made great strides when it taught production workers about the chemical reactions associated with their work. Another company wound up with very inexpensively automated operations after employees were taught how to make simple electromechanical devices. All employees must be well versed in the basics of the business.
- **The use of data**: We need to do a better job of building and continually refining measurement systems that help us learn. The emphasis must be on learning, not on reward and punishment. If we use data and measurements to reward and punish, we will never have openness and honesty. People will tell us what we want to hear; they will distort the figures to make sure we see what we want to see. If we are to challenge what is and find better ways of doing business, we must use data as a diagnostic tool, to find out where we are doing well and where there are problems, not to blame people.
- **Teamwork and change**: People working together with a common aim not only produce better results but also get much greater satisfaction from their work. And when the challenge of continual change is added to seamless teamwork, true joy in work often results in a way that is not possible through adherence to the status quo.

Taking action

Whether or not you are in a position of authority, you can take effective action. We all need to be leaders. We all need to welcome openness and discovery. We all need to be willing to engage in dialogue about 'the moose' or anything else that matters. We all need to be open to feedback on our own behavior. We all need get much better at using data for learning and discovery.

4   IMAGINE WHAT WILL BE

For many years, the Royal Dutch Shell company has been using a technique called scenario planning to great strategic advantage. They imagine different scenarios of what might happen in the future and then envision, in some detail, what it will take to thrive under those conditions. For example, years before it happened, they imagined the possibility of a dramatic rise in the price of crude oil. As a result, in their scenario planning, they developed strategies that allowed them to come out of the 1970s in much better shape than most other oil companies. This example epitomizes several key aspects of leadership: First, it requires a deep understanding of the oil business. Second, it incorporates both wild, crazy ideas and practical skills such as scenario planning. These helped them move beyond what *could* be to what *will* be. This balance between imagination and knowledge is key to doing a good job of Imagining What Will Be.

Creating the environment

We all know how to create an environment where imagination and creativity are stifled. We've all heard expressions like, 'That's a dumb idea', 'That won't work here', 'We've tried that before', 'Who asked you for your opinion'?, 'That's not your job'. Our challenge is to turn these around, to create an environment where curiosity and forward thinking are eagerly welcomed parts of everybody's job. And the best place to start, as always, is with ourselves. As de Bono (1985) points out in his book *Six Thinking Hats*, simply pausing a few minutes from time to time and saying, 'We need some new thinking here' helps. New knowledge and skills, coupled with serious intentions to achieve new thinking can go a long way.

Developing knowledge and skills

Perhaps not too surprisingly, there are strong parallels between the knowledge and skills needed to Challenge What Is and those needed to Imagine What Will Be:

- **Customer needs and values**: Imagining What Will Be requires a deep understanding of our customer's future. Some of the most successful companies are those that are able to anticipate or predict needs their customers aren't even aware of yet. To do that we must learn our customer's agenda—where they are trying to go, not just where they are today. If we know where they are trying to go, we can be of higher value to them than we can by merely reacting to their current needs (Joiner 1994).
- **The 'technologies' of your business**: To help you look out towards the future, it helps to benchmark the best. Who is the best in the world at some key aspect of your future? Not just the best in your industry or your region, but the best in the world. How good are they? How do they do what they do? What are the technologies of the future? What can you do to learn today? To promote learning?
- **The use of data**: Effective use of data often stimulates new thinking by forcing us to abandon old assumptions. As one manager put it, 'Data has destroyed a number of great truths around here'.
- **Creativity techniques**: In recent years, Nadler (1990), de Bono (1992), and others have done some very exciting work developing specific techniques for helping us stretch our awareness and thinking. Many of these techniques are easy to learn and quite effective. They can help anyone become more creative and innovative provided a conducive environment is developed.

Taking action

Again, we can all take responsibility for changing the environment. We can all censor from our own vocabulary and our own thought patterns expressions such as 'That won't work here'. We can instead use open-ended questions and dialogue to learn more: 'Can you tell me more about that'?, 'And how might that work'?

We can learn creativity techniques and use them ourselves–then we can help others learn and use them. We can get more knowledgeable about our customers, about the technologies of our business and about how to use data. Then we can put all this together to flesh out new futures that we *will* help to make happen.

5   MAKE IT HAPPEN

Most of us think that once we've decided what changes to make the biggest part of our job is done, but in fact it is just beginning. The great bulk of change efforts fail to achieve the desired results more from poor quality of execution than from poor design. (See also Zangwill 1995.)

To make change happen, we can't just announce our great idea, nor can we merely see that a change effort is launched and walk away. To be successful, we must stay with it, providing ongoing support and follow up. We must Make It Happen.

Creating the environment
When done well, the creative work required to Imagine What Will Be leaves people with a sense of energy and excitement. Unfortunately, that energy all too often fades when nothing happens quickly with the ideas generated. People are left with broken dreams. We can't settle for dreaming; we must move to action. We must use the ideas to generate a new vision, a clear picture of where we are going and how that vision fits into the larger context in which we work.

An environment supportive of making the desired changes has several important characteristics:
1) An energizing atmosphere built from a sense of community
2) A sense of challenge and support; the ability to challenge one another and to support one another
3) The honesty and openness discussed earlier
4) Clarity of the vision of where the organization as a whole is headed
5) Clarity of what the change will look like when it is done

Item 1 is particularly important, for even the best blueprint for change is only as good as the willingness of people to support it. To have a sense of community, employees must understand and see the need for change and feel comfortable working to make it happen. Such a sense of community does not happen overnight. With any given change its best to start upstream, from the moment a change is conceived, to involve people in deciding how the change will happen. Even better, involve them in deciding what changes to make, if that is possible. Once the basic details are in place, work with employees to identify *specifically* what effect the change will have on them. Who will be doing what on the other side of this change? How will that be different from what they are doing now? What level of resistance can be expected and why? Work to develop a common understanding and language about the nature of the change and the ways that groups of people commonly react when confronted with the demands of change. Then formulate and implement specific commitment-building strategies that resolve the anticipated barriers.

Developing knowledge and skills
The particular knowledge and skills that need to be developed will depend on the particular change. If we're switching technologies–for instance, from one computer type to another– people will need to understand the new hardware and software. If the proposed changes will affect products and services that our customers purchase, people will need to know how to explain the changes to customers, how to answer customers' questions, and so on.

The ability to develop, document, teach, and use new approaches is thus a component of every change effort since the very definition of change is that people will no longer be doing what they used to do. Widespread knowledge about how to make improvements is also needed since whatever changes we make will always need to be continuously refined and improved, both to fine-tune them to their new context and then to continually upgrade them over time.

Taking action

Two aspects of change to keep in mind when working to Make It Happen are that
1) The design of any change will have flaws, aspects that were either not clear in the design or aspects that will not work as conceived. Many of these flaws will only be repairable by the manager in charge of the change. If they are not fixed, the implementation will slow down until it eventually stops entirely and the change efforts dies. (Zangwill 1995)
2) There is a great element of emotional involvement in change. People will have fears and doubts. A leader's job is to help them work through those natural reactions and grow in confidence and capability by successfully making the change.

One extremely useful approach that helps a leader ensure that changes are made is described by Zangwill (1995) as 'active follow up, correction and support'. We have for years called it the 'Review Process'. (See also Joiner 1994.)

An effective way to do this is to meet regularly with those directly involved in making the change happen. Typically, these meetings might be once a day, once a week, or once a month: in general, the faster the change needs to happen, the more frequent the need to meet.

Here's an example of how this approach works. Several years ago, the World Trade Center in New York City was bombed. There was much structural damage to the facility and people thought it might take years to put everything to rights. But to the surprise of almost everyone, the towers were put back in operation much faster than anyone believed possible. A woman associated with this reconstruction described a key factor in the rapid progress as a twice-daily meeting between those doing the work and the project manager. As a group they discussed the problems they were having and what was getting in their way, mutually decided on the priorities and figured out how to help each other, and moved on. Whenever necessary, the leader would take action to remove some obstacle, but most times the group could solve these issues themselves.

The general principle is that leaders must actively follow up to see that things are on track, make corrections if changes need to be made, and provide support both emotionally and by helping to get obstacles removed.

Some people think this sounds like micromanagement. They firmly believe that once the direction of the change is decided, the leader should turn it over and walk away. But the Hersey-Blanchard model for situational leadership (Hersey 1988) pointed out years ago that most people need additional support when they are doing something new. And every change involves something new. In such cases, frequent open communication and support is key.

6   LEADERSHIP AND DEMOCRACY

As the pace of change continues to accelerate, we must increasingly all become leaders. Traditional reliance on formal leaders and formal organizational structures becomes more and more obsolete. The need for involving more people, for sharing leadership responsibility throughout the organization, continues to increase. Reliance on any formal organization chart is far too cumbersome. It is too slow at decision making and especially at implementation.

In his book *Creating*, Fritz (1991) describes an encounter with an executive who was disappointed that people weren't taking more initiative. The executive said that everyone agreed with him that risk taking and initiative were important for the company, but people still waited for him to take the lead. Why was this happening? This executive hired only the 'cream of the crop' among college graduates, ostensibly those with high scores in cooperation, adaptability, and cleverness. He then rewarded high performers, admitting that 'we don't like [failures]'. The contradiction was obvious–but not to this executive. He hired smart people who knew how to avoid failure and rewarded them for not failing. Hence, a company of people who played it safe.

Have we forgotten something we once knew? In the 1830s, Alexis de Tocqueville, a young French politician, visited the United States for the first time. The outcome of his visit was an important book called *Democracy in America* (1835, 1840). He noted that American democracy was very different from European democracy. American democracy, he said, had an incredible feature that ordinary citizens would take it upon themselves to identify what *they* considered to be problems or opportunities for improvement. Not only that, they would then decide what needed to be done and go ahead and do it! While European citizens might go so far as to identify the needs, they relied on their governments, nobility and experts to do something about it. These spontaneous, self-organizing initiatives were apparently unique to America and fundamental to the functioning of American democracy in those early years.

If de Tocqueville visited America today, he might see more parallels with the Europe of the 19th century than with his observations in the 1830s. Throughout America today there is an expectation that those with official power are responsible for identifying and fixing problems and for taking advantage of opportunities that come along. John McKnight, an expert in community development, has observed that the difference between healthy and not so healthy communities is whether the citizens manifest de Tocqueville's style of spontaneous democracy or just grouse about what "They" should be doing to fix problems. McKnight's belief is that too much power and control by formal organizations tends to undermine and destroy these critically important grassroots initiatives. (McKnight 1995)

A paradoxical aspect of spontaneous initiatives is that they won't happen if you try to organize them. You will just create unnecessary bureaucracies that hinder the rapid change that is needed in today's dynamically changing environment. We need a better balance between formal and spontaneous organizations. The formal organization is needed but will never be able to do enough by itself. Likewise, grass roots initiatives alone will never be enough. We must create space in our formal organizations to welcome, support and celebrate grass root initiatives. As Margaret Wheatley told me recently, we need to develop '**leaderfull organizations** ', organizations full of people who can and do regularly Challenge What Is, Imagine What Will Be, and Make It Happen.

7   REFERENCES

Argyris, C. (1991) Teaching Smart People How to Learn. *Harvard Business Review*. May-June 1991.

Argyris, C. (1993) *Knowledge for Action*. San Francisco: Jossey-Bass.

Covey, S. (1989) *The 7 Habits of Highly Effective People*. New York: Simon & Schuster.

de Bono, E. (1985) *Six Thinking Hats*. Toronto: Key Porter Books, Ltd.

de Bono, E. (1992) *Serious Creativity*. New York: HarperCollins Publishing, 1992. (Principles and techniques to systematically foster creative thinking.)

Deming, W.E. (1986) *Out of the Crisis*. Cambridge, MA: M.I.T. Center for Advanced Engineering Study.

Fritz, R. *Creating*. New York: Columbine. 1991.

Joiner, B.L.(1994) *Fourth Generation Management: The New Business Consciousness*. New York: McGraw-Hill.

Kearns, D.T. and Nadler, D.A. (1992) *Prophets in the Dark: How Xerox Reinvented Itself and Beat Back the Japanese*. New York: HarperCollins.

McKnight, J. (1995) *The Careless Society: Community and Its Counterfeits*. New York: HarperCollins Publishing. (Provides a series of examples of how we destroy "community" and what we can do about it.)

Nadler, G. and Shozo, H. (1990) *Breakthrough Thinking*. Rocklin, CA: Prima Publishing & Communications. (Principles and techniques for developing breakthroughs.)

Oestreich, D. (1995) The personal transformation of leadership. (Seminar materials, August 1995).

Senge, P. et al. (1994) *The Fifth Discipline Fieldbook*. New York: Doubleday.

Tocqueville, A.de (1835, 1840) *Democracy in America*. (See 1st Perennial Library edition, J.P. Mayer, ed. New York: Harper & Row. 1985).

Zangwill, W.I. (1995) "Active Feedback, Correction and Support" (unpublished manuscript).

8   BIOGRAPHY

Dr. Brian L. Joiner is a leading consultant to North American companies on managing for quality and productivity. He is co-founder and Chairman of Joiner Associates Incorporated, a management consulting and product development firm. He is author of *Fourth Generation Management: The New Business Consciousness* (McGraw-Hill) and lead developer of the video-based seminar entitled Fundamentals of Fourth Generation Management. He was one of the original nine judges for the Malcolm Baldrige National Quality Award and has received numerous awards including the W. Edwards Deming Medal, the Wiliam G. Hunter Award, the Frank Wilcoxon Prize, and the Shewhart Medal.

4

The system works . . . only through co-operation

J. Carlisle.
John Carlisle Partnerships.
44 Dover Road, Sheffield, S11 8RH, U.K.
Tel: 0114 2678 689, Fax: 0114 266 0188

Abstract

One of the two key factors working against successful Total Quality initiatives in Britain has been the extent to which organisations conduct their businesses in an adversarial fashion. The other has been complacency at the top, as the RSA Report "Tomorrow's Company" (1995) states: 75% of the directors questioned thought their company was world class, only 3.2% were actually world class! This is a deadly cocktail for the stifling of continuous improvement.

This paper examines the first of these; but the complacency runs like a thread through the whole presentation.

INTRODUCTION

In the early 1980's the late Nicolae Ceausescu paid a state visit to Britain to receive, amongst other honours, a knighthood for his independent stand in the communist bloc. He was a guest of Her Majesty the Queen at Buckingham Palace while he was there, and she very quickly developed an intense dislike for him. The reason? He brought his food-taster with him, and would eat nothing until the man had passed it as safe! Such a blatant lack of trust between two nations who were meant to be developing an understanding was unthinkable to Her Majesty. (She must have stripped him of his knighthood in 1989 with some degree of grim satisfaction.)

In industry, we too instituted food tasting, which we called, for example, goods inward inspection, or audits, or one way open book accounting.

We did not regard the practice as unusual. We, in the West, in so far as business is concerned, have grown used to having low expectations of each other, or in fact, operating in a climate of mistrust. We have the equivalent manufacturing "nations" - the automobile industry, electrical goods, pharmaceuticals, construction, and so on - many of whom have, or have had, that mediaeval look about them. They have built walls and moats, which we call contracts. They have guards to defend them called lawyers, inspectors and tender boards, and, in some cases, some really hard-bitten gatekeepers called traditional buyers ("Even if you are a preferred supplier, don't try to go round me, mister!").

As a result, over the years, the behaviour of these "nations" has become more and more remote from the wishes of their people, the needs of their customers, and from the support of their real allies, their best suppliers and contractors. Consequently they lost their customers, their market share, and their profits. Two victims in particular were the British car manufacturing industry and construction. The largest British car manufacturer today probably makes 700 cars a week, while the largest British construction company, Wimpey, is valued at a third of its French and German rivals, and a seventh of the largest Swedish competitor, Skanska. It is estimated that the construction industry has shed 500,000 jobs since 1990, and it is not all due to the economic slowdown.

What on earth had happened?

1.	They had forgotten, or, indeed some had never realised, that whoever raises consumer expectations, and then unfailingly fulfils them, is going to gobble up market share, e.g. Japanese cars. PIMS calls this "Relative Perceived Product Quality", which in their opinion is the major factor behind productivity and growth. Consumers have now become a lot more discriminating, and producers who anticipated this were pulling away fast from the rest of the field.

2.	They used an inappropriate model of business, that of deadly competition. The more accurate model of business is that of a fraternity, not combatants engaged in a war. There should be a healthy balance between cooperation and competition; what Hayes and Wheelwright call *"the manufacturing confederation"*. The cooperative element which works best in this new world of business is that of a *Collaborative Venture* between all those with shared interests in serving the customer best.

Nowhere is this practice of acknowledged shared interests more vital than in a company that is going into total quality. (It is worth noting that, among all the hype about Japan, what has been seldom mentioned is the MITI Annual Report on Small Enterprises in 1984, in which it was stated that "Japanese manufacturing industry owes its competitive advantage and strength to its subcontracting structure".)

W. EDWARDS DEMING

The last contribution that Dr Deming made before he died in 1993 was what he called *Profound Knowledge*, which he felt every leader should have if their organisation was to compete in the global economy. A key feature of this is the ability to appreciate the organisation as a system. When this happens the leaders come to understand that their company is interdependent internally on its people and functions, and externally on its suppliers, customers and community. And it is only at this point that process-driven management, and, especially outsourcing strategies can actually work! (Figure 1).

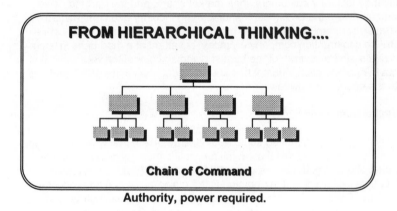

Authority, power required.

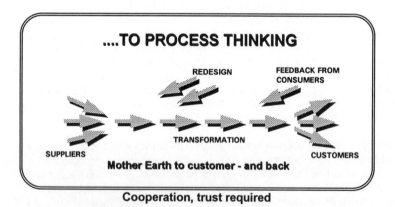

Cooperation, trust required

Figure 1 From hierarchical thinking to process thinking.

The cost of coercion and conflict

If there are doubts that cooperation, or at least fair treatment, is fundamental to successful company performance then it becomes worthwhile looking at the downside of bad relationships.

(a)　　The cost of quality: British Leyland had a terrible relationship with their suppliers even as late as the early 1980s. One of the results was that in **one month** they had to return over 22, 000 defective parts to their suppliers - a real lose/lose. This was at a most critical time, when they really needed to win back customer confidence.

The latest news is that the Rover Group really are taking serious steps to help their suppliers and develop the right relationships, i.e. make it two-way. It is called "Best Practice", and seems to be making headway. However the question is: will the buying culture change?

(b)　　In 1990 the Channel Tunnel project was in dire straits. It was 50% over budget halfway through its life (nearly £2.4 billion) and work was halted by its bankers. The reason? The conflict-ridden relationship between the customer, Eurotunnel, and the contractors Transmache Link. They have had to bring over an American from Bechtel, John Neerhout, to restore and manage the relationship! I want you to compare that with the Esso Chemical success story I shall recount later. In 1991 history repeated itself, and shareholders today must be distinctly uncomfortable!

(c)　　Finally, within the marvel of the space shuttle triumph, let us never forget that this year is the tenth anniversary of the tragedy of the tenth Challenger mission: a direct consequence of the buyer (NASA) riding rough-shod over its supplier.

It can be fairly said that bad supplier relationships really do poison organisations, particularly those with a Total Quality culture. Having healthy systems in your own organisation which convey supplier defects means, ultimately, having an unhealthy organisation. But the answer is not to install food tasters, as in Ceausescu's case; it lies in giving suppliers the confidence to invest in putting their "kitchens" right, so that customers can have confidence in the goods received.

Rewards of relationship management

The Xerox and Honda stories are becoming legendary, as is Motorola because buyer/supplier partnerships have been an integral part of their Total Quality drives from the beginning.

However, there are many others who also deserve mention: NCR in Dundee, Nissan, and Asda and Slough Estates, who are developing an exciting pioneering approach with their contractors.

Nevertheless, I would like to add to those a little-known success of one of my outstanding companies, Exxon Chemicals, which occurred in Britain in the early 1980s, in that least promising sector, construction.   In the days when it was still Esso Chemicals, there began a project, in Mossmoran, Scotland shared by Esso and Shell called the Fife Ethylene Project. The main contractor Lummus, (urged on by Essochem) and Essochem, set themselves the mission of meeting *"The last chance for British Construction Industry to change its world image,"* and called it "Flagship Fife" .

They agreed principles and ways of working, and set up systems and structures in which key relationships could be "mirrored."   They also held joint team building sessions to develop the right relationship skills across both organisations, and so on. In other words they planned, not just the `what', but the `how' as well, and worked very hard at it. In so doing they built a strong contractor/client team of equals characterised by close/effective counterpart partnerships .

The result was:

•   Field productivity was 20% higher than historical prediction for Esso projects in UK.

•   The Project was completed five months ahead of schedule and 10% under budget.

•   Safety was four times better than the US standard for construction i.e. six times better than UK.

•   Labour relations - lowest strike rate for a UK large project in more than 20 years. Approximately 1% of field man hours was lost due to disputes in four years.

Here is an outstanding success story, and one which illustrates the fact that *cooperation is not a Japanese patent.* It is just that we have not seen fit to reward it in this country, because, perversely, we seem more comfortable with adversarial behaviour.

There is an even more outstanding success story in Shell Holland, today, with NAM, the drilling company with whom we have been working. In the first 18 months of their partnership in 1992, they increased efficiency by 31%, saved £19 million, AND shared £3.5 million with their partners. They continue to prosper in every way. But then they have an outstanding leader, Tom Bakker - and they are Dutch. . . .

So, these are some obvious reasons why customer companies and their most important suppliers should work as partners; but why is it taking so long? Let us look at the length of the journey, and the extent of the learning curve.

Partnership - a developing relationship which has to be worked on.

The way ahead

The good news is, of course, that work on Western better buyer/supplier relationships has already begun, and it is no coincidence that trailblazers such as Xerox Reprographics and Motorola were winners of the prestigious Malcolm Baldrige award for quality in the USA in 1989. (Cadillac's award in 1990 was a real fillip for the USA auto industry, and Bill Scherkenback.)

Many companies are now coming round to the view that suppliers have to be partners in the business, and many are beginning to reap great benefits in a very competitive world. But it is a hard, long road, needing fundamental shifts in individual and organisational thinking.

Figure 2 shows the changes that must be undergone in order to move from the old-fashioned coercive relationship to that of genuine partnership. It is a movement from the more powerful party's right to dictate, to a conscious obligation to support its most important suppliers in their efforts to meet the customer's needs . In short it represents a growth in consciousness in what is meant by a relationship which is good for both parties. The basic principle here is one which the best buyers and suppliers have intuitively understood for a long time, i.e. **Your ability to influence the other party is determined by their perception of your organisation's willingness and capability to help them meet their needs.**

The diagram also illustrates, therefore, how you need to shape up to be perceived as helpful, and the kinds of developmental crises you have to manage on the way. It also shows that you cannot change overnight.

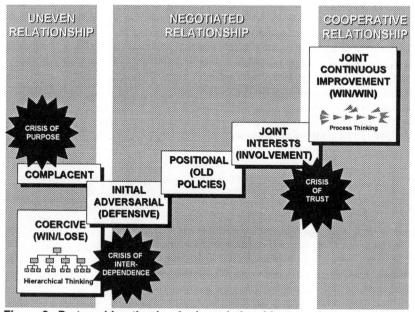

Figure 2   Partnership - the developing relationship towards cooperation

(Interestingly enough, in my research twelve years ago it was the buyers who told me of their unhappiness with the arm's length relationship, and of the wasted opportunities they thought these adversary policies of mutual suspicion caused. It was also the buyers, particularly in Rank Xerox, Rolls Royce and Motorola, who responded most positively to being trained in my Win/Win negotiating programme ten years ago. But it was senior management who very often had the most trouble practising the approach. After all, so much had been invested in building all those hierachial silos!)

Three major shifts towards cooperation

Three things need to happen, on the surface, in organisations who wish to develop real partnerships with their suppliers and customer companies.

1. Recognise the "chain of cooperation" from mother earth to consumer.

Total Quality has demonstrated that paying attention to the processes of industry has real payoff. It is not good enough merely to attend to what happens in your department or your company; you also need to attend to what happens between. Any chain is as strong as its weakest link, and pulling product through just does not work if you pull so hard that you break any link in the chain.

What is needed is both strong links - with controlled processes - and strong, but flexible, connections. This is what good relationships provide, responsive connections, which give reliable performance, good communications and flexible response to special causes. This is the way we learn and continuously improve together, and it is impossible without a cooperative relationship, because all the organisations in the chain must see that there is something in it for them.

2. Overcome unconscious incompetence

The sad fact is that the importance of this fundamental relationship to successful businesses is still largely misunderstood or unrecognised by the business media and top management; with the honourable exception of the Financial Times. It is not a seductive term in the way marketing or technology are, and therefore is not visible enough for popular understanding.

For example, in the 1989 description of the top five companies in Great Britain, published by the magazine *Management Today*, it was clear that they had all worked hard on their relationships with their suppliers. In fact, Toshiba's Managing Director described the suppliers as "part of our team", while Sony and Rank Xerox both mentioned the importance of suppliers in their JIT organisation. But, in over 1200 words of commentary by the staff of the magazine on these successes, fewer than a dozen referred to this vital relationship. The focus was technology, cellular manufacturing, participation and product quality. All the *visible* things.

The same lack of recognition occurred in the 1990 awards article. Only recently has it begun to correct this neglect.

This lack of awareness about the importance of the system understanding is one part of the national incompetence, and it means that public recognition for all the hard work has been slow in coming. (*Pace* the CBI, CRINE and The Reading Construction Forum.) This might have made the job harder for some organisations because it did not have that public image element about it. However, for others this absence of attention could be an advantage, as it is so easy for the executive to take on board the superficial message, for example, a cost-cutting culture will welcome the idea of outsourcing because it will see it as an opportunity to push costs upstream, and will miss the real benefit which is (a) reducing variation to increase quality, and (b) developing closer working relationships to jointly reduce costs and increase innovation.

The other part of the syndrome is the fact that many of our top executives today in customer and supplier firms still do not understand the importance of good relationships in their value net. (See Figure 3) This means, at best, that work on good relationships is not recognised (How many company reports write about cooperation? Very, very few.) and, at worst, that the organisation exercises policies which work directly against cooperation. How many companies actively discourage relationship-building because it infringes their ethics policy? I know of at least two vast organisations who send out clear messages to their employees saying: "You are untrustworthy", because of the ludicrous application of ethics policies. The same message goes to suppliers and contractors. How on earth can one empower people to take risks with each other or their suppliers for the sake of quality? Contracts departments and tender boards and simplistic directives have a lot to answer for!

Many Quality managers and line managers in the field need to work hard on educating their top management in the need for trust and cooperation. As long as the executives do not really understand how important relationship are, the harder it is going to be to take those steps to set it up in a sensible way, a way that promotes continuos improvement and innovation.

And his brings us to the third factor that needs to happen to improve relationships and performance.

3. Develop a "leadership" strategy.

Internal coercion leads to external coercion, just as internal cooperation leads to external cooperation. We have seen how the relationship towards partnership evolves (Figure 2) , and in looking at how the more powerful or conscious party influences this, we have what I call the "Leadership" strategy. In other words, **Get your own house in order first!** Do not ask others to do what you are not already doing well. As a customer organisation you need to be at least two steps ahead of the other organisation in order to "pull" it along, so that they can then be the mirror of your activities the model of what they need to be, and, by your skill and care you can reflect back to them what they need to **do** to get there. So as a supplier, you probably need to be ten steps ahead!

Risk-Trust - Large British Company

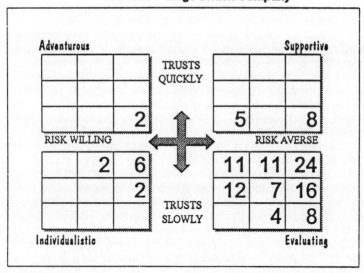

Figure 3   Risk-Trust diagram.

The diagram shows:

        Trust Only 13% thought **Trust** was encouraged
        Risk   Only 10% thought **Risk-Taking** was advisable - with the
unusual situation that 50% are <u>very</u> averse to risk. (extreme right)

This compares with an equivalent sized successful USA computer company;

        Trust 35% thought Trust was encouraged
        Risk   31% thought Risk-taking was advisable

They are making great strides with their alliances.

You also need to pay particular attention to, and invest time in, **communication**. When Phil Condit, the current chairman of Boeing who master-minded the highly successful Boeing/Mitsubishi Alliance, was asked his advice on partnering, he said: There are four things - communications, communications, communications. Then the fourth does not really matter!"

The key message is that good internal relationships lead to good external relationships. Thus if you are hoping to really influence the other party you need to work on your own organisation first, then you can "pull" the other organisation along by:

(a)   Having the climate that encourages productivity and innovation and can therefore deliver.

(b)   Understanding what it takes to set up change processes and structures - of which the most important is effective teams. The more people you have talking to each other the better, and the more the empowered teams talk to each other the better the thinking is. Combine this with good implementation and you have established the basis for trust. Ultimately what we are looking for is the key players in the two organisations talking to each other with the buyer and sales executive acting as "relationship managers".

Quality leadership in the 1990's

There are two key lessons today that organisation leaders must learn:

1. Understand your organisation as a system

Deming says that there is no knowledge without theory and prediction. Therefore experience, or experimentation (which is what you are doing when changing the organisation), teaches nothing without a clear understanding of the system you are trying to change. How many times have we seen people struggling under the weight of meaningless reorganisations which, contrary to the edicts from the top, are not customer-friendly, do not make processes more efficient, and are not helping real profitability? I have seen far too many repetitions with beleaguered middle managers asking despairingly why nothing has been learned from the last disaster. My heart goes out to them as they welcome their delayering redundancies with a resigned sigh of semi-relief.

Before you alter it or realign it decide exactly what theoretical construct you are working from - if any. Then check it against reality. Study it, talk about it, and when you feel confident enough in it, use it for prediction. Then make your plan by starting with improving processes by beginning with removing special causes, followed by reducing common case variation - and always with your eye on what is most important to the customer.

2. Create a climate of trust in your own organisation

If there is one common theme emerging in business today it is the need for **trust**. Trust-building is the single most important issue in business relationships, because it brings about the freedom in people, groups and organisations to do their best work. It is also one of the most difficult, as we found in our 1988 studies in Detroit - and we have paid dearly for it's absence!

This is not just an intrinsically good thing to do, it also has bottom-line benefits, e.g. Jim Sierk of Xerox USA reckons the bureaucratic structure created to handle the lack of trust in their buyer/supplier relationships cost them around 7 cents in the dollar, i.e. about 14 million dollars in 1981. I think the same could be saved in most companies, and that is a lot of money.

To achieve trust means working with attitudes, behaviour **and** structure; which means that leaders in potential partnership organisations need to work at four levels to develop a trust-building strategy.

1.   Accept the evidence that shows that trust and cooperation work better than suspicion and minimum risk tactics.... It is overwhelming. And accept the fact that ultimately the only way to build trust is to **ensure** a series of agreements which work as planned all the time every time. Implementation failure is the biggest source of organisational mistrust after downright proven dishonesty, as the Detroit study shows; so you are simply going to have to take the risk to trust your partners!

2.   Reward your people for taking risks to build cooperation for better performance .

        (a)   Make your internal customers and suppliers feel good about being open about the organisation's needs with those organisations that are important to yours.

        (b)   Encourage your top team to display confidence in their people's judgement, and educate them in the principles of relationship management. Give them feedback on how they are perceived to behave in this respect.

3.   Provide internal and external structures that facilitate trust, i.e.

        (a)   Set up cross-functional improvement teams

        (b)   Provide plenty of opportunity for communication and feedback both ways and **never** use the data as a reason for blame or punishment. It's main purpose is continuous improvement.

4.   Invest time and money in openly supporting your partners' aspirations. Take risks with each other on areas of common ground or joint interests. Do not expect people to take risks with your company if they cannot see some clear payoff for them. In many respects the Preferred Supplier and Partner jargon has a lot to answer for here. Our experience is that it can be a one-way street if the customer company is not working intelligently and consistently on reducing their variation, and involving their partners early. They become the frantic, and expensive, crisis solvers

Also, be flexible with your qualifying criteria. Do not crush smaller contractors under your bureaucracy. And, finally, if you say long term, mean long term. Do not have 30 day and 60 day termination clauses, no matter what your lawyers say; because all you have then is a one or two month contract in reality. Why should your contractors believe that you really trust them? And why should they then do their very best for you? Would you?

In a sentence: get **yourself and your own** organisation organised before expecting others to make that extra effort for you. And making that extra effort together means trusting people and becoming the deserved leaders in your industry today, and in the year 2000.

©John Carlisle, John Carlisle Partnerships.

REFERENCES:

Carlisle, J.A. and Parker, R.C. (1989) *Beyond Negotiation*. Wiley, Chichester.
Hayes, R., and Wheelwright S. (1984) *Restoring Our Competitive Edge - Competing through Manufacturing*. John Wiley, New York.
RSA (1995) *Tomorrow's Company* RSA, London.

BIOGRAPHY

John Carlisle started his working life on the cooper mines in Zambia, and after various posts in England became head of Personnel for Booker McConnell in Malawi. He settled in England in 1970 and in Sheffield in 1976 where he headed up the UK and European operations of Huthwaite Research Group for several years.

He encountered "Quality" in the mid 1980's, and is a consultant in the field recommended by the late Dr W Edwards Deming. His book, *Beyond Negotiation*, on improving buyer-supplier relationships in a Total Quality environment, was published in March 1989.

John Carlisle Partnerships is the leading provider of partnership launching workshops in Britain today.

5

A strategy for nurturing a culture of continuous improvement

[a]T. G. Wheeler - [b]R. W. WELLS
[a]Director, [b]Manager T.Q. and Systems Development
B.S.S.P. Coated Products, Shotton Works, Deeside, Clwyd. U.K.

INTRODUCTION

Changing the culture of an organisation is like turning an oil tanker around. You can't do it in ten minutes. The case study that follows illustrates B.S.S.P. Coated Products attempt to "turn the oil tanker around" to develop a culture of continuous improvement which will be better equipped to meet the demands of today's customers in today's market. How long will this take? There is no absolute end point, only targets, measures and milestones to achieve along the way.

PROGRAMME

By July of 1993 British Steel Strip Products (B.S.S.P.) Coated Products had completed its initial programme of Total Quality Performance (T.Q.P.) awareness workshops.

Over 2000 employees had been indoctrinated into the principles and philosophy of Total Quality and some customers and suppliers had also attended the workshops. During the eighteen months that it took to do this, in excess of a hundred Quality Improvement Teams had introduced new ideas which generated well over £5 million of savings for the business. A management structure to support the programme was well established and in good working order with the Director of Coated Products chairing the Steering Group of Works Managers:

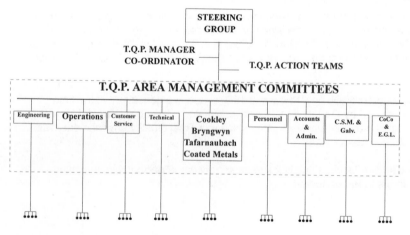

QUALITY IMPROVEMENT TEAMS

Figure 1. Management Structure to Support T.Q.P.

Many other changes which had emanated from the T.Q. programme had, by this time, also taken shape and were in place, e.g. Communication Policy, but despite the obvious success and strong mechanisms firmly established, it was recognised that culture change, the attitude of mind that determines "the way we do things around here" would take more than had already been done if "real" continuous improvement was to become daily business and part of every day life.

To produce a strategy for Total Quality and move forward and develop, the Works Management Committee of Coated Products spent a weekend to discuss the time honoured process of questioning: "Where are we now?", "Where do we want to be?" and "How do we get there?".

During this process there was an awareness of our own research that told us that the main pit fall in implementing a total quality philosophy is the lack of organisational speed in managing change. Amongst the causes of this lack of response are:

(i) the absence of an internally consistent and focused manufacturing strategy,
(ii) conflicting objectives within the functionally oriented organisation,
(iii)personnel blindly influenced by old ideas.

Conversely, successful T.Q. programmes also had certain common characteristics:

(i) an emphasis on tangible results and performance measurement,
(ii) an integrated programme which orchestrated all initiatives,
(iii)a clear, demonstrable commitment from top management.

There are many issues that impact on the culture of the organisation and affect "the way we do things around here". In the case of B.S.S.P. Coated Products, the W.M.C. discussed the ones considered to have the greatest influence :

Customer satisfaction
Team Oriented Programme of Improved Customer Service (Team working)
Communications
Cross Functional Teamwork
Management Style and Values
Employee Satisfaction
Education and Training
Strategic Goals and Vision
Empowerment

The last issue on the list, "Empowerment", is a much abused, misused and misunderstood concept. It means different things to different people. For B.S.S.P.
it's about training and developing people to reach their full potential, accepting responsibility for the quality of their own work, which is a reflection of their ability, confidence, and competence.

A clear vision for the business, easily understood by everyone, had to be established. Hard objectives against which the organisation could measure itself needed to be developed. The PA Improvement Grid* was used as a mechanism to facilitate the "where are we now?. Where do we want to be? How do we get there?" and pick out precise objectives to determine when the goals were reached. Examples of these objectives are :

Every department can measure its operations based on internal and external customers requirements and target improvements.
All employees have been trained in problem solving/quality improvement.
Annual appraisals include performance against the Vision, Mission and implementation of Total Quality.
All employees understand the concept of variability and the need to control and reduce it.

Five works manager led teams were given the task of providing a framework for the organisation to move forward to achieve these objectives, using five key themes as the focus:

Customer awareness
Process simplification
Values and Beliefs
Rewards and recognition
Education and training

CUSTOMER AWARENESS
"The only thing that matters is how good your customers think you are.
Its unfair. Its unreasonable. But it is a fact". So said Clive James, the C.E.O. of Milliken in accepting the European quality award in 1993.
  The team took this to heart and developed a questionnaire which was completed by customers via a lap top computer. Responses on disk were fed into a central database for analysis. Delivery to time came out as the number one priority for customers which B.S.S.P. Coated Products then took as one of its critical success factors.

  Also, small teams of people, multi function/multi status, have been formed to visit customers and gather information about them to raise the general awareness level of all employees through a variety of communication media back at the work place.

PROCESS UNDERSTANDING
  Techniques such as process mapping, deployment mapping and benchmarking were adopted and adapted to suit requirements and came into there own in analysing the Key Business Processes (KBP) Order to Cash and Procurement of Materials to Distribution (Supply chain management), two processes which have great influence over Delivery to Time.

  Nineteen quality improvement teams were set up to pick up the recommendations of the high level team, who became coaches to the new teams. £1½ million pounds was the estimated savings that this work generated.
  The works manager led team developed a process for benchmaking based on the experience of other companies and enabled an exercise to be carried out examining the storage and control of stock.

*PA Consulting Group   123 Buckingham Palace Road, London.

VALUES AND BELIEFS

An outside facilitator from the Industrial Society conducted discussion groups amongst a variety of employees from a horizontal and vertical slice through the organisation including the Works Management Committee. A report was widely published outlining the values and beliefs people felt were appropriate to a Total Quality company. There were no real surprises, the attributes of "fair, honest, trustworthy, etc....." being what would be expected from any "good" employee, but it was a worthwhile exercise in that it established that there was no difference in the perception of managers or shopfloor.

The Works Management Committee also took part in a team building process, again facilitated externally, and the actions from that exercise were policed internally over eighteen months.

Also, to monitor the perceived change in management style and organisational change, two exercises are carried out annually, surveying around 10% of employees:

Management Style - employees are asked to rate their manager against the following criteria, a clear definition being given for each:

Commitment
Leadership
Ownership
Teamwork
Right First Time
Action On Quality
Motivation
Involvement
Prevention
Awareness of Customer/Supplier Requirements

Characteristics of a Quality Company - the same sample of employees rate the whole organisation against these criteria :

Emphasis on integrity
Belief in the company
Welcomes new ideas
Teamwork
Clear standards
Planned development
Good supplier relationships
Customer first/meet customer requirements first time
Quality before quantity
Good leadership
Investment in people

Year on year the perception of employees, in general, is that movement in all areas has been positive.

Regular employee surveys monitoring the effectiveness of communications direct efforts and resource to areas of perceived weakness.

REWARD AND RECOGNITION

The team examined the effectiveness of the suggestion scheme and, indeed, if a suggestion scheme was still appropriate in a Total Quality culture. It was decided that, in an old industry with old traditions, it would be too big a step to disband the scheme. The effort, therefore, went into improving the administration and encouraging better use of it. The effort has proved successful in that the number of suggestions has doubled, but the target of one per employee per year (average) is yet to be achieved.

Presentations have been held to give further recognition of employee involvement in continuous improvement, both as a result of suggestions and success in academic achievements.

Quality improvement teams regularly present their work to the Director and Works Managers as further recognition and encouragement.

EDUCATION AND TRAINING

The foregoing, plus other initiatives such as TOPICS (team oriented programme for improved customer service) in particular, is underpinned by employee education. Focused training, delivered as and when required, is fundamental to quality improvement. The problem solving process and the quality improvement process have been the subject of workshops facilitated internally. Teams have been coached in tools and techniques such as process mapping, S.P.C., design of experiments, etc., as and when appropriate. The education and training budget for the year 1995/96 in B.S.S.P. Coated Products was £6 million and an average of twenty four days per person per year has been delivered.

In recognition of the quality and quantity and education, the Training and Enterprise Council awarded Coated Products the Investor in People Standard at the beginning of 1996.

TEAMWORKING PROGRAMME

TOPICS has been referred to several times already, running in parallel with the other initiatives under the umbrella of Total Quality, and a brief outline follows:

FIVE SHIFT TEAMS

Five integrated manufacturing shift teams involving around 1,000 employees in the main Shotton production units, are being developed from Key Tasks Analysis work. This is a collaborative effort between management, trade union representatives and process, engineering and technical employees.

All production employees were asked to apply for team positions and members were selected from people already employed in existing production areas, plus others with appropriate specialist skills. An agreed selection process was followed, shown in Figure 2 which involved occupational testing, numeracy, verbal and mechanical reasoning, as well as face to face interviews.

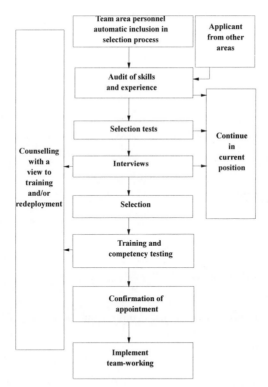

Figure 2 TOPICS selection process

Through this process, team composition is a blend of people who were previously regarded as specialists in their own right, such as time served craftsmen, technical staff and quality control experts alongside experienced production operators.

This has resulted in true multi-skilled teams with a capability to cope with most contingencies, although further training and coaching is an essential and dynamic supporting process. Initially, teams follow an intensive programme averaging 13 weeks over one year, 10 weeks of which is classroom-based off-the-job.

For example, training for Team One - the first of the five to become operational in August 1995 - was delivered as follows:

- Phase one: core science, engineering and chemistry.
- Phase two: plant-based training averaging five hours a week over a two-to-four week period.
- Phase three: plant process technology training.

The training programme relates back to new skill profiles developed from the Key Task Analysis for each team position and the development of the team model in Figure 3.

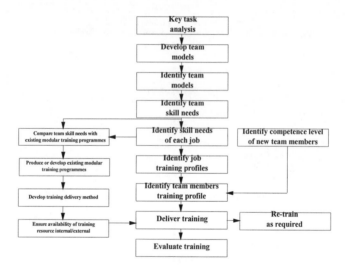

Figure 3 TOPICS training activity model

Training modules are also being examined in order to link them to the UK's National Vocational Qualifications structure.

The team grading structure has been simplified into a shift manager supervising working section leaders and operatives in three grades, all of whom have the support of day managers and specialists from disciplines such as engineering and technical, as shown in Figure 4.

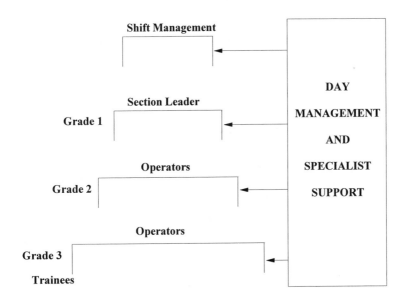

Figure 4 Team structure

Team membership and subsequent promotion is based on competence rather than length of service, as was the historical position.

Continuous learning by team members in their own time is recognised as an integral part of the training process and can lead to financial reward. It certainly places individuals in a favourable position with regard to promotional prospects.

Over time, specialist support is expected to be required less as teams grow in experience and confidence following the self-sufficiency model in Figure 5.

Fig 5. TOPICS shift team skill development

For this to be achieved, training continues to be high on the agenda to enable the full benefits of team-working to be realised.

Also, section leaders are given a week's off-the-job training on the appropriate management skills to help them deal with issues such as individual and group briefings, creating reports, solving problems, improving quality and understanding team dynamics.

TEAM-BUILDING

INDIVIDUAL PERFORMANCE APPRAISAL

QUALITY IMPROVEMENT PROCESS

LEADERSHIP/ TEAM TRAINING

PROBLEM SOLVING PROCESS

REGULAR BRIEFINGS

NEWSLETTERS/ FACTSHEETS

UNIT PERFORMANCE REVIEWS

Figure 6 Ensuring team leaders are prepared

Now, there is a good understanding at all levels of what the Business and Coated Products Works is trying to achieve.

Great emphasis is placed on ensuring that the Business, Works and departmental objectives are aligned and that all employees understand them.

Team-working through the TOPICS programme is just one approach to achieving them, albeit involving major change.

Raising customer awareness, examining reward and recognition and articulating the values and beliefs of a quality organisation - backed by focused training - are playing their part in taking the business towards its vision of becoming the preferred supplier of coated steel products.

6

T I Europe - "Strategies for Excellence"

D. Antcliffe
Texas Instruments Ltd
800 Pavillion Drive, Northampton Business Park, Northampton,
NN4 7YL. Tel +44 (0) 1604 663045, Fax +44 (0) 1604 663047

Abstract

Texas Instruments Europe adopted the EFQM business excellence model in 1993, and in the same year its entire European operations underwent a Self assessment to the model's criteria. The company applied for the European Quality Award for the first time in 1994 and achieved finalist status. In 1995, it was named winner of the European Quality Award.

BACKGROUND

Texas Instruments is a high-technology company with manufacturing operations in 18 countries and marketing or engineering services in more than 30 countries.

Our products and services include semiconductors; defense electronics systems; software productivity tools; printers, notebook computers and consumer electronic products; custom engineering and manufacturing services, electrical controls and metallurgical materials.

Each of these businesses is also represented in Europe. We've been a part of the European economy for nearly 40 years, and were the first US semiconductor company to manufacture in Europe. Today, TI operates in 16 countries in Europe and has more than 5000 employees

- TI Revenues for 1994 topped a record $10Billion.
- In Europe our Revenues rose to nearly $2Billion.

1994 was clearly our best year in history. Revenues and profits hit record levels, and all of our main lines of business showed strong progress toward their strategic goals.

It's clear that 1994 will be remembered at TI Europe for much more than financial results. We made real progress in teamwork, quality, customer satisfaction, and cost reduction.

Like other companies, we have been faced with a number of challenges and opportunities. Technology leadership has carried us far in the last few decades. But our customers and markets are changing and we know that winning in the marketplace requires a lot more than technology innovation.

EFQM ADOPTION

We began a strong focus on quality in the early 80's with Dr Juran, Crosby and other concepts. It has developed over time and Total Quality has permeated all our organisations. Our quality journey took a major step forward in 1993 when we adopted the EFQM model for TI Europe.

Despite much good progress on TQ on a site basis, the building of a new, stronger, more competitive European Business Structure meant we needed a harmonised approach with a common framework and language. We needed to accelerate our rate of improvement.

On 18 June 1993, in a meeting we have named **L'Accord de Paris**, all TI Europe businesses and support function managers made a collective commitment to business excellence, and the willingness of management to dedicate time and resources to it.

This was a commitment to evaluate and raise our performance across **all** organisations, using the EFQM model for Self-Assessment and Award application.

Unlike past programs that had a country by country approach - we made a decision to apply the EFQM criteria to the entire region, making it a single, common framework for all of our quality initiatives. It would become our tool to bring the organisation back to competitiveness. The various diverse quality initiatives could come together under this single common EFQM framework.

A comprehensive communications package with the objective to create awareness, understanding, acceptance and active participation of the organisation at all levels was developed.

It included:

- Action Logo and Slogan
- Letter from the President
- Special EFQM Newsletter; 8 issues to date
- Bulletin boards
- Awareness booklets
- Department meeting foil presentation
- Badge stickers

All of that translated into 6 languages, and together with this, we produced a 76 page score-book on the EFQM programme and the criteria to help with Self-Assessment.

The package was created, designed, translated, produced in two months, and shipped to 30 different organisations and over 6000 people across TI Europe.

SELF-ASSESSMENT

In our first year with EFQM, all 31 business groups and support organisations in TI Europe completed self-assessment and scoring against the 9 excellence criteria. This involved at least 3 days of solid management commitment, all day meetings, going through each of the 76 pages of the score-book we had prepared, one by one. For TI Europe, that meant more than 7000 hours of management dedication and 2500 pages of score book.

All Business and Support organisations of TI Europe completed Self-Assessment against the EFQM criteria and sub-categories recording strengths and areas for improvement, loading their Self-Assessment scores to a secure database. Each organisation has prioritised its areas for improvement into **Excellence Gaps** based on points lost and business relevance.

Improvement action plans for each prioritised gap have been defined and are being executed through Policy Deployment.

In summary, this showed us major changes were needed in our processes and structure - in particular, the need to meet corporate profit goals and to focus on Europe-Wide business units with less emphasis on a country infrastructure.

TI Europe had performed unsatisfactorily for several years. Our market and customer requirements were changing and we needed to quickly adapt. We had a high cost structure with multiple layers, which greatly limited our flexibility.

The EFQM methodology gave us the tool we needed to fully evaluate our organisation and processes and launch a major restructuring plan across Europe.

Key elements of the plan were to focus sales and marketing functions closer to the customer; concentrate on our core competencies and create a pan-European structure.

Today we have streamlined organisation with business centers strategically placed to serve the whole continent, but with local marketing and sales organisations that ensure strong technical support to our customers.

Along with the re-engineering of our businesses and support organisations, we also re-designed our management structure. The new European Strategic Leadership Team operates on the basis of 8 Quality Steering Teams, along with the managers of our business and support functions.

This team is based on the EFQM categories and ensures a clearly focused, quality-driven approach to business excellence across the different organisations and countries in Europe.

RESULTS

We are seeing the results of our commitment to excellence through EFQM:

- We have increased revenues, sales and market shares.
- We have reduced overhead costs and substantially improved our profitability.
- We have a new semiconductor design win initiative that continues to gain momentum.
- Our manufacturing operations are making significant gains in productivity, cycle time and yield improvements, and we are making major investments in expanding and upgrading our manufacturing plants to better meet customer requirements.

And our customers are noticing the difference. The results of our 1995 Customer Satisfaction and Expectations Survey shows the % of **Very Satisfied** and **Satisfied** Customers rose from 71.8% in 1994 to 79.4% in 1995. We are working on raising that level quite a bit further.

This year, TI Europe received the Vendor of the Year award from Dataquest, a leading market research company. We're seeing our entire organisation rally around a single cause: Total Customer Satisfaction. And we're using EFQM as the tool for continuous improvement.

EFQM is now the key process behind our quest for business excellence and the umbrella for all our quality efforts. The EFQM methodology fits well with our company-wide business excellence process, built on 3 main concepts: Customer-Focus, Continuous Improvement and People Involvement. Implementation is through an annual improvement process, which for Europe is self assessment and the filing of an application, using the EFQM model. Policy

Deployment, and the use of both internal and external stretch goals are amongst the tools we use in working to close our excellence gaps.

In addition, strengths from our Self-Assessments are being loaded to a central Lotus Notes Database and shared a best practices with our TI Colleagues around the world.

BENEFITS

In our case, the EFQM initiative has given us:
- A common language
- A Roadmap for unification and synergy
- A common purpose and direction
- Shared objectives
- A framework for all our quality initiatives
- Comparable business processes
- Defined measurements or metrics
- A base for continuous improvement, and
- A tangible chance to achieve Business Excellence

Figures in Appendix 1 show our road to Business Excellence in order to meet the EFQM challenge.

AUTHOR

Dave Antcliffe, Business Process Re-Engineering Manager TI Europe tells the story of TI Europe's EFQM programme; why it was adopted, how it was executed and the benefits that the organisation has gained from it. He also describes the annual improvement process used by TI Europe on a pan-European basis, integrating EFQM as a tool to define priorities and provide a common language across borders, cultures and businesses.

The Need for Change

- **Business Excellence**

Growth

- **Sustained Profitability**

- **Satisfied Customers**

RADICAL CHANGE

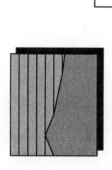

- Changing Marketplace

- Demanding Customers

- Tough Competition

- Unsatisfactory Performance

EFQM - Focusing Quality Efforts

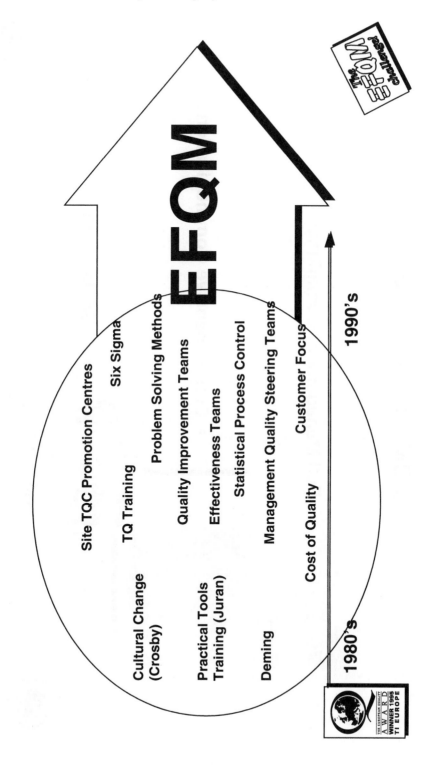

EFQM - Making It Work

- **Full Management Commitment**

- **Comprehensive Communications**

- **Expertise in Process and Criteria**

EFQM - External Process
Applying for the European Quality Award

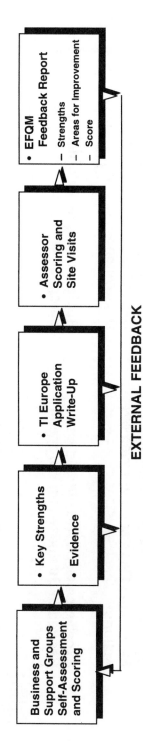

- Business and Support Groups Self-Assessment and Scoring

- Key Strengths
- Evidence

- TI Europe Application Write-Up

- Assessor Scoring and Site Visits

- EFQM Feedback Report
  - Strengths
  - Areas for Improvement
  - Score

EXTERNAL FEEDBACK

Reasons for Applying

- **External Perspective**
  - Are We Doing the Right Things?
  - Objective Assessment and Feedback From Outside
  - Benchmarks

- **Confirms or Uncovers Excellence Gaps**

- **Accelerates Rate of Learning, Deployment and Improvement**

- **Develops Teamwork, Involvement, Common Goal and Winning Spirit**

- **Provides a Measure of Improvement**

EFQM - Internal Process
Self-Assessment and Improvement

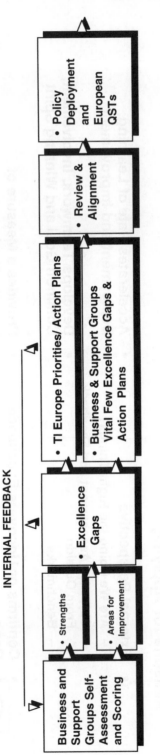

INTERNAL FEEDBACK

Business and Support Groups Self-Assessment and Scoring
• Strengths
• Areas for Improvement

• Excellence Gaps

• TI Europe Priorities/ Action Plans

• Business & Support Groups Vital Few Excellence Gaps & Action Plans

• Review & Alignment

• Policy Deployment and European QSTs

• Cycle of Assessment, Defining Excellence Gaps and Improvement Actions

• Business Priorities Aligned and Cascaded Through Policy Deployment

• Excellence Gaps Are Filtered and Ranked at Business and European Level

• Regional Enabler Priorities Driven by European QSTs

TI Business Excellence Process

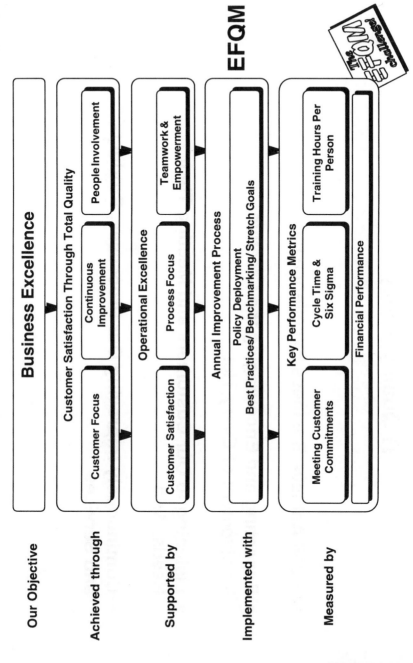

Our Objective — Business Excellence

Achieved through — Customer Satisfaction Through Total Quality
- Customer Focus
- Continuous Improvement
- People Involvement

Supported by — Operational Excellence
- Customer Satisfaction
- Process Focus
- Teamwork & Empowerment

Implemented with — Annual Improvement Process
- Policy Deployment
- Best Practices/ Benchmarking/ Stretch Goals

Measured by — Key Performance Metrics
- Meeting Customer Commitments
- Cycle Time & Six Sigma
- Training Hours Per Person
- Financial Performance

EFQM

The EFQM challenge

TI Quality Policy

We Will Achieve Business Excellence by:

- Expecting and Encouraging the Creative Involvement of Every TIer,

- Listening to Our Customers and Meeting Their Needs, And

- Continuously Improving Our Processes, Products and Services

7

Doing quality from the middle: the Sheffield experience

D. Gilks, J. Grogan, D. Miller, A. Nash, D. Patmore, A. Tomes
Managers and internal consultants
Sheffield City Council, Town Hall, Sheffield, S1 2HH
Telephone: 0114 273 6328   Fax: 0114 273 6657
E-mail: p.services@sc001.sheffield-city.gov.uk

Abstract
The paper gives an account of how the present position of Sheffield City Council has been reached in trying to improve the quality of service to its citizens. It outlines the training initiatives that have enable it to reach that position and details the impact of these initiatives in one particular department.

Keywords
Sheffield City Council, Agenda for Change, service user focus, process improvement, employee involvement, leadership, Investor in People, national standards, NVQ.

---

1.   INTRODUCTION AND BACKGROUND

1.1   Historical Background

In the autumn of 1993 Sheffield City Council signalled its plunge into the world of quality in the document *Agenda for Change*. This was prepared by the organisation's Chief Executive Officer and proposed that a cultural change was to be sought across the organisation through a number of different initiatives. It was intended that the result of this would be a greatly enhanced quality of service to Sheffield's citizens and Council Tax payers.

To support the CEO and her management team, a 'Service Quality Sub-group' was formed whose purpose was to pursue initiatives that would encourage the understanding and application of quality philosophies and systems. In the autumn of 1994, the *Agenda for Change* programme was bolstered by the recruitment of two dedicated project officers whose task was to provide, support and monitor change initiatives.

In late 1995, following further progress, the corporate management team of the Council, meeting from time to time in 'quality mode', took on the role previously carried out by the Service Quality Sub-group.

A 'Best Practice Forum', made up of quality practitioners, managers with a specific quality remit and corporate officers concerned with quality, was also formed to learn from one another and from external applications of quality principles.

A guiding principle behind this initiative was the relationship between quality systems and productive cultures. Experience indicates that this holds good, but that in a large bureaucracy it is the sub-cultures which change through quality work rather than the corporate culture[1].

The following analysis and description are designed to form the basis of comparative discussion with other local authorities and public sector organisations concerning the contrast between the theory of total quality implementation and the actual reality.

1.2   *Sectionalisation*

Most quality textbooks at the beginning of the 1990s advocated the implementation of quality through a series of top-down, cascading teams, whose members swung into action following education in quality theory and practice[2,3].   This approach, strongly propounded by Deming, presupposed a fairly homogeneous and culturally uniform organisation.

In Sheffield it quickly became apparent that this approach held little attraction for the organisation. Like many large bureaucracies, the City Council is divided into a number of large groupings, each of which fiercely, if not always consciously, defends its own traditions and ways of working. These differences are reflected in the behaviour of the leaders of each group, who make up the authority's top management team.

For these reasons it soon became obvious that a uniform approach would not be supported and that even the promotion of quality at a senior management level was itself debatable. In the event, external pressures came to bear and drove forward quality primarily as a competitive weapon.

Thus, in the social services area some form of quality improvement was required to cope with increasing central government assessment and the inspection of services. Clear-sighted leadership resulted in a coherent and consistent organisational culture that developed quality in an understated but nonetheless appropriate and effective way, albeit with few links to other departments.

In the area of housing, the threat of compulsory competitive tendering overcame a highly sceptical leadership. It resulted in the installation of an effective infrastructure to turn around threatened areas through careful analysis and improvement programmes driven by wholesale training.

Finally, in the City Treasury, again with the threat of CCT looming large, the combination of this factor with a highly energised leadership resulted in an extraordinarily strong emphasis being placed on customer relations systems and process improvements.

So, in this large bureaucracy, it is the leaders of the constituent groups that have set both the tone and the pace of improvement. Change programmes have taken on the image of these individuals, their preferences and prejudices. Suspicion and opposition have been broken down in the first instance by some form of external threat. Once change is observed other areas tend to follow suit, although occasionally as a result of the 'me too' syndrome, and in a superficial manner.

1.3   No Common Starting Point

In Sheffield it gradually became apparent that, apart from the presence or absence of leadership knowledge, one of the key issues was 'from where do we start?'. To help overcome this the Council developed a simple process of assessment based on the work of Paul Goodstadt in Bedfordshire[4]. However, having assessed themselves, many areas had difficulties with that old problem area: action.

It is clear that the traditional power structure within the organisation, that is the hierarchy of members - chief officer - staff, has had very little influence on moving sections forward. This in turn reflects two factors: first, the lack of involvement of elected members (the equivalent, in this case, of non-executive directors) as a result of both limited interest and the absence of any training in quality thinking; second, the limited real influence of the CEO beyond the areas of elected member priority.

Different divisions have entered the quality circle at different points of causation, at different moments in their 'personal history', and at different levels of expertise and capability.

We have yet to find the solution to the 'non-starters', but the feeling lingers that the answer revolves around the presence of the two factors already touched on: leadership and knowledge.

1.4   Leadership

As with the 'cascade' model of implementation, the textbooks maintain that committed leadership is essential for the successful implementation of quality practice[5,6,7]. The absence of this in the group culture, and the predominance of sectional cultures, has allowed a varied set of sub-cultures to develop, each of which is determined to 'do its own thing'. Diversity has become a way of life. It is leadership at this level that has resulted in change.

The intermittent corporate focus upon quality has been further emphasised by a continuing preoccupation with structural change, allied to persistent financial crises. The consequence of the relationship between these two factors, acting at times like demonic 'gemini', is a climate of uncertainty which has never allowed the validity of quality systems to gain a firm foothold, although change as understood by 'quality' is actually what is required to achieve true organisational development.

The persistent uncertainty and anxiety stimulated by these factors have forced quality down the agenda and often out of sight in some areas. Change in these circumstances is seen as being delivered through structures rather than behaviour. This runs against quality theory and practice.

1.5   Knowledge

The experience in Sheffield has definitely indicated that the will to change, added to the possible desire to acquire knowledge, can achieve powerful and positive outcomes. These are illustrated later in this paper.

Furthermore the thirst for knowledge and change can be acute in the middle strata of the organisation, where considerable levels of motivation, and impact may be attained. Supportive and consistent leadership in such circumstances can unleash hither-to unsuspected sources of energy.

However, at the same time initial reluctance and the difficulties around having the time and intellectual 'space' to absorb new ideas to the point whereby they can be translated into action appear to render true change both difficult and unlikely.

Where those at the very top of an organisation have strongly committed to change, for instance in the London Borough of Brent, the results are impressive if not without human cost.

Again our experience has been that there exists a broader openness to learning and to change in the middle levels of the organisation as well as a willingness to experiment with training in a wide variety of forms and topics. This often results in the acquisition of the knowledge and self-confidence necessary to commence the drive to change.

2.   TRAINING IN QUALITY IN THE COUNCIL

2.1   *The Beginning*

The first thing to say is that, initially at least, we did not have a corporate strategy for tackling training in quality or continuous improvement. It really began in 1993 when, as part of a pilot management training programme based on MCI management standards, two internal trainers ran a day workshop on the basics of *Managing Quality*.

At that time, the Council had a single training officer ploughing a lonely furrow trying to introduce national standards of competence and National Vocational Qualifications; one or two departments, dealing directly with external, quality-conscious organisations, were exploring or working for BS 5750/ISO 9000 accreditation; one or two others were considering or had committed to the achievement of the *Investor in People* award.

2.2   *What we have done*

Early in 1994, in an endeavour to improve the competence of managers, the Council bought into a skills-based training programme from *Times Mirror Training Europe* (formerly *Zenger Miller*). Two unique features of the training that made an immediate impact were its foundation on a clear, simple value system - the Basic Principles - and the consistency of its learning objectives with its methodology: skills are improved through structured skills practice rather than instruction or exhortation.

The Basic Principles

1   Focus on the issue, situation or behaviour, not on the person.

2   Maintain the self-confidence and self-esteem of others.

3   Maintain constructive relationships with customers, suppliers and colleagues.

4   Take the initiative to make things better.

5   Lead by example

During 1993 the City Council launched a major programme of empowerment under the banner *Agenda for Change*. Under headings of Service User (Customer) Focus, Process Improvement, Employee Involvement and Leadership, staff and departments have been challenged to make a significant shift in the whole approach of the Council. Based on work pioneered by Paul Goodstadt in Bedfordshire, the Leader of the Council and the Chief Executive now conduct a *Quality Health Check* of each area of activity every six months against the headings given above.

This organisational development has created the opportunity for the various disparate activities mentioned earlier to begin to be co-ordinated and taken on further.

Achievement of *Investors in People* is now a corporate commitment rather than a piecemeal patchwork of the more enlightened departments. It is closely linked with work being done on the rights and responsibilities of staff and provides the basis on which the Council can honour its commitments under a recent national agreement about the training and development of staff and ensure a "quality" workforce.

Measurement against standards of personal competence has moved towards the centre of human resource development in the Council and is linked to both the *Investor in People* commitment and an increasing emphasis on performance management as a tool for continuous improvement.

Although some departments are still seeking quality assured status for commercial reasons, the quality thinking within the authority is more and more based on the European Foundation for Quality Management model.

The specific training responses to these developments have been:

*   consultancy work with senior managers to foster an understanding of quality and continuous improvement and the role they play in "bottom line" performance;

*   a corporate continuous improvement programme designed to help individual activity managers to assess the issues in their area of responsibility and to plan for change;

*   the training of over a hundred managers as facilitators for the *Times Mirror Training Europe* materials (an effective quadrupling of the Council's training resource).

The impetus for this last point came from the discovery that TMTE provided skills training materials in the quality/continuous improvement area. These skills, ranging from awareness of the roles of the individual and the leader in quality programmes to analysing work processes and problem-solving techniques, have now been widely used in situations as varied as improving existing commercial viability, internal restructuring and as the basis for a successful bid under a compulsory competitive tendering regime.

All of this is very much the start of a process that is still being developed "on the hoof" rather than being a carefully planned strategic initiative. It is slowly being adopted, however, by the strategic movers and shakers with the formation of a corporate Best Practice Forum as a sub-group of the corporate management team and is supported by an informal "quality practitioners' group" that offers an arena for sharing information, grief and successes as quality is introduced from the middle of the organisation.

3.   THE CITY TREASURY: A CASE STUDY

A nightmare scenario for any business is to have its mistakes highlighted in court by its customers. Yet this is the prospect routinely faced by local authorities nation-wide. A summary procedure takes 'reluctant' council tax payers to court where a simple error can become a public indictment of the service.

Identifying your customers, clarifying their needs and improving services for them are usually key elements of any quality initiative, but it was clear from the beginning that this approach was going to have to be a little bit different. Even so, all customers, reluctant or not, have a right to efficient processes, accurate recording of information and good customer service. They also have a right not to be taken through the courts as a result of out of date records or clerical errors. This is not to say that these are regular occurrences, but there is always room for improvement.

3.1   *What happened*

Prior to April 1994 some limited quality seminars had been held in City Treasury, mainly for senior managers. In April 1994, delayering of the department's structure, combined with the creation of a quality manager post and the corporate *Agenda for Change* initiatives allowed a real impetus for change to start in the department.

Throughout the summer of 1994, the City Treasurer fronted sessions for all staff where the departmental vision, pledge and mission were devised, together with sectional mission statements which are now on display in all sections of the department. Around this time, the slightly whimsical but memorable acronym TICIT (Treasury Implementation of Continuous Improvement Techniques) was conceived.

TICIT teams were set up to function as quality circles in each functional area. The teams consist of staff drawn from all levels who work on initiatives to improve services. An Image and Marketing Group produced a new logo for the department, did some work on competitor analysis, produced a customer care booklet for every section and also a guide to Treasury services. Further work continues on a booklet on effective writing, on questionnaires and some design work on Council Tax leaflets and financial accounts.

Much time has been spent on trying to improve communications within and outside of the department. A Communications Strategy Group was set up which, amongst other initiatives, has implemented a system whereby all information discussed at Policy Team is relayed to all staff in the department within a week, with facilities for feedback upwards. The suggestion scheme enables staff suggestions for work improvements to be replied to within a week. 'Treasury Notes', the departmental newsletter is issued once a month. ICL have recently helped us with a communications review with 25 recommendations. At a recent away-day for activity managers, all but three recommendations have been approved, with plans in place to implement them.

At each enquiry point customers have access to customer care cards and posters encourage them to complete them to help us to improve the service. In the first year we received 313 completed cards, of which 225 were positive about the service.

In terms of process improvement, RIP (review and improve processes) exercises are carried out in the department. Small teams of people from sections work with a facilitator (a *Times Mirror Training Europe* part-time trainer) to completely dismantle processes and then rebuild them to optimum effectiveness. To date we have conducted thirteen such RIPs and have two more planned.

Two surveys have been sent to staff with a seven month interval to test staff views on TICIT and the training. Although the level of response was not as high as we would have wished, 38/40%, the trends of the results were encouraging.

To support this activity, a 1995 training and development prospectus was prepared called 'A Toolbox of Opportunities'. Four distinct strands of training were outlined: management development, core skills, TICIT training and sectional plans. Voluntary, 360-degree appraisal has been undertaken by many managers. All managers in the department have completed four *Times Mirror Training Europe* quality units: Quality:

The Leadership Role; Leading Quality Problem-solving Sessions; Analysing Work Processes, and Tools and Techniques for Solving Quality Problems. Over forty other staff who are in work improvement groups have also completed four similar TMTE quality units. All departmental staff have attended a two-hour introductory session on quality and have completed two TMTE units. Further training has been provided on other topics and the department has committed itself to achieving *Investor in People* status.

3.2   *The Present and Future*

The British Quality Foundation has recently published a local authority version of the European Quality Foundation Model which it is calling the Business Excellence Model. We have set up teams of staff at all levels to work on each element of the model. Use of the model enables an organisation to self-assess itself in terms of quality, obtain an overall score at a point in time and then set plans in motion to improve continually on the score.

Already we have found the model very beneficial, although the work has only just started. Its great strength is that it will allow us to measure tangibly and to set targets for improvement as well as permitting us to compare ourselves with other similar and diverse industries.

Future initiatives, based on the EFQM model, will enable us not only to measure our performance, but also to publicise our successes by continually assessing, re-evaluating and improving our service to our customers.

4.   IMPLICATIONS

The implications thus far are simple:

*   it is generally external pressure which has stimulated internal moves to a 'quality' agenda;

*   the wide variety of departmental cultures has led to a diverse range of quality improvement initiatives, with many different starting points;

*   continuing corporate preoccupation with structural as opposed to behavioural change, especially when combined with financial pressures, may drive quality down or off the agenda;

*   the real push to quality comes from positive sectional leadership, and structured training which in particular stimulates learning;

*   in these circumstances the effective drive for change is often found within
        the middle of the organisation, particularly among middle management.

5.   REFERENCES

1   Patmore, D. and Tomes, A. (1994) 'Quality: the engine of cultural
        change'. Local Government Policy Making Vol.21 No.2.

2   Walton, M. (1986), the Deming Management Method, New York: Dodd,
        Mead

3   Walton, M. (1991), Deming Management at Work, New York: Perigree
        Books/Putnam

4   Goodstadt, P. (1994), Quality Self-Assessment, Bedfordshire County
        Council

5   Bennis, W. (1983), 'The Art-form of Leadership'. In: Srivastva and
        Associates (1983), eds. 'The Executive Mind', San Francisco, Jossey-
        Bass.

6   Kotter, J.P. and Hesket, J.L. (1992), 'Corporate Culture and
        Performance', New York: Free Press.

7   Schein, E.H. (1985), 'Organisational Culture and Leadership', San
        Francisco, Jossey-Bass.

6.   BIOGRAPHY

David Patmore is Director of Arts and Museums with Sheffield City Council
and chairs the Best Practice Forum. David has a long-standing interest in quality
and recently completed an executive MBA with a dissertation on the relationship
between organisational culture and quality systems.

David Gilks, and **Alan Nash** are senior trainers and internal consultants in the
Council's corporate *Training for Change* team. Both have been involved with
training for quality for some years and are the Council's lead trainers for the
Times Mirror Training Europe programmes referred to in the paper. David is a
Licentiate of the Institute of Quality Assurance.

Jenny Grogan is currently Assistant Director (Quality and Support Services) with Sheffield Works Department, a direct labour organisation. Jenny was formerly the Quality Manager with City Treasury, where she and David Miller were responsible for the programme described in the case study.

David Miller is also a senior trainer and internal consultant with the corporate *Training for Change* team. David was formerly the Training Manager in City Treasury. Currently he is co-leading work to improve the quality of functional managerial skills in the Council.

Dr Anne Tomes is a lecturer in the Management School of the University of Sheffield. She specialises in marketing, operations management and quality and has published widely on all these topics.

FOOTNOTE

The authors would welcome discussions with other organisations forced into unconventional approaches to the implementation of quality/continuous improvement programmes, particularly those who are surviving the experience!

8

Quality deployment in the service sector

Dr J. J. E. Swaffield,
Head Of Corporate Quality, Royal Insurance Life & Pensions,
P.O. Box 30, New Hall Place, Liverpool L69 3HS, England.
0151 239 4592 (Tel) 0151 239 3624 (Fax)

D Graham MA FFA MCIM
Market Development Manager, Royal Insurance Life & Pensions
PO Box 30, New Hall Place, Liverpool L69 3HS
Tel: 0151-239-3808 Fax: 0151-239-3231

P. McBeth MIPD, MIM
Managing Partner, Wood worth McBeth Young Consulting
The World Trade Centre, Exchange Quay, Manchester, M5 3EQ
Tel: 0161-877-6600 Fax: 0161-876-7788

J. Dotchin B.Sc MBA
Centre for Quality and Innovation, Sheffield Hallam University
100 Napier Street, Sheffield, S11 8HD
Tel: 0114-253-3162 Fax: 0114 253 3161

Abstract

Some companies seek to implement Total Quality as a tangible programme of specific actions and events, often to improve customer service. Within Royal Insurance Life & Pensions, the view is that quality must permeate all that we do. The holistic approach is taken. Quality Function Deployment (QFD) has been used for new product development in this setting. Specifying products designed using QFD cannot be done effectively using traditional methods, however. Some criteria for an effective solution, and a framework designed to help produce effective specifications are described. The paper also discusses how QFD can contribute to the resolution of the apparent clash between the creative process of new product development, which requires divergent thinking, and project management, which which seeks convergence.

Keywords

TQM, total quality management, continuous improvement, QFD, Quality Function Deployment, service, product, development, design, specification, Project Management, estimating, risk management.

1. INTRODUCTION

This workshop is based on Royal Insurance, Life and Pensions' recent experiences of using Quality Function Deployment (QFD) concepts and techniques in the development of a new service product. QFD's many strengths have been well publicised and compared to traditional sequential approaches to New Product Development (NPD) these strengths include decreased start up problems, more effective internal communications, better use of market and competitive information and the realisation of significantly better products. Products are better because they are based on a thorough understanding of customers and their needs.

Many of the applications which have been discussed in the literature describe manufacturing situations. A team at Royal have pioneered an approach to developing services in which QFD is a primary tool.

Each of the three contributors to this paper address a distinct aspect with particular relevance to the work. In section two the context is described by summary of Royal's approach to Total Quality Management (TQM). This is followed by an examination of some of the challenges which are faced when attempting to specify service products and a framework, designed to help overcome some of the difficulties which arise, is presented. Finally the scope of QFD to resolve some evident conflicts between the creative processes of NPD and the demands of project planning and control are addressed.

2. THE APPROACH OF ROYAL INSURANCE LIFE & PENSIONS TO TOTAL QUALITY MANAGEMENT

2.1 Royal Insurance Life & Pensions

The company forms part of the world wide Royal Insurance Group which celebrated its 150th anniversary last year. The group employs over 23,000 people in over 60 countries making it one of the largest providers of general and life insurance products in the world.

Royal Insurance Life & Pensions employs over 2,000 and provides a complete range of pensions, investment, protection and mortgage related products through a variety of distribution channels.

2.2 Background

The Trading Environment
Throughout the 1980's, various economic, market and regulatory pressures combined to generate the change imperative:
- well publicised financial services irregularities had caused the public to be extremely suspicious of the sector
- the economy was in a period of recession
- fewer endowment policies were needed due to the reduction in house moves

- customers were becoming more sophisticated and educated in their demands
- the industry significantly tightened its regulatory procedures which produced onerous requirements in a time of declining sales

Strategic Review

To meet the challenge of improving customer service whilst managing down the cost base, the Board undertook a major strategic review in mid 1991, with specific issues to be examined including distribution and products, management style, organisation structure, costs and productivity and future IT direction. The output from the review was a Business Improvement Programme designed to deliver benefits across the wide range of activities subject to the review. One consistent theme running through all the improvement effort was that of Quality of service, of products, of distribution, of sales and of advice to customers.

Mission Statement

The Board decided to adopt a philosophy of Total Quality Management in the autumn of 1992, and the commitment to quality was articulated in the Mission Statement which was issued during the year. It reads:

- The Mission of Royal Life is to satisfy the protection and savings
- needs of our customers, profitably.

- We shall do this through

- Our **TEAM** of well trained, highly motivated staff and sales
- associates, providing
- Courteous, efficient and effective **SERVICE** to all our customers with
- Attractive products offering **VALUE** for money, and
- Superior **PERFORMANCE** for our shareholders and policyholders.

- In short, through the delivery of **QUALITY.**

2.3 Total Quality Approach

Definition of Total Quality

"Total Quality is both a management philosophy and a practical working process for achieving distinctive quality products and services at lowest cost to the company, which 'delight' the customer."

   The principle underpinning this phrase is a recognition that specific, practical changes need to go hand in hand with cultural and behavioral changes. Achieving one without the other would fail to maximise the benefits to customers

Making it Happen

From its inception, the TQM programme has sought to engage the workforce in the process of change and development, by involving staff in improvement initiatives and harnessing their creative and innovative capabilities.

As TQM philosophies and practices cannot become embedded in all parts of a company overnight, two initiatives - Critical Business Processes and 'Brainwaves' - were employed to provide momentum to the TQM programme and accelerate progress towards the required 'critical mass' of continuous improvement activity, and they are worthy of specific mention.

2.4 Critical business processes

In 1993, Business Processes were identified which the General Management team considered to be critical to the achievement of the Mission and corporate goals. In 1994 they were subject to a systematic review and refocusing as part of the Operational Plan review process. Eight of them were created on a cross functional basis, to:
* identify and prioritise improvement opportunities within each process
* sponsor Continuous Improvement Teams to investigate and recommend actions
* implement process changes
* hold post implementation reviews

Their creation recognised the difficulty of realising major process improvements within a vertically aligned functional organisation and was a pragmatic, short term step pending transition to a process based structure.

Each CBP was led by a Single Point Owner within a Steering Group which contained management representatives from every function involved and received guidance and facilitation from a manager from the Quality function.

Each Steering Group chartered Continuous Improvement Teams which involved staff at all levels from relevant functions. Again support from Quality staff was available and, through the use of Quality tools and techniques within the teams, such skills were migrated into the business areas.

2.5 The 'Brainwaves' programme

'Brainwaves' is the name of the programme, launched in September 1993, designed to realise the innovation potential of all staff by involving them in improvement initiatives. The need at that time was to increase the 'critical mass' of people involved in such initiatives. Although the Critical Business Processes had spawned many Continuous Improvement Teams, their infrastructure meant that no more than 10% of the workforce were generating improvement ideas at any one time. The 'Brainwaves' programme, a response to that need, contains 3 distinct strands:

Company Initiatives
These are company wide, mostly behavioural, initiatives - eg. Effective Meetings, Telephone Manner - which are mandatory. Although individually they involve only minor, incremental improvement, collectively they provide a more professional, quality image.

Local Initiatives
Local Initiatives relate to continuous improvement ideas generated at a local level. The main aim of this approach is to make team working and systematic problem solving a way of life within the workplace. Within the first 2 months of 1994, over 800 ideas were generated locally and implemented immediately.

Suggestion Scheme
The scheme gives staff an opportunity to make suggestions outside their normal work area. Cash awards are made and over 2000 ideas have been received since the scheme was launched at the end of 1993.

2.6 Restructuring to a process based organisation

During the first half of 1996 the whole organisation is involved in a complex series of structural changes which, by the Summer, will result in Royal Insurance Life & Pensions being a truly process based company. The Board recognised that the previous functional structure was a serious obstacle to the low cost, high quality company espoused in the Mission Statement; also, that the creation of Critical Business Processes and the 'Brainwaves' programme, whilst of value at the time, were pragmatic ways of mitigating the conflicts inherent in a functional structure, and were incapable of delivering radical change or quantum process improvement.

A high proportion of activity and staff will reside in a series of customer facing, end to end processes, with a small number of compact Corporate Units setting policy and monitoring standards throughout the organisation. In fact Royal's use of Quality Function Deployment, and the way in which the Marketing and Quality functions worked together to develop an emerging technique for the benefit of the Product Management process, is a prime example of the new synergies available by successful management of the Corporate Unit:Process interface. Details of how QFD has been applied to a specific project follow.

3. SPECIFYING SERVICE PRODUCTS USING QFD

3.1 QFD and Services

QFD is a technique designed to support an effective new product development process. This process, like all good processes has inputs, actions and outputs.   The inputs are the organisation's knowledge of their customers and their needs, and the expertise and creativity of its staff. The QFD matrices are designed to facilitate the design process itself. The outputs are the specification of the new product.

No matter how good the design, it will be useless unless it is implemented effectively. And this is where services are liable to run into particular difficulties. Unlike engineering design, where QFD originated, services cannot be specified in terms of weight, power, strength, size or tolerance.

Royal Insurance Life and Pensions has been experimenting with QFD for a little while now, and we have given quite a lot of thought to the problems of specification. To understand this issue more fully, we need to identify why Royal have found their traditional approach to specification is not appropriate.

3.2 The traditional approach

In Royal's business, much of the effort in the 'build' phase has traditionally gone into developing IT systems for the new product. When problems arise with the IT build phase, they can usually be traced to deficiencies in the specification. This results in pressure for ever more comprehensive, more detailed specifications. Although this seems perfectly rational, in practice this is an unrealistic goal, for a number of reasons.

First, it requires design work to be completed before IT can start work in earnest. This precludes any concurrent development and runs totally counter to QFD design philosophy.

Secondly, as the specifications get longer and more comprehensive, it is harder to ensure that they stay consistent. This may be a variant of Heisenberg's Uncertainty Principle - it seems to be impossible for a product to be specified both completely and consistently at the same time.

Thirdly, much practical experience shows that the wording of a carefully thought out specification can be interpreted differently by intelligent people coming to them fresh. It seems that the clear and obvious meaning is not so clear and obvious after all to those with no prior background knowledge.

Finally, and most tellingly, IT professionals have been trying to make this approach work in countless projects round the world - and not just for new product developments - for decades. But if anyone has been able to succeed consistently, Royal has yet to hear of it.

3.3 Requirements for effective specifications

If the traditional way of specifying the product doesn't work, how should we go about it? Our ideal solution should have a number of characteristics:

- It should be true to QFD philosophy. And it should cover all aspects of the product: contractual terms; regular information; ongoing service; promotion and distribution.
- It should facilitate, rather than hinder, concurrent development.
- It should provide only as much detail as will be needed for the build phase, avoiding inconsistencies.
- There should be no scope for ambiguity or misunderstanding.
- It should take a minimum of effort to produce, and to understand, the specifications bearing in mind that they are only a means to an end, and not an end in themselves.

Clearly, this is quite a tall order, and at Royal we do not claim to have found a solution that meets all these requirements. However, we do believe we have developed a framework which will produce a much more effective solution than the traditional approach.

3.4 Towards a better solution

Give the background
The first step Royal has taken is to recognise that if the people building and running the new product or service understand the customer background better, then they will do a better job. We have therefore introduced a customer specification which is cross-referenced to the more traditional product and service specifications. This aims to give the reasons for design decisions to augment the description of what needs to be built.

A secondary benefit of this approach is that it provides an excellent basis for future product improvement activity.

The QFD documentation provides most of the information to develop these specifications. One area for future improvement is to look at how the QFD documentation itself can be adapted to become the required specification.

Communicate better
A second important step is to regard the written specification as no more than evidence of the understanding built up by the members of the design team. This implies that the specifications must be accompanied by teach-ins and workshops to ensure that this understanding is shared with those responsible for building the new product. The design team also have a crucial role both in resolving ambiguities and misunderstandings in the specifications, and in ensuring that the product when built is true to the original design concept and to the customer's requirements.

Don't over-specify
Another hard lesson, but one which fits well with the QFD philosophy, is to avoid making specifications too prescriptive. Of course, the design team have a responsibility to ensure that their design can be implemented effectively. But it is important to concentrate on specifying what is required for a successful product rather than how it should be built.

Being over-prescriptive can cause two types of problem. Just because the design team verified that a particular solution would be satisfactory does not mean that a different one may not be even better. Too much detail can stifle the creativity of the people involved in the implementation.

Conversely, by specifying how a feature should be built, it is easy to lose sight of what you are really trying to achieve. Then, what gets built may meet the specification, while missing the original intention.

Consider the Company structure
Finally, it helps a great deal if the company is structured so that there are clear owners for each element of the new product. Royal is restructuring around customer focused processes, and

this fits well with separate specifications for the product itself, service, promotion and distribution.

It also makes the QFD process much easier to use, as there will be ready-made definitions of the main processes and their key performance indicators. Attention can then focus on how these processes and indicators need to change to accommodate the new product.

3.5 Summary

Finding an effective way of specifying new products is far from easy. However, it is important to give this careful thought, or else all the good design work could well be spoilt by poor implementation.

The QFD design team have a crucial role as well as a keen interest in seeing that this does not happen. They must take this role seriously, and the Company culture must encourage and support them in doing so.

4. THE CREATIVE PROCESS AND PROJECT MANAGEMENT

4.1 Divergence and convergence

The creative process of New Product Development(NPD) needs time and space to be successful. Divergent thinking, where lines of thought go in different directions and where the options they create are kept open until the last moment, can be a fundamental part of this creative process. The length of time required to produce the optimum result is, because of the nature of the process, difficult to estimate.

NPD is a critical part of the life of any customer facing organisation. Project status gives it special focus. But project management is essentially a convergent process ie lines of thought coming together and decisions being made quickly.

4.2 The Clash

There is an apparent clash between the needs of the divergent process of New Product Development and convergence needs of a Project.

What contribution, if any, can Quality Function Deployment make to resolve this apparent clash?

4.3 QFD As Part of the Solution

In reality NPD projects are made up of a combination of deliverables, some of which require divergent thinking and some which are more convergent. QFD supports the early identification of these different deliverables. This helps the Project Manager to target time and resources specifically at the areas where the effort using divergent thinking will be of most benefit, and to reduce the time for the convergent areas, these having been agreed quickly and passed on to other specialisms for their work to commence.

Using a more rigorous approach such as QFD gives the Project Manager greater confidence that the decisions taken and deliverables produced will not be subject to as much rework as under previous methodologies. This means that the Project Manager has more control, and hence more chance of delivering success, than under previous methodologies.

In a situation where time, cost and hence budget are finite, being able to prioritise effort against anticipated benefit is of tremendous advantage to the Project Manager. Having 'the voice of the customer' built in to the QFD process provides a means of prioritising competing work against perceived benefits to the customer. This contributes to a quicker and more confident decision making process, as compared to other methodologies, where 'he/she who shouts loudest' is often the main means of prioritisation. Apparent progress is at the cost of either later rework or failure of the product to meet customer needs.

The problem of estimating for deliverables which use divergent thinking still remains. Reverting to the fundamentals of historical data, scientific formula, standards or intuition does not give much comfort within an immature QFD set up. Intuition remains as the only approach. The highest risk combination associated with intuition is to 'guess' on your own. If intuition has to be used, then as many people as possible must be involved to inform the guess. Having a QFD team together provides an opportunity to use that team to assist with the estimating. Using Risk Management, the Project Manager can attempt to manage the other risks created by the immaturity of the QFD estimating process.

Over time metrics can be established which could be used in formulae based around cells in the QFD matrices, to increase the accuracy of the estimates produced.

4.4 Summary

In a NPD Project, QFD can assist the Project Manager to identify deliverables which need divergent thinking and deliverables which can quickly be closed off and passed to other specialisms for further work. The QFD team itself can be used in the estimating process for those divergent deliverables and Risk Management techniques can be used to minimise the potential effects of other risks associated with the immaturity of the process. Metrics should be built which will enable a more data based estimating process in the future.

5. CONCLUSIONS

In the preceding discussion some aspects of Royal's approach to QFD for the development of new services have been set out. Success of this pilot project has depended, in part, on the background of TQM initiatives in which Royal are engaged.

Preparation for QFD has also been thorough. Three two-day seminars were used to introduce QFD concepts to management and team members. The team's commitment to the project has been maintained at a very high level throughout a nine month period of regular meetings. Independent facilitation was used to guide the process for all this time.

It is still too early to decide objectively about the effectiveness of QFD for Royal. Team members, however, have little doubt that compared to some other new product development programmes the QFD pilot has been able to cope better with the divergent activities of idea generation and communication, has produced more comprehensively considered specifications which are clearly aligned to the satisfaction of customers' needs and has facilitated project management.

6. BIOGRAPHIES

John Swaffield has worked in both the telecommunications and financial services sectors and has extensive management experience in the fields of Engineering Design, Human Resource Planning and Development, Business Strategic Planning and Market Research, as well as managing large line departments. Over the past 10 years, he has held senior management appointments in British Telecom, Eagle Star and Royal Life implementing Total Quality Management as an integral part of business strategy. During this period he has extensively researched the application of TQM to service sector industries - both in the USA and Europe - as well as lecturing and writing on the subject. John holds degrees in management studies and business administration and in 1981 was awarded the MBE for services to industry.

After obtaining a Mathematics degree at Cambridge in 1972, **David Graham** qualified as a Fellow of the Faculty of Actuaries in 1975 and became a Member of the Chartered Institute of Marketing in 1980. Since joining Royal Insurance Life and Pensions in 1981 to design a new range of investment products, he has held a variety of marketing and customer servicing roles. In his current role as Market Development Manager, he is responsible for strategic marketing as well as researching customer needs for new product developments.

Paul McBeth is a specialist in Project Management and has undertaken numerous consulting assignments with a with many internationally recognised organisations. He is the Managing partner of Woodworth McBeth Young where he provides consultancy, education and training in many Management and Quality topics including project management, service quality improvement and quality function deployment.

John Dotchin is a graduate of Leicester University and Bradford University. He worked equally in engineering and services before adopting an academic career in 1990. He has done research and taught at Bradford University, University College Salford and now at Sheffield Hallam University. As a member of the Centre for Quality and Innovation, he is an active teacher on undergraduate, post graduate and post experience courses and conducts research in services management, quality, new product development and teamwork.

9

Onwards and upwards - building on business excellence

T.W.Boon
BT Group Quality
PP: B2005, Westside, London Road, Hemel Hempstead, Herts., HP3 9YF UK
Tel: 01442 295699   Fax: 01442 248363

1 INTRODUCTION

The European Model for Total Quality Management underlies the European Quality Award, organised by the European Foundation for Quality Management (EFQM) - of which BT was a founder member. One of the nine criteria of the model, now widely used for self-assessment by organisations of all types, is named "Impact on Society". In this criteria, self-assessment should "demonstrate the organisation's success in satisfying the needs and expectations of the community at large".

The purpose of this paper to put forward a view on how an organisation, in this case BT, can approach this subject, by building on excellence to satisfy the needs and expectations of the community at large. Or, to put it another way, to move onwards and upwards in the search for excellence.

2 ONWARDS AND UPWARDS - BUILDING ON BUSINESS EXCELLENCE

"make a fitting contribution to the community in which we conduct our business"

These words, taken from the BT Mission statement, are the driving force behind it's corporate community programme and the many activities and services which BT, and the people who work for the organisation, provide for the community at large. In some ways it may be seen as BT's contribution to the "stakeholder society" which has recently become a feature of political debate in the UK The statement itself actually raises very important questions: just what is a "fitting contribution to the community" for a major global corporation? How much resource should actually be devoted? What should the approach be?

Few other industries have a greater impact on society than telecommunications. It is an industry on which other industries depend for their success, and has revolutionised both economic and social life in the twentieth century. BT is the UK's major supplier of telecommunications services and one of the leaders in research and development in the area.   By their very nature, BT's activities have a profound impact on interpersonal communications, on the UK economy, and on the delivery of public services. The efficient and effective running of BT undoubtedly benefits the whole community. Indeed, to do this and provide a good return to it's shareholders, many of them institutions controlling personal investments and pension funds covering a good percentage of the general populace, would to some people appear sufficient in itself as a "fitting contribution to the community".

BT's own view is that it can and should do more. To do so, BT has developed a wide range of community and environmental programmes, costing over £15 million in 1994/95, as well as putting in place the enablers for it's people to make their own individual contribution - either through the provision of facilities or by support. The aim of these programmes is to ensure BT is seen as a responsible and sensitive organisation, in social, economic and environmental terms - and it's success in doing so is a key corporate measure. The programmes operate at corporate, divisional and unit levels, many of them inspired at a local level.

Licence Requirements

It cannot be denied that some of the services BT provides are based on the requirements of the licence under which it operates in the UK. BT's approach to these has not been to reluctantly embrace them and perform the bare minimum to meet the requirement, instead it has welcomed them as an opportunity to fulfil it's social responsibilities by either operating the required service with maximum efficiency or by far exceeding the requirement. Good examples in this area include:

- access to the emergency services (999 and 112), where BT not only provides a highly efficient service, but filter some 11 millions hoax calls (including some 9 million made by children) which would otherwise swamp the emergency services;
- a blind & disabled directory assistance service, where to comply with the licence BT would only have to provide free local area numbers to people unable to use a phonebook - instead BT provides a free national service.

The BT Community Programme

The BT Community Programme helps with both finance and expertise on a wide range of projects. The programme aims to involve the widest range of people possible, rather than concentrate purely on just a few high profile events. To ensure help is targeted effectively, the programme is structured into six key areas:

- Arts - sponsoring innovative dance and visual arts projects, bringing high-quality performances and exhibitions to communities which might otherwise not have the opportunity to enjoy them;
- Environment - backing a wide range of schemes to improve the UK environment, including BT Environment Week and BT Environment City, BT Young Naturalist of the Year and BT/WWF Community Partnership Awards designed to promote good environmental practice;

- People with disabilities - sponsoring sporting and outdoor projects, encouraging easier access to buildings and the countryside, supporting training courses and providing awards for achievements;
- Economic regeneration - supporting schemes which improve inner-city areas, which offer employment training for disadvantaged groups, which provide workshops and advice for start-up businesses;
- People in need - tackling major social themes such as homelessness, medical research, alcohol and drug addiction, caring for dependants;
- Education- offering communications services to schools (most recently Campus World linking schools from around the world), helping with teacher training (over 200 industry experience placements annually), and work experience for students (since 1986 over 30 000 placements).

In addition, a number of activities are undertaken which do not fall immediately under the auspices of the community programme, including the work of the BT Action for the Disabled Customers unit.

Divisional and Unit Initiatives
Programmes in support of the community are not restricted to the corporate level. BT's Divisions and smaller Units undertake their own activities, examples include:

- The "roots and wings" initiative, providing mentors for inner-city school students;
- The provision of telephone boxes in areas which are not commercially viable - over 7 000 of these sites exist but are retained as part of BT's commitment to the community;
- Provision of the Malicious Calls Bureau at a cost of over £10 million, and £3.7 million annually, to help the victims of these calls. In 1994 the service traced 2 661 offences leading to prosecution or police caution.

Support and Facilities for Individuals
Many thousands of BT's people are involved in an enormous range of charitable activities and fund-raising activities of their own. In many cases the money raised is topped up by the company through the BT Community Challenge scheme which recognises and rewards individual employee achievements in the six key areas of the community programme. Another example of support is the Give As You Earn (GAYE) scheme, actively promoted by BT and which has one of the highest percentage memberships of any company. This matches employee payroll contributions pound for pound and to date the total (after the match) has reached a total of nearly £8 million, currently contributing some £1 million annually to charities. Other enablers include support for over 1 000 BT employees who are school or college governors, plus Justices of the Peace etc. including special arrangements for time off to pursue their duties. BT also encourages it's people to become involved in corporate initiatives, such as the BT Swimathon - which in 1995 involved over 43 000 swimmers and raised over £1.5 million pounds for such charities as the British Heart Foundation and the British Sports Association for the Disabled.

Self-Interest or Altruism?

How much of this activity is driven by self-interest? It cannot be denied that a positive public image is (at least indirectly) beneficial to any organisation, nor can it be denied that it makes good business sense - BT's business depends considerably on the health of the community. If that health is adversely affected by deprivation, crime, vandalism, racial tension, inner-city decay, homelessness and pollution, so too is BT's own business health. Opportunities are reduced, problems increase, costs rise. Yet BT does not forget that it's people, from the boardroom down, are also members of the community, with their own desire to live in a healthy and desirable environment, who on their own initiative are involved with both local and national activities that help everyone to live in a better world. If BT were to undertake none of these activities it is very doubtful that the business would collapse. Outside of the corporate programme (which contains many elements that are known to relatively few people), there is no defined requirement on any of the Divisions or Units in the business to undertake community activities. Altruism may not be particularly fashionable these days (although it does seem to be making a comeback), but it is still alive and well in BT!

3   WIDENING THE QUESTION

At Total Quality in Action, BT ran an interactive workshop to explore the question of contributing to the community at large on a wider basis. The questions addressed included: Is there a requirement to make a contribution to the community at large? Does this apply to all major organisations (however these may defined)? Does this also apply to medium and small enterprises? If so, to what degree? Is the degree of contribution driven by the type of organisation, whether they are "public" utilities, educational establishments, government organisations, service or manufacturing? Are there any benefits for the organisation in actually doing so? The data gathered will be provided to participants, and forwarded to the EFQM and the British Quality Foundation as input to their reviews of the Total Quality Management model.

4   BIOGRAPHY

Trevor Boon has spent 25 years with BT and it's predecessor, the Post Office. Following a career on the computing side of the business, he was most recently the Total Quality Programme Manager for BT Operator Services, in which role he was responsible for the implementation of Total Quality and the self-assessment process. He was project manager for the Operator Services European Quality Award application in 1995, reaching the short-list of finalists. He is now a Quality Manager in BT's Group Quality Unit, where he is responsible for integrating the activities of Quality professionals across the company, particularly organisational self-assessments.

10

Achieving excellence in small and medium sized enterprises

A. Dodd and M.J.Pupius
Sheffield Excellence
c/o Royal Mail Sheffield
Sheffield S1 1AA, UK

Tel: +44 (0) 114 273 3228, +44 (0) 113 244 7431
E-mail: 100747.3265@compuserve.com, pupiusm@royalmail.co.uk

Abstract

The European Foundation for Quality Management (EFQM) European Quality Award is becoming established as the model for Business Excellence in Europe. This paper explores the opportunities for larger organisations to work in partnership to introduce the European Quality Award model to Small and Medium Sized Enterprises (SMEs). The paper describes Sheffield Excellence, a community quality project funded by the European Regional Development Fund.

Keywords

EFQM, European Quality Award, Total Quality Management, continuous improvement, business excellence, community quality, SMEs

1   INTRODUCTION

This paper outlines an approach to achieving excellence in SMEs through the transfer of knowledge from larger organisations using the EFQM model as a framework. An understanding of the interdependence between the enablers and results areas can be used to demonstrate the opportunities for promoting Total Quality and business excellence principles and practice in the community for the benefit of SMEs, schools and community organisations.

2   BACKGROUND

The Royal Mail has used benchmarking to develop the process for implementing Total Quality throughout the organisation. Extensive benchmarking was carried out in the United States against companies that had won or had been prize winners in the Malcolm Baldrige National Quality award. Benchmarking was also used to develop a strategic framework for promoting Total Quality in the community.

From benchmarking and a survey of available literature it concluded that:

- Total Quality principles can be applied at community level and in virtually any organisation including all types of business, schools and community organisations
- it is relevant for organisations aspiring to become Total Quality organisations to become involved in community-based, quality management activities
- involvement in community activity can be seen as an extension of customer/supplier partnership principles
- leverage can be applied to help organisations such as schools and smaller businesses become better by improving management effectiveness
- inclusion of Total Quality principles in the school curriculum will enhance the awareness of young people prior to entering the world of work
- involvement benefits all partners involved
- whole communities will gain if the organisations within them begin to perform with greater effectiveness

In 1992, the Royal Mail adopted the European Foundation for Quality Management (EFQM) model (Figure 1) of Total Quality and has focused on three areas: leadership, business processes and self-assessment. The model allows for the measures of the performance of an organisation to be considered for its stakeholders: the customer, the employee, the shareholder and the community.

In 1992, the Royal Mail was one of a number of Sheffield organisations which created the Sheffield and South Yorkshire Total Quality Forum. The Forum provided a regular opportunity to receive presentations on Total Quality and to share good practice. From this base a training approach was developed for schools and three Sheffield schools were taken through a training programme to introduce the teachers to Total Quality principles. Further work funded by the European Commission demonstrated that the EFQM model could be applied in an educational environment.

A partnership between Avesta Sheffield and Sheffield University piloted an approach to introduce Total Quality to a group of Small and Medium Sized Enterprises (SMEs).

Two initiatives have been created out of this pilot activity:

- the development of the **Sheffield Centre for School Improvement** which seeks to apply the principles of continuous improvement to schools in terms of curriculum development, school management and sharing good practice
- **Sheffield Excellence,** a project aimed specifically at the introduction of Total Quality principles to SMEs in the city of Sheffield.

3   UNDERSTANDING THE DYNAMICS OF THE EFQM MODEL

The EFQM model is shown in Figure 1. The community, as a stakeholder, is dealt with in the Impact on Society result area of the model. The guidelines for assessment suggest that areas to address include involvement in education and training.

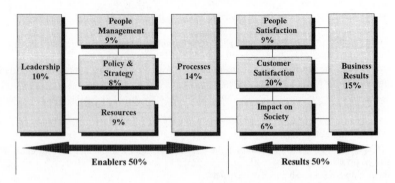

Figure 1   EFQM model

The lines that join each of the boxes in the model are important in that they imply connectivity or interdependence beyond just the clear link between enablers and results. Thus there are links across the model between the Leadership criterion of the model which includes (at sub-criterion 1f) the external promotion of Total Quality through such activities as conferences, seminars and support for the community featured in Impact on Society.

Some other linkages have been realised as a result of the pilot activity and business experience:
- there is a link between Leadership and the external promotion of Total quality and People Management in that managers can become involved in external activity as part of personal development
- such involvement enhances self-esteem and external awareness of customers which links to potential improvements in People Satisfaction and Customer Satisfaction
- support for Impact on Society can be dealt with as a sub-process of the people management process
- whilst difficult to measure in direct terms there is an intuitive link between support for organisations, their performance and our performance. In the case of Royal Mail 'everyone is a customer'. If we help our customers, this will enhance their perception of us, their business performance and ultimately our business performance.

Looking at the positioning of the EFQM model in system level terms Figure 2 shows how the EFQM model is being applied at different levels in the Royal Mail.

In Royal Mail the EFQM model has been developed for self-assessment at business unit level and at unit level. Typically a business unit or division would have a turnover of £500m and 18,000 employees. A unit by contrast could have between 10 and 1000 employees. Some early work has been undertaken to apply the concepts of the model to personal development.

At community level the pilot activity in Sheffield has shown that the EFQM model applies to smaller organisations such as SMEs and schools.

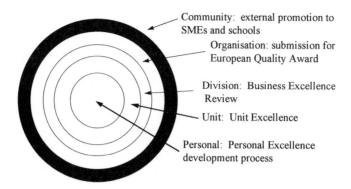

Community: external promotion to SMEs and schools

Organisation: submission for European Quality Award

Division: Business Excellence Review

Unit: Unit Excellence

Personal: Personal Excellence development process

Figure 2 Circles of excellence. The EFQM model can be used for self-assessment at different levels within the system.

4   SHEFFIELD EXCELLENCE

During 1992 a number of people involved in Total Quality Management established the Sheffield and South Yorkshire Total Quality Forum. This group met regularly to hear presentations and share experiences related to Total Quality issues.

This group identified that the introduction of business excellence techniques was, in general, restricted to the larger organisations. Many smaller organisations had received BS5750 or ISO 9000 accreditation, but this had been largely driven by the demands of their large business customers to obtain consistent quality. Few then moved on into a permanent continuous improvement culture.

Two of the reasons for this were:
- a lack of awareness of the principles and techniques of business excellence
- the high cost of learning and applying the techniques

Whilst the Quality Forum members were attempting to address the awareness issue by their very existence, lack of resources made this an impossible task. In early 1995 an opportunity was identified to access European Regional Development Funds (ERDF) to allow both of the above issues to be addressed. This would allow activity in SMEs. If Business Excellence could be introduced into the community via SMEs, community organisations and schools then Sheffield would have taken the first key steps towards becoming a 'quality' city.

The pre-requisite to accessing the ERDF was a strong commitment from the Sheffield business community to providing resources and assistance to ensure the project's success. This commitment was obtained. The support from the partners and the ERDF means that the services and support given to small and medium sized enterprises is heavily subsidised. Typically a recipient organisation pays around 25% of the total cost of the support provided.

The contributing partners are from a wide range of organisations, from large public bodies, large businesses to some smaller businesses who have already committed to the approach.

The central framework of all Sheffield Excellence activity is the EFQM model. There are numerous activities either operating or planned which have the common aim of inculcating a culture of self assessment against the model and continuous improvement.

These activities include:

Awareness Raising
This is fundamentally the marketing activity of Sheffield Excellence and is aimed at introducing organisations to the concepts of business excellence and the benefits which can be obtained from the approach. This is one of the key start points for identifying organisations who then go on to the full training and implementation programme.

Training programme
Comprising 6 days training spread over a 2 to 3 month period. It commences with an introduction to the EFQM model and an initial self assessment against the model to identify the strengths of the organisation and improvement opportunities. This assessment is refined over the rest of the training programme and an action plan to address the improvement opportunities is developed. The rest of the training programme covers the tools and techniques which are needed to develop and implement the action plan. A key element of the programme is to allow improvements to be introduced from the organisation's first contact with the approach.

Implementation support
Following on from the training programme this is split into two elements. Firstly, two one-day workshops with other organisations to share implementation experiences; the second workshop is held some months after the first. Secondly, three days of one-to-one support for each organisation. The aim of this support is to prevent any feelings of isolation once the training is complete and to ensure successful implementation.

Sheffield Excellence Award Scheme
Based on self assessment using the EFQM model but specially adapted for small and medium sized businesses. All organisations taking part in the training programme will be encouraged to consider applying when they feel they are ready for external review of their assessments. This award will also be open to organisations who have not been through the Sheffield Excellence programme.

Resource for Excellence
A central repository for Quality related items. Includes books, articles, best practice information, case studies, training materials and videos and is available to any organisation involved with Sheffield Excellence. Normally a wide selection of this type of material would be beyond the reach (and pocket) of many smaller organisations. Many of the contributing partners are also making their quality libraries available as satellites of the Resource for Excellence. The opportunities being offered by new technology are also being assessed.

Sheffield Excellence Forum
The Quality Forum has now evolved into the Sheffield Excellence Forum. It exists to provide networking and learning opportunities for all organisations in the Sheffield area. Regular meetings and workshops along with a monthly newsletter provide ample opportunity to seek help or offer assistance to others. The Forum is also a key element of the awareness raising activity.

5   CONCLUSION

From our experiences in Sheffield there is growing evidence that the EFQM model can be applied to organisations of all sizes and at all levels. Larger organisations can work in partnership with SMEs to transfer knowledge and experience. In so doing they fulfil some of the criteria for assessment in the Impact on Society criterion of the EFQM model.

Sheffield Excellence is pioneering this approach with help from the European Regional Development Fund. Throughout the life of the project great care will be taken in gathering data to provide clear evidence of the impact this type of approach on both the participating organisations and the local community.

Sheffield Excellence is also positively seeking out relationships with other bodies with similar objectives both in the UK and abroad to share experiences and to learn from each other.

5   BIOGRAPHY

Tony Dodd is the project manager of Sheffield Excellence on secondment from Royal Mail. A qualified accountant, he has held management positions in finance, facilities and distribution within Royal Mail.

Mike Pupius is Co-Chair of Sheffield Excellence and Co-Chair of the Sheffield Centre for School Improvement. He is Director Quality of Royal Mail North East, one of the nine operating divisions of Royal Mail. He is a member of the Impact on Society Strategy Steering Group of Royal Mail.

11

Overcoming the barriers to TQM

Professor D. S. Morris and Professor R. H. Haigh
Sheffield Business School
Sheffield Hallam University, Sheffield, UK.

There have been many approaches to the study of management ranging from the Classical School, with its two components of Scientific Management and Classical Organisation Theory, through to the Human Relations School and its successor, the School of Management Science (Stoner 1982). To these Schools must be added the integrative approaches of systems theory and contingency management. None of these approaches has achieved mutual exclusivity and each has taken something from one or more of its predecessors and added something original. Total Quality Management follows in this tradition. It has adopted an integrative approach and added the unique element of holism. Whilst all of the Schools of management have sought to delineate a rational approach to the attainment of increased productivity, enhanced effectiveness and efficiency and greater economy, TQM has emphasised the attainment of those objectives through the concept of continuous quality improvement. In addition, TQM can claim, because of the holism which it advocates, to be distinctive in affording a strong philosophical underpinning to its prescriptions. (Kanji , Morris & Haigh 1993)

TQM has attracted both praise and criticism. Praise for the benefits which it can bestow upon enterprises in both the manufacturing and service sectors; with the Japanese economic miracle being often cited as the most manifest example of its bounty. Criticism for the fact that some 80% of all TQM initiatives result in complete or partial failure.(Voss & O'Brien 1992)

Two conclusions may initially be drawn from the praise-criticism dichotomy, namely that:

1) 20% of organisations which have sought to implement TQM have either (a) not encountered any barriers to its implementation, or (b) they have encountered barriers which they have successfully surmounted

   and

2) 80% of organisations which have sought to implement TQM have encountered barriers which they have failed to surmount.

Whilst it may be reasonably contended that those who have failed should learn and/or have learnt in advance from those who succeeded, the central thrust of this workshop is to identify the origin and nature of the barriers which have been encountered and then to analyse these as a basis from which to either prevent their occurrence or surmount them once they arise. Clearly, it is far more in keeping with the philosophy of TQM to prevent the emergence of barriers than to respond to them, no matter how positively, once their presence has become manifest.

Surprisingly, given the high failure rate of TQM initiatives, little has been written about the character of the barriers which impede the implementation of TQM. Many reasons could be cited for this omission: few wish to speak of failure and many wish to talk of success; the message of TQM is positive and barriers are negative; failure does not lead to analysis but to neglect etc.

Let us attempt to consider what appears to be one of the major barriers to the implementation of TQM, namely, the work of the so-called Quality Gurus. Whilst it is easy to contend that writers such as Deming, Juran, Crosby, Feigenbaum, Imai and others have left a rich legacy of advice on the essence of TQM, it is equally possible to contend that they have done far too little to aid the practising manager to implement their insights. (Morris & Haigh 1995) In essence, the Gurus have offered only prescription, prescription which is often contradictory; and have abdicated responsibility for delineating a comprehensive and coherent pattern of implementation:

Figure 1 (Oakland 1990)

	Crosby	Conway	Deming	Juran
Definition of quality	Conformance to requirements	No definition, incorporated in definition of quality management	A predictable of uniformity and dependability at low cost and suited to the market	Fitness for use
Degree of senior management responsibility	Responsible for quality	Bottleneck is located at the top of the bottle	Responsible for 94% of quality problems	Less than 20% of quality problems are due to workers
Performance standard/motivation	Zero defects	Remove waste, measure on monthly basis	Quality has many `scales'; use statistics to measure performance in all areas; critical of zero defects	Avoid campaigns to `do perfect work'
General approach	Prevention, not inspection	`Right' or `new way' to manage, Deming `disciple' `imagineering'	Reduce variability by continuous improvement; cease mass inspection	General management approach to quality, especially `human' elements
Structure	14 steps to quality improvement	6 tools for quality improvement	14 points for management	10 steps to quality improvement
Statistical process control (SPC)	Rejects statistically acceptable levels of quality	Advocates use of simple statistical methods to identify problems and point to solutions	Statistical methods of quality control must by used	Recommends SPC but wams that it can lead to `tool-driven' approach
Improvement basis	A `process', not a programme; improvement goals	Constant in all areas; statistical and industrial engineering basis	Continuous to reduce variation; eliminate goals without methods	Project-by-project team approach; set goals
Teamwork	Quality improvement teams; quality councils	Human relations skills	Employee participation in decision making; break down barriers between departments	Team and quality circle approach
Costs of quality	Cost of nonconformance; quality is free	Measure waste in all areas, includings inventory	No optimum, continuous improvement	Quality is not free, there is an optimum
Purchasing and goods received	State requirements; supplier is extension of business; most faults due to purchasers themselves	Call for improvement includes suppliers; use statistics	Inspection too late; allows defects to enter system through AQLs; statistical evidence and control charts required	Problems are complex; carry out formal surveys
Vendor rating	Yes and buyers; quality audits useless	Statistical surveys	No, critical of most systems	Yes, but help supplier improve
Single sourcing of supply			Yes	No, can neglect to sharpen competitive edge

What is the practising manager to make of the differing definitions of quality, the differing performance standard/motivation, the differing general approaches, the differing structures, the differing emphasis upon SPC, the differing improvement basis, the differing interpretation of teamwork, the differing assessment of the costs of quality and the differing vendor rating offered by Crosby, Conway, Deming and Juran? How is such variety, such variance, to be managed and, more importantly, to be used to guarantee a barrier free implementation? Confronted by such a wealth of well intentioned, but largely unhelpful advice, where does the practising manager begin and to where does he proceed? In short, prescription which falls short of offering a modus operandi is itself a potential barrier to the implementation of TQM.

Clearly, the way out of this dilemma is to develop a model for the implementation of TQM which adheres to its underlying philosophy. Such models are notable for their paucity but two are offered below:

Figure 2 (Kanji & Asher 1993)

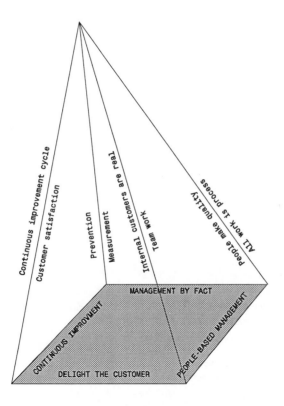

Figure 3 (Morris & Haigh 1994)

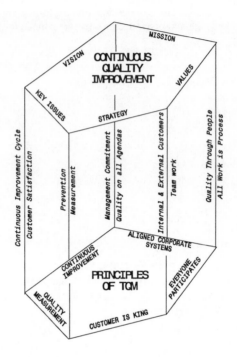

We would contend that both of these models, by their emphasis upon the key implementational aspects of TQM, direct attention to the areas in which barriers are most likely to emerge. These areas may be distinguished as those which are concerned with the implementation of TQM at the:

1) macro level, or context level: the level concerned with the questions of vision, mission, values, strategy and key issues

and

2) micro level, or content level: the level concerned with the operational activities essential to make the philosophy of TQM manifest: teamwork, process, prevention, measurement etc.

What we do know is that the implementation TQM is not something which is an instantaneous event but is rather something which is phased throughout an organisation over time. It would, therefore, appear reasonable to contend that barriers to the implementation of TQM differ depending upon which phase the implementation of TQM has reached. If we think of any TQM initiative as progressing through four phases, set up, get up, stay up and move up, then the following pattern of barriers may be discerned:

FIGURE 4

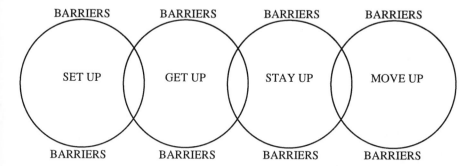

Such a contention is supported by the work of Munchi, who offers not four but two helpful scenarios as to the nature of barriers to the implementation of TQM (figures 5 and 6): (Munchi) 1992)

Such an analysis raises two further questions:

1) is it possible to identify all of the barriers which might arise in implementing TQM?

   and, if this is possible,

2) can these barriers be divided between the various phases of implementation?

Let us take the first question and offer the following as a response. Barriers can arise from the following causes: (Schoonmaker 1989)

- **organisational**:   lack of management will

  lack of a properly discernible and properly managed implementational vehicle ie a comprehensive and coherent model

- **executional**:   problem statement contains inherent flaws eg the statement of the quality problem is too broad and/or implies cause-effect and thus prevents systematic diagnosis and rational solution

  teams lack appropriate training and education are improperly constructed and their activities are improperly coordinated

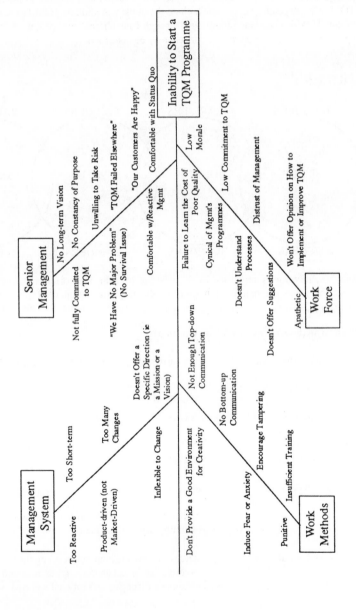

FIGURE 5

SCENARIO - A

FIGURE 6

SCENARIO - B

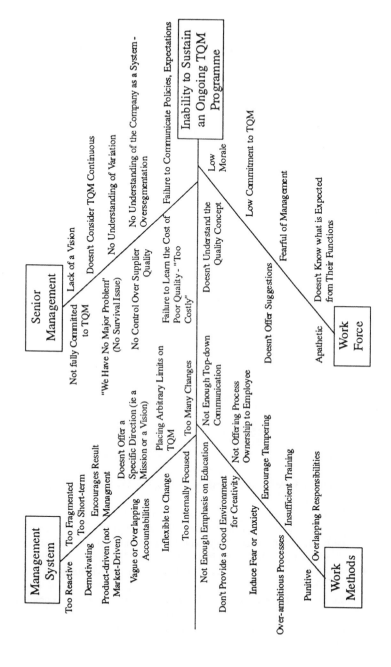

past practice and experience limit solutions

solutions only work in the short term because of a failure to appreciate that there is a hierarchy of desirable solutions involving quality and acceptance.

- **perceptual**:   stereotyping of problems generates incomplete problem identification, incomplete solution generation and incomplete solution implementation

- **emotional**:   fear of taking risks

                   no appetite for uncertainty

                   judging rather than generating ideas

- **environmental**:   autocratic supervision

                   lack of trust and cooperation

                   lack of support: monetary, moral, physical and emotional

Other barriers undoubtedly exist which are less readily categorised but which warrant mention. We have designated these adverse features as "traps" because they have the potential to become barriers. They are as follows: (Algoma Steel 1989)

- **Training Trap**: where the only tangible result which can be defined is the number of people trained
- **"For the Troops" Trap**: where the responsibility for poor quality has been passed to those at the lowest level of the organisational hierarchy
- **Technique Trap**: where some technique is thought to provide the answer to quality improvement eg SPC, Taguchi etc
- **Technology Trap**: where some technology is thought to provide the answer to quality improvement eg JIT
- **Hawthorne Trap**: since any management focus yields a short term improvement in results, this causes many organisations to believe that they are on the right track
- **Doldrums Trap**: when the organisational enthusiasm and commitment to the process falls off; typically, after the initial training period has been completed
- **Measurement Trap**: where the approach is to put measurement charts on everything that moves
- **Management Isn't Committed Trap**: an almost universal complaint of a lack of tangible action on the part of senior managers
- **Doing Quality Trap**: the idea that quality improvement is something outside the realm of people's real jobs

- **Participative Management Trap I**: management unwillingness to let go of the reigns of power/control and embrace employee participation
- **Participative Management II**: the failure to adopt a pro-active strategy to cause participative management to become manifest and the assumption that it will occur as a natural consequence of a quality improvement initiative
- **Quick Fix Trap**: where a TQM initiative is seen as affording a swift solution to any organisational problem
- **Quick Return Trap**: where a TQM initiative is seen as providing instant cost savings, increased market share etc

Obviously, the above list can be extended almost infinitely. However, the intention in considering the barriers to the implementation of TQM has been to raise awareness of some of the more common ones, the recurring ones, so that they can be prevented. As to the means of prevention, these must be located in the effective management of the operational principles which are at the centre of the philosophy of TQM.

REFERENCES

Algoma Steel (1989). Ontario, Canada.

Kanji, G.K, Morris, D.S, and Haigh, R.H (1993) Philosophical and System Dimensions of TQM: a further education case study. Proceedings of the Advances in Quality Systems for TQM. Taipei, 123-141.

Kanji, G.K and Asher, M (1993) Total Quality Management Process: a systematic approach. Carfax. Abingdon.

Morris, D.S, and Haigh, R.H. 1994.

Morris, D.S, and Haigh, R.H (1995) The Development of a Generic Model for the Implementation of TQM in Kanji Gopal, K. (Ed). Total Quality Management. Proceedings of the First World Congress. London 85-94.

Munchi, Kersi.F (1992) Averting a Reversal of TQM. Transactions of ASQC Quality Congress, Nashville 1161-1169.

Oakland, John.S (1990) Total Quality Management. Butterworth-Heinemann. Oxford.

Schoonmaker, Amanda.L (1989) Creative Block-Busting. Transactions of ASQC Quality Congress. Toronto 249-254.

Stoner, James.A.F.(1982) Management. Prentice Hall International, New York

Voss,C and O'Brien,R.C (1992) In Search of Quality. London Business School, London

12

Planning for excellence

Ann Liston,
Post Office Counters Ltd.
Northern House, 7 King St, Leeds LS6 3QE, England
Tel. 0113 237 2741, Fax 0113 237 2798

Abstract
This paper outlines the work carried out within Post Office Counters Ltd to integrate the Business Excellence self assessment process with the business planning process.

1. BACKGROUND

Post Office Counters is a wholly owned subsidiary of the Post Office Group. It is the largest retailer in the UK, with almost 20,000 outlets, serving 28 million customers per week. These outlets are run by 14,000 directly employed staff and over 18,000 agents. Post Office Counters deals with over 160 different transactions, on behalf of over our clients. Through our network, we handle £140bn in coin and notes each year making us the largest handler of cash in the UK. The business is divided into twelve business units - seven geographical regions, three business centres, a central services group and head office.

Post Office Counters Ltd began its quality journey in 1989 with the introduction of Customer first. Since that time all staff and agents have been trained in the principles and application of total quality.

In 1994, in order to ensure the integration of Customer First into business as usual activities, a self assessment process for business units was established. This is known as the Business Excellence Review (BER), is based on the European Quality Award (EQA) model (figure 1) and uses the same scoring framework.

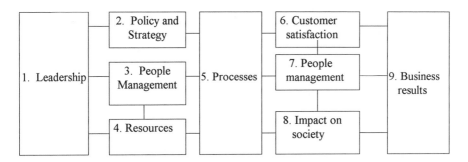

Figure 1. The European Quality Award model

The review process provides a useful picture of a business unit's current performance against the model but in itself will not produce improvements. It is therefore essential that the process is linked closely to the existing business planning process.

2. PLANNING AT NATIONAL LEVEL

From 1990 onwards, a five year Masterplan had provided a high level framework for Customer First activities throughout Post Office Counters Ltd. In 1995, this plan was renamed the Route to Excellence and, for the first time, included target EQA scores. The plan is now produced in the format of the nine EQA criteria.

Following the introduction of the business excellence review, the twenty most senior managers within Counters visited four companies who had won a European Quality award or prize in order to benchmark their approach to self assessment. One of the learning points was that all the companies visited had a 'champion' for each of the EQA criteria. Criterion sponsors were subsequently appointed within Counters with the role of promoting activities which would ensure that Counters achieved its stated aim to be in a position to win the European Quality Award by 1997.

For each criterion part, a 'current state' and a 'future state' description was prepared. Detailed plans were then drawn up to bridge the gap between the two descriptions. For the most part, the plans consisted of development of new national approaches to be deployed at business unit level. The plans were reviewed as a result of feedback from a 1995 UK Quality Award application. The revised plans were communicated to all business units by means of a series of best practice workshops to ensure that deployment of the new approaches in included in the next three year plans. Progress against the national criterion plans is reviewed and communicated quarterly.

3. PLANNING AT BUSINESS UNIT LEVEL

Until 1995, there was no standard business planning process at business unit level, although all plans were produced in a standard format for collation by the national Business Planning team. Each business unit had developed its own process, resulting in a variety of formats. Mindful of the requirements of the EQA model for a soundly based systematic approach, a cross-functional working group was set up to develop a process for planning within business units. Customers were consulted and a step by step process was developed to enable business units to amalgamate the feedback from a business excellence review with requirements of the existing planning process. The business process is shown diagrammatically at figure 2. The individual steps in the business unit planning process are at figure 3.

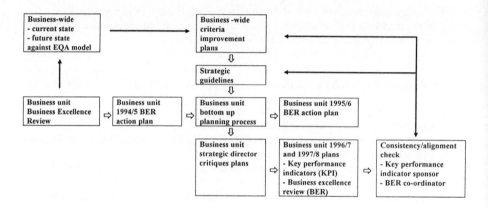

Figure 2. The business level planning process

Step 1	Timetable and responsibilities agreed

⇩

Step 2	Strategic review of business unit

- STEP factors and benchmarks
- KPIs: targets and improvement opportunities
- Top objectives and strategic priorities
- Year 2 of last year's plan
- Strategic guidelines: other priority activities
- National criterion plans
- BER feedback

⇩

Step 3	Turn into actions

⇩

Step 4	Code to BER format (enablers only) to produce a comprehensive list of potential actions

⇩

Step 5	Business unit's objectives and strategic direction

⇩

Step 6	Prioritisation

⇩

Step 7	Lead responsibility identified and planning task communicated

⇩

Step 8	Team tactical plans developed

- Cross-functional plans for new approaches
- Functional plans for business as usual/deployment issues
- Timescale/costs/measures.

⇩

Step 9	Consolidate team tactical plans

⇩

Step 10	Prioritisation and resource allocation

⇩

Step 11	Plan submitted to strategic director

⇩

Step 12	Plan approved/amended by CEC

⇩

Step 13	Check against plan as submitted

⇩

Step 14	Re-prioritise as necessary

⇩

Step 15	Communicate to teams

⇩

Step 16	Year 1 = current operating plan and budget (OPB) Year 2 = will become next year's OPB

Figure 3. The business unit planning process

The process was communicated as a supplement to the annual strategic guidelines, by means of presentations to quality managers and through business excellence review workshops. A review early in 1996 indicated that, in many cases, the principles had been adopted, although the exact process had not been followed. Research is currently underway to refine the planning process and define the common principles required in business unit planning processes. From 1996/97, it is intended to synchronise the business excellence review process with the business planning cycle to ensure full integration.

4. PLANNING AT TEAM LEVEL

The 1995/96 business excellence review process included a facilitated workshop at team level, in which each team could assess its own performance compared to the EQA model. The focus of the workshop was measurement of deployment of national and local approaches. A simplified deployment planning process was defined for use within teams to assist them to make use of the output from their workshops. This process has not been widely used and little progress has been made in improving deployment of approaches at team level. . The reasons for this are not clear at the time of writing, although it is clear that planning skills at team level are less developed within teams than at business unit level. The process is currently under review.

5. SUMMARY OF EXISTING PROCESSES

Planning process have now been developed at three levels in the organisation. All have been linked to assessment against EQA standards, although each level has a different focus (see figure 4).

Level of planning	Review process	Planning activity	Focus of plan
National	UK Quality Award application	Route to excellence National criterion plans	Framework Development of national approaches
Business Unit	Internal Business Excellence Review	Three year business plans	Deployment of national approaches Development of local approaches
Team	Team workshop	Deployment plans	Deployment of national and local approaches

Figure 4: Business planning processes

6. THE FUTURE

As we begin to use the EQA model increasingly as a framework for managing our business, we recognise that the links between self assessment at all levels of the business and planning activities must become closer. The introduction of policy deployment techniques appears to be an attractive option. Some of the building blocks are already in place, for example all our staff and agents have been trained in the use of tools and techniques and we have a sound total quality culture. However, we have as yet insufficient data on our key processes to operate the techniques effectively, our planning activities are not yet aligned to our processes and planning skills among middle managers are not well developed. In the short term, we are continuing to put the building blocks in place and are testing some of the principles of policy deployment in our current planning activities. In the longer term, we hope that policy deployment will be our path to even more effective planning.

BIOGRAPHY

Ann Liston has worked for Post office Counters Ltd for sixteen years, initially in personnel and latterly as a quality manager. She is currently Business Excellence Manager responsible for the development and implementation of self assessment techniques within Counters.

13

Forget managing change - get back to managing the business

John Macdonald
Chairman
John Macdonald Associates Ltd, 16 Woodcote Avenue, Wallington,
Surrey, SM6 OQY, Tel and Fax: 0181 647 0160

FORGET MANAGING CHANGE-
GET BACK TO MANAGING THE BUSINESS

The last decade has been characterised by a mounting clamour for change. The siren voices of revolution seem to permeate every aspect of life. In religion, politics, society and business the past is derided. The future is declared to be uncertain and unpredictable. A plethora of gurus and change masters offer tempting panaceas for managing the revolution of change. At their behest all manner of organisations are abandoning old verities, methods and values. They are caught between gods. The change masters are causing havoc. It is time to call **halt** or at the very least take a pause for thought.

The world of business does not exist or operate in a vacuum. It has to comprehend and adapt to the changing circumstances in which it operates. So business is always about change. But the need for **radical** change in the way business is organised and managed is being exaggerated. There is evidence that a lot of damage is being caused to organisations (and to the men and women who work in them) by frequent knee-jerk reactions to this clamour for change. This paper argues that:

- a healthy dose of common sense is long overdue.
- many businesses are throwing out the baby with the bath water.
- executives are loosing sight of the simple truths of business.
- the secret of successful business is nurtured evolution rather than revolution.

The conventional wisdom of the change masters tends to concentrate on examples such as Xerox and now IBM. These case histories explain how these great corporations recognised the need to change and then glory in how they went about it. In other words the traditional scenario of Phoenix rising from the ashes. But in truth these case histories are more pertinent as evidence of the earlier catastrophic management failure to understand the evolutionary nature of markets and business.

Based on a book *Call a Halt to Mindless change*, to be published by American Management Association, New York

Most businesses need evolution not revolution. The scope and reverberations of radical change are extremely hard to control. As a consequence the results are rarely as envisaged. Throw a pebble in the pool and the ripples will quietly touch and influence every corner of the pool. Throw in a damn great rock and the results are usually chaotic. The water is displaced, the banks are damaged, the fish are stunned and the ecology will take a long time to recover. Business should avoid the temptation to throw rocks and encourage a continuous pattern of pebble throwers.

Business has more to learn from the substantial number of great firms who appear to sail serenely through all the storms of change. They continually grow and encompass the changes around them without sacrificing or perhaps because of their original values. From the outset these companies created organisations that anticipate change. They do not need revolution or re engineering. They educated and empowered their people before the words became management jargon. They drove the technologies rather than being driven by them. They practised prevention and managed quality long before the quality guru Philip Crosby wrote a book. They understood that the paradox of change is that it always takes you back to where you once were.

In reality most of the revolutionary changes which are said to threaten modern enterprises are nothing of the sort. They are relatively slow moving evolutions taking place well within the perspective of intelligent executive decision making cycles. They only appear fast when we use false analogies with the time measures of past ages. People have adapted to change and have at their command technologies which make those measures irrelevant.

All this change and uncertainty provides an ideal environment for the growth of false gods and gurus. Each new utopia or technique introduced helps to mould the perceptions of management and people to create a company culture. All too often the culture tends to obscure the fundamental purpose of the organisation and to bring about a general lack of focus. In that culture, change is more seen as a threat rather than as an opportunity. Sooner or later a new chief executive or other officer recognises the need for change. Unfortunately it usually is implemented as another revolution, which brings disruption and chaos in its wake.

The growing influence of technology has ushered in a quasi scientific language for business communication. Each functional specialisation now has its own brand of management **sciences** or jargon, with which to confound its internal competitors. Much of the new language is incomprehensible but few managers are prepared to admit openly that they don't understand the new terminology. The CEO has stolen the emperor's clothes!

Now the lexicon of management includes meaningless philosophies and techniques as well as phrases. Once the simple rules of business were breached a whole host of messiahs were free to parade their flavour of the month. Bemused by the complexities of managing the present many executives fall prey to consulting academics and gurus with their latest quick fix route to the future. Many of these management philosophies do contain a germ of truth but they are not seen as only part of the greater whole and are then implemented without due care and attention.

The trouble with most of these management fads is that they concentrate on only one facet of the management process. They are often implemented by enthusiastic apostles with an uncritical belief that they represent a management break-through or a magic cure-all. There is never time to consider how these new techniques or approaches are to be integrated with or replace existing procedures. Doubters are derided as **ye of little faith** or as traditionalists who are **past it**. All of this creates conflict and resistance throughout the organisation. In some cases the specific concept or technique is in itself an agent of conflict, fear and resistance. Management by Objectives and most Performance Appraisal Systems fall into this latter category but seem to have a longevity in management practice.

TOTAL QUALITY MANAGEMENT

Since the late 1970s thousands of Western companies have woken up to the competitive challenge, originally from Japan, and launched some form of quality initiative. As a result, organisations have not met with the same measure of success.
many have become world class competitors but unfortunately it is also true that the majority of Success is a comparative term. Almost without exception, every company that launched a quality drive has improved; for in business terms quality has been in focus and has shown a positive return. Those companies considered themselves successful. But the real measure of success should be against competitors, and customer expectations. Seen in that light many have reasons for disappointment.

The really successful companies understood the word **total** and recognised that TQM could provide a holistic approach to managing their companies. They used TQM and the readily accepted need to improve as the change agent to evolve out of **Taylorism** to a new management culture.

THE FALSE GODS OF BUSINESS

As I said earlier, over this century we have steadily made the practice of business so complicated and devisive that most individuals cannot see the wood for their own favourite tree. Successive waves of consultants and gurus have proclaimed a multiplicity of isms and false gods that have confused management and gnawed away at the simple truths of organisation and business.

In the main, executives, managers and other employees want to do a good job. There will be some personal agendas, but generally they are united in that they want their company to be successful and respected. Yet despite this unity of purpose, organisations lose sight of their changing marketplace and are plagued with turf wars and adversarial relationships. The activities of business have become so complicated that individuals are lost in a maze of procedures and other barriers to communication and action.

THE GOD OF SPECIALISATION

The intriguing fact is that step by step this over complication of business has all been done on purpose in the name of enlightened management. It all started when first Adam Smith and then Frederick Taylor and countless apostles demonstrated to businessmen that if they divided major processes or work activities into a host of small specialised activities they could achieve massive increases in productivity. They were proved right and the era of mass production began.

The pioneers of modern industry and commerce were right **at the time** and in the conditions in which they promulgated their ideas. But the conditions changed and the process of specialisation created other problems which were not recognised at the time. Now the progress of technology, education and the expectation of both customers and employees have evolved to a stage that demand a re-evaluation of the **science of management**.

One result of pursuing the **truth** of specialisation has been the steady division of business operations both vertically and horizontally. A vertical division between **the thinkers and the doers** and a horizontal division between departmental functions. Over time each division has created barriers to communication and understanding of how the business is operating. The phenomenon of **them and us** is much broader than that between managers and workers. On the people front the confrontation is layered between boss and subordinate at every level. On the business activity front functional departments have become fortresses to be defended at any cost. Ultimately in this environment the organisation sees their customers and suppliers as combatants to be overcome.

As the channels of communication and action became more complex and time consuming the thinkers needed people to advise them and to help control the disparate elements of the business. These advisors were soon organised into staff groups who exercised power and control on behalf of (and often instead of) the executives and senior managers. Their customer is senior management rather than the actual customer of the business. As the eyes, ears and voice of management they serve to reinforce the separation between management and worker.

Even more important this trend has divided management from the customer and the real issues of the marketplace.

In most businesses today a substantial proportion of managers and employees have little or no contact with the customer. At the same time they also have little or no contact with the people who make products or deliver services. They live in their corporate chateaux (like the Great War Generals) and spend their working hours with other managers or **members of staff**. They are far removed from changing customer perceptions and the **insignificant** problems of the workers and **difficult** customers. Too often their energy is expended **Haig like** on jockeying for political position and extending their privileges rather than on improving the business. Management becomes immersed in pointless detail and the business is slowly frittered away. In this environment few will take risks and opportunities are missed. The fear of not being able to see the wood for the trees has misled many business leaders into believing that the wood was composed of sturdy oaks when in truth it was merely brittle fir saplings.

Four is too many

It doesn't have to be like that. Business is quite simple; managers have made it appear complex. In functional terms only three positions really matter in the business process. These are the:

- Chief Executive, who is responsible for determining the strategy of the business (or resolving the inherent conflict between the other two) and organising the resources and support.
- Head of Marketing, who is responsible for defining customer needs and wants and then designing the products and services to delight the customers.
- Head of Production or Operations, who is responsible for developing the capability and then delivering the product or service to the customer.

All other functions in the organisation are only there to support these processes. This original rock steady triumvirate of management based on the purpose of business has been distorted. This is to the detriment of long term decision making and the management of organisations. The clouding of these simple principles has led to the relative decline of Western industry. This can be illustrated by the following tendencies:

- The rise in the power of the financial directors in the fifties and sixties led to an obsession with quarterly results and short term financial thinking.
- The rising influence of the HR or personnel directors in the seventies (largely caused by government interference in industrial relations) sapped management's will to manage people.
- The eighties and nineties are witnessing the growing influence of the lawyers and the public relations **spin doctors** on business organisations. They are now also seeking a seat at the strategic business decision making table.

These and other tendencies have created habits of thought which are obscuring the true purpose of the key processes of business and public sector organisations. None of these functions represent key business processes. A moments consideration of how businesses start and indeed any small business makes this clear. Those functions just do not exist in the small business; when skill or advice is required in those areas it is sourced outside.

As we examine these issues we realise that the focus on the purpose of the organisation provides many reasons for radical change. However, these attitudes have evolved as successive managements launched initiatives and chased false or only partially true gods. Their tentacles are buried deep across the organisation and embedded in the culture. In the social language of today the business body may need therapy and de-toxification rather than surgery. But one issue is clear. The purpose of business is to understand customer needs and fulfil them. That does require that we break down the fortress walls within the organisation.

Management cultures still differ widely but most are now agreed that Taylor's theories are no longer applicable to today's work environment. We now know that a participative style of management is better suited to achieving competitive performance. However, we find it very difficult to change the daily small habits of a lifetime. We preach participation but practice command and control and seem a little surprised that the workers are not compliant. Most management practices are still anchored in these traditional behaviours.

We need to evolve our management style and become constant pebble throwers. Evolution not revolution.

AUTHOR

John Macdonald is the best selling business author and chairman of John Macdonald Associates Ltd., the international consultancy group.

PART TWO

Community and Education

14

Principles of quality in the community

J. Marsh
Total Quality Partnerships
10 Charles Avenue, Stoke Gifford, Bristol, BS12 6LW, UK,
Tel +44 (0) 117 9492119, Fax +44 (0) 117 9497784,
EMail john@marshj.demon.co.uk

Abstract

Through the careful application of the principles and tools of total quality, involving all the relevant stakeholders, deeply entrenched community wide problems can be identified, analysed and addressed thus making real, sustainable improvements to our quality of life. This paper presents a view of the community as a system and summarises the principles of community wide improvement.

Keywords

Total Quality, Community, Quality of Life, Stakeholders.

1   INTRODUCTION

A dramatic shift is going on concerning our understanding of effective management. Traditional ideas are being challenged and new ways of working, such as total quality, are being developed in many organisations. People are asking if these principles could be applied more widely to the systems that make up our communities. This is bringing new opportunities to tackle and reverse systemic decline. This movement is underway across the UK.

2   THE COMMUNITY AS A SYSTEM

Figure 1 shows how a community functions as a system. Many linkages have been left out for clarity. It highlights the need for all components to work together to improve the quality of life. Details will vary according to the social, economic and political environment of the community being considered.

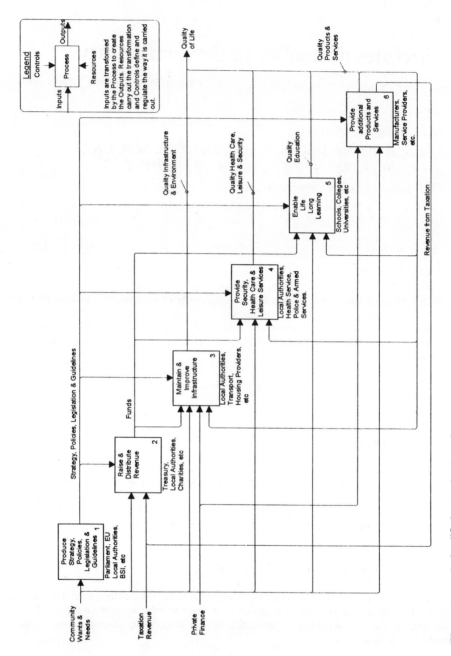

Figure 1   A simplified systemic view of a community

Parliament and the European Union own the processes for generating legislation which then defines and regulates all other parts of the system. Other bodies, such as the British Standards Institute, government departments and local authorities, produce standards and guidelines which again guide parts of the system.

Once the strategies and policies are clear, within a legislative framework, priorities for funding can be established. The Inland Revenue and Customs & Excise are responsible for collecting revenue from individuals and organisations, but the Treasury controls its distribution. Once central government and the Treasury have decided on overall allocations many other bodies such as local authorities and an ever increasing number of quangos decide on more detailed funding priorities. Charities redistribute wealth independently.

These funds are then used, often along side private finance, to provide products and services to the community. The foundation of the community is provided by the maintenance and improvement of the infrastructure. This includes the provision of housing, transport systems and electronic infrastructure. These processes may be initiated by public bodies but will involve public / private partnerships. The infrastructure is not only used by the citizens, but also by all other community organisations such as schools and businesses.

Certain organisations are concerned with the provision of health care, leisure activities and ensuring that the community is safe. These include hospitals, leisure centres, the police, prisons and the armed services. They depend on funds and products and services to ensure a safe and healthy community.

All community members should have equal access to life long learning. Schools, colleges, universities and employers provide this opportunity. They are becoming more and more conscious about improving standards and reducing costs. They, like all the other organisations, can only do this in partnership with other community stakeholders. This process is likely to be the key differentiator for communities as they struggle to gain or retain the highly skilled jobs.

Finally there is a raft of community businesses which provide products and services direct to the public and to other organisations in the system. They need to ensure that they are continually improving their products and processes to ensure profitability and employment. By this means government is able to raise the revenue, so critical to keeping the system functioning and improving.

3   PRINCIPLES OF QUALITY IN THE COMMUNITY

Many organisations across the UK are experimenting with the concepts and tools of quality in the community (Marsh, 1995). There is no clear pattern. Sometimes enlightened businesses take the lead, other times it is innovative local authorities. Schools can be natural 'hubs' in the community and many are addressing total quality. Other catalysts include Training and Enterprise Councils, the police and voluntary organisations. Despite the difficulty of seeing patterns in the diversity of quality in the community projects under way some common principles are emerging.

Create a shared vision

All successful initiatives have a strong sense of shared vision between the stakeholders. This can take considerable effort to achieve. The writing of a vision statement is the start of the process. Once a clear vision has been generated this can be translated into prioritised actions. The vision must be driven by understanding the community's wants and needs. Strategic planning is continuous.

Work on community wide processes

Real systemic improvement can only be achieved by working on the whole process, involving all the key stakeholders. Communities are made up of complex processes which cut across private, public and charitable organisations. Therefore before community wide improvement can start, the process under consideration needs to be defined and understood. Flowcharts and process models (Marsh, 1993) can be used to highlight community wide processes.

Develop a common language and way of working

In order for many stakeholders to work together effectively they need a common language. The language and tools of total quality, once learnt, provide a universal approach for people from very different backgrounds to work together.

Deal with root causes

As community processes start to be understood and the stakeholders learn the total quality approach they will have to focus on root cause issues. They will have to distinguish between special and common causes and adopt suitable approaches (Deming, 1993). There is no point throwing resources at the symptoms whilst the root causes go unchecked.

Optimise the whole

Solutions to root causes must aim to optimise the whole process. Consider the example of a city. It comprises a complex series of processes involving wealth creation, infrastructure provision and transportation, and many others. If each is regarded as independent then decisions made to optimise a single component may have very negative effects on the other components of the system. Improvement actions must be taken in the light of the whole process and not any one component.

Build respect and trust through understanding

Community wide improvement starts to break down many of the barriers that exist between stakeholder groups. Working together in a structured, focused way helps to improve the respect and trust between the different groups.

Empowerment

Any successful approach must be based on the principle of empowering the people being served by the initiative. Improvements to services for disabled people must actively engage them in defining their wants and needs and throughout the whole process of improvement. Reducing truancy must engage the students and their parents. Regeneration initiatives should be driven by the needs of the inner city residents. The 'customer' is the most important part of the process. This is true community empowerment.

4 REFERENCES

Deming, W.E. (1993) *The New Economics for Industry, Government and Education.* MIT, CAES.

Marsh, J. (1995) Quality in the Community - an Overview of Progress in the UK, *Proceedings South African International Quality Convention,* SAQI.

Marsh, J. (1993) *The Quality Toolkit - an A to Z of Tools and Techniques.* IFS International Ltd.

5 BIOGRAPHY

John Marsh has many years experience of implementing total quality in business, government, education and more recently with whole communities. Whilst based in the UK he regularly works in the US. He has written two books, many papers, and co-authored several British and International Standards. He is a passionate enthusiast for using total quality to develop new solutions for whole communities.

15

Quality management systems in HEIs in the UK: an empirical study

K. Narasimhan
Bolton Business School, Bolton Institute,Deane Road, Bolton, UK, BL3
5AB.Fax:01204 399074, e-mail: KN1 @ Bolton.ac.uk

Abstract

In response to the changes in the structure of higher education some Higher Education Institutions (HEIs) both in the UK and abroad have started on a 'quality journey' using various approaches. This study reports on an investigation carried out, in 1994, to discover the practices in the HEIs in the UK.

Keywords

Quality, higher education, total quality, business management

1   INTRODUCTION

The staff and students in Higher Education Institutions (HEIs) are affected by the re-emphasis on the three A's: accessibility, autonomy, and accountability; the five E's: economy, expansion, efficiency, effectiveness and empowerment; and last but not least the Q: quality of the product and service. No none of these can be considered in isolation as the A's, the E's and the Q are interrelatred. However, this paper concentrates on the quality aspect.

2   THE CHANGING AWARENESS OF QUALITY IN HEIs

Succesive Government reports on all stages of education have signalled the priority to be given to Quality as an organising concept for the reform of educational organisation and practice (Marsh,1992). Following Further and Higher Education Act, the Higher Education Quality Council (HEQC) was established in May 1992. Its principal services are quality assurance and quality enhancement.

There is wide spread interest in the aspect of 'Quality' in higher education as evidenced by the number of studies in progress in the UK: for example, the major research project on "Identifying and developing a quality ethos for teaching in higher education" by the Centre for Higher Education Studies, (Loader, 1992); a Quality in Higher Education Project launched in 1991 to develop a methodology for assessing quality in higher education (Harvey, et al. 1992).

However, there is not much research done on what exactly are HEIs in the UK doing to enhance quality. This paper which is work-in-progress is intended to address that void.

3   METHODOLOGY

This interim report is based on the findings of a postal questionnaire survey carried out in 1994. The main aim of the survey was to discover the current position regarding quality management practices in the Higher Education Institutions (HEIs) in the U.K. excluding Northern Ireland.. Questionnaires with a covering letter were sent to 146 HEIs predominantly funded by the HEFCs of England, Scotland and Wales but not Northern Ireland. Colleges that are part of universities established on a collegiate basis have been included in the relevant sector.The analysis that follows are based on the positive usable responses from 60 HEIs and may not be representative of other. HEIs.

4   THE INTERIM FINDINGS

Status of Quality Systems in (QS) in institutions

- Under 50% of the pre-1900 universities are engaged in research or consultation activities in the field of quality and 31% have no involvement. Over 70% of post-1990 universities and NUHEIs are engaged in research and/or consultancy. Within the institutions that responded quality systems are in use more in the academic area than either in the faculty, or central, administration.
- A majority of the institutions that responded (69% pre-1990 universities, 95% post-1990 universities and 96% NUHEIs) have quality co-ordinators or someone with separate responsibility for quality across the institution.
- Only 15% pre-1990 universities, 32% post-1990 universities and 46% NUHEIs have used, or are considering the use of, external consultants to assist in the introduction of QS. 69% pre-1990 universities, 68% post-1990 universities and 50% NUHEIs have not used, or not considering the use of external consultants.
- Majority of post-1990 universities (74%) and NUHEIs (64%) have QS "Champions," (that is, a person committed to the idea of 'Quality Service' and who is assigned the task of implementing the Quality System'). Only 38% of pre-1990 universities have such a person.

The extent of commitment to QS at institutional level

- In all NUHEIs, in 95% post-1990 Universities and in 77% of the pre-1990 universities there is a statement of policy on academic quality matters in their plan. However, on non-academic matters (that is, matters concerned with administrative and support services) a majority of NUHEIs (86%) and post-1990 universities (74%), but only 46% pre-1990 universities have such a statement. In the other institutions, however, steps are under way to include a statement of quality policy.
- The quality policies of various institutions identify both external users and/or customers. NUHEIs seem to be in the forefront in this connection, followed by post-1990 universities. In under 40% of the Pre-1990 universities their customers are identified in the quality policy.
- In over 90% of the three types of HEIs there exists a 'quality improvement process'(QIP) sub-system covering academic matters. However, for non-academic matters only 38% of pre-1990

universities have a QIP sub-system as against 71% of NUHEIs and 84% of post-1990 universities that have such a sub-system.

- In nearly 65% of the three types of HEIs Staff Councils or Committees with clear responsibility for quality on academic matters exist or are being established. NUHEIs lead in the use of Joint Staff and Student councils or committee for quality issues (61% NUHEIs, 47% post-1990 universities and 31% pre-1990 universities). For non-academic quality matters the use of such committees is less prevalent.
- Pre-1990 universities lag very much behind post-1990 universities and NUHEIs in the use of external publication for making the quality policy visible.
- Post-1990 universities and NUHEIs lead pre-1990 universities in the use of separate budgets for such quality related activities. There is a separate budget in a higher proportion of HEIs for activities relating to maintaining and enhancing quality of academic matters than for non-academic matters.
- In 60% of the institutions, faculty or school or departmental teams, and institution wide teams, are used for improving quality related to academic matters. The use of such teams is less prevalent for for non-academic matters.

Institutions' use of feedback systems (that is, stakeholders' views)

- A majority of HEIs (62% pre-1990 and 63% post-1990 universities and 57% NUHEIs) extensively use current student opinion for modifying curriculum. The use of students' views for improving services is marginally lower.
- A majority of all types of institutions make some use of the views of academic staff for modifying quality policy and curriculum, improving services and staff appraisal. Support staffs' views are used less extensively than the academic staffs' views. However, the views of such staff are used more in the universities than in the NUHEIs.
- Employers' views are made use of more in post-1990 universities than in other institutions for modifying Quality Policy and curriculum and for improving services. Industrialists' views are used more for modifying curriculum than for either modifying policy or improving services.
- All types of institutions make some use of research funding bodies' views more for modifying quality policy. 31% pre-1990 universities make extensive use when compared to 11% each of the post-1990 universities and NUHEIs.
- 46% of pre-1990 universities, 26% of post-1990 universities and 39% of NUHEIs make extensive use of HEQC's opinion for modifying Quality Policy. Pre-1990 universities are again in the fore front (31% as opposed to 11% of post-1990 universities and 18% of NUHEIs) in using HEQC's views for improving services..
- 53% of post-1990 universities and 31% of other institutions use professional institutions' views extensively for modifying curriculum.

The extent of training received by various groups of staff

- All the senior managers in 15% of pre-1990 universities, 47% of post-1990 universities, and 25% NUHEIs had received training in general principles of quality management.
- In no institution have all the staff had customer awareness training. However support staff, in a significantly higher proportion of post-1990 universities than other HEIs, received training in user awareness (15% pre-1990, and 48% post-1990, universities, and 25% NUHEIs).

In no institution have all the staff had training in the application of quality improvement tools. None of the top mangers of pre-1990 universities have had this training. In 21% of post-1990 universities all senior managers had this training. In 7% of pre-1990 universities the academic and support staff had this training. In under 50% of post-1990 universities and NUHEIs the middle managers and other staff had such training.

Methods of obtaining views of stakeholders

- 8% of pre-1990 universities, 95% post-1990 universities, and 79% of NUHEIs use 'satisfaction' surveys for soliciting stakeholders' expectations. Benchmarking is used by 21% of post-1990 universities and 18% of NUHEIs. 31% of pre-1990 universities, 53% of post-1990 universities and 39% of NUHEIs do not use benchmarking.
- Except for one NUHEI all institutions have formal procedures for course reviews. Universities use faculty panel more than the other two types. NUHEIs use a central panel rather than a faculty panel or review by the course tutor. Other methods adopted for obtaining students' opinions are: questionnaire survey, feedback forms, lecturer ratings, exit interviews, and complaint cards.
- A questionnaire survey is the most popular form of obtaining students' opinions of their experiences. Students' rating of lecturers is used more by pre-1990 universities (85%) than post-1990 universities (53%) or NUHEIs who use the least (32%). In about 40% of the institutions that answered the questionnaire exit interviews are also used.

5   REFERENCES

Marsh, Peter, (1991, 1 Nov.) Bounce in Showroom. *The Times Higher*, 16.
HEQC (1995) Annual Report 93-94. Higher Education Quality Council, London.10.

Loader, Cari, (1992 Feb.) Identifying and Developing a Quality Ethos for Teaching in Higher Education. *CHES Newsletter. No. 2.* Institute of Education, University of London.

Harvey, Lee, et.al. (1992) Someone Who Can Make an Impression: Report of the Employers' Survey of Qualities of Higher Education Graduates. QHE, Birmingham.

K Narasimhan, holds Bachelor degrees in Science and Engineering, and a Masters in Management. He worked in both manufacturing and service industries before switching to teaching in 1987. He teaches strategic and operations management related subjects. He is conducting research on 'quality' in HEIs at macro and micro levels.

16

Implementation of a holistic quality concept at a university as a tool for increasing efficiency and effectiveness

M. Carlsson
School of Applied Engineering and Maritime Studies, Department of
Mechanical Engineering, Chalmers University of Technology
S-411 05 Gothenburg, Sweden. Tel: +46 31 772 5025.
Fax: +46 31 772 2689. e-mail: maca@ios.chalmers.se

Abstract

Within western-world industry, the work to implement holistically related quality concepts has been going on for more than a decade. The second wave of quality programmes undertaken on a larger scale within different types of service-producing companies began in the early 1990s. These programmes are being carried out within the framework of ISO 9000, different quality awards or in the form of more or less developed TQM-concepts.

For several hundred years now, Swedish universities have, with one or two exceptions, been owned and controlled by the State. In July 1995, two of the largest universities in Sweden were privatised, Chalmers University of Technology being one of them. At the operational, practical level, this change brought about, among other things, a new board of directors including representatives from business and industry. These representatives started to introduce the same type of thinking in terms of efficiency as have been applied in industry for many years.

The College of applied engineering and maritime studies, a school sorting under Chalmers University of Technology, became interested in quality issues in 1993. This interest originated in, among other things, the development and introduction of several major quality programmes during this period. During the spring of 1993, the first systematic course on the subject of quality was introduced aimed at the management group of the school.

During 1995, a more stringent economy was imposed on Chalmers. The management decided to economise by means of a proactive efficiency programme, while still maintaining or even raising the quality level of its operations. Based on the introductory course in quality, a discussion was started during the spring of 1995 regarding the possibilities of conducting the efficiency efforts within the framework of a quality development project. The board came to the decision that the quality efforts should be started in June of the same year. It was also decided that the work should be documented from an analytical scientific perspective.

This paper presents the approach adopted in the work with the quality development project carried out at Chalmers. The principal considerations made initially regarding the choice of concepts are treated as well as the practical work with the project. Concrete results in the form of different empirical data are presented and discussed. Both the positive and negative experiences made so far are analysed and the qualitative conclusions regarding the continued conduct of the project described.

Keywords

TQM, efficiency, effectiveness, university

1   INTRODUCTION AND BACKGROUND

In the early nineties, Sweden was struggling through a deep recession, which threatened the international competitiveness of our industry. In an effort to overcome this serious situation, the Swedish Government initiated a number of different investigations. Of these, the so-called "Productivity delegation" received the greatest attention. This investigation emphasised the importance of dedicated programmes focusing on quality issues: "Highly productive, leading companies are characterised by their continuous, intensive work efforts to enhance quality in all parts of their operations... Quality is a question of producing what the customer wants and is prepared to pay for... It presupposes close contact with the market coupled with the ability to react quickly in response to new signals... A company's quality work is closely connected to its work organisation. A prerequisite is motivated and committed personnel who can spur the quality work forward... Key is here that both the authority and responsibility for quality improvements are invested in the employees. This is true of the private as well as the public sector, of services as well as industrial production" (the Swedish Government Official Reports, Drivers of productivity and prosperity, report of the Productivity Delegation, SOU 1991:82).

Interest in different quality development concepts has been steadily increasing in Sweden. There are several forces behind this development; apart from the above-mentioned investigations, the main force is the increasing spread of the ISO-system as well as the establishment of a Swedish quality award. There also exists today a special award for schools, "the Swedish school award". Further, every other year, a major conference focusing on quality is held within the public sector.

In line with the harsher economic conditions, extensive cutbacks have been imposed on Swedish universities, cutbacks which are assumed to be met partly by increased efficiency. In an attempt to rationalise, various measures have been taken - in some cases in the form of quality programmes.

2 DEVELOPMENT OF MODELS AND WORK PROCEDURE FOR THE QUALITY WORK

In order to meet the increased demand for cost reductions, an extensive quality development project was initiated in the autumn of 1995 at the School of Applied Engineering and Maritime Studies, Chalmers University of Technology.

At the request of the School's President, a project proposal was presented during the spring of 1995, which was subsequently approved by both the President and the chairman of the board. After this, a detailed plan was prepared showing how the work should proceed, and a kick-off meeting with the key personnel to be engaged in the project was arranged.

The overriding goal of the project was to increase the efficiency of the internal processes of the School in order to better meet customer demands and expectations by focusing on quality. In order to reach this goal, the project has been designed from a chain perspective; by clarifying the goal of the activities, both the customers and those processes that create added value to them could be identified. By securing the involvement and commitment of the employees, knowledge of the processes and their improvement potential will increase, which in turn enhances the possibilities not only of improved efficiency but also employee commitment, customer satisfaction, finally resulting in improved competitive ability. See figure 1 below.

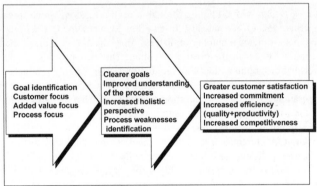

Figure 1. Means and goals of the project.

The project has been built up and organised partly based on results from research carried out on the implementation of ISO 9000 (Carlsson & Carlsson, 1996) and different TQM-concepts (Carlsson, 1995) and partly based on the way in which other, similar projects have been conducted within the academic world (e.g. Oakland). As a result, the following structural frameworks were applied:
-   the top management were to carry the overall responsibility for the project as well as take an active part in it;
-   the project was to be carried out at a rapid pace, the steering group meeting frequently;
-   the managers carrying the operative responsibility were to be included in the steering group to enable decisions to be taken quickly and efficiently;
-   the operative work was to be delegated to the employees concerned;
-   as many employees as possible were to be engaged in the work;
-   the project was to be started as a pilot case in one department for a period of 4 months, after which the whole School was to be involved;
-   a project leader was appointed as a support and sounding board for the work.

Based on results from research carried out concerning similar change projects, it was expected that certain steps would be difficult and require a great deal of work:
-   identifying overall goals and visions;

- finding suitable, operative goals, result measurements and control points within the process;
- mapping out of existing processes;
- documentation of the new or improved processes;
- implementation of the improved or new processes.

Today, few models exist providing concrete guidance for the implementation of quality work. The different quality awards, ISO 9000 and the principles put forward by e.g. Crosby, Deming and Juran act more like evaluation instruments for the progress of the quality work or as normative check-lists of what should be taken into consideration in the performance of this work. Therefore, in order to attain a structured approach to the quality work, a model was developed aimed at providing a better description of the work procedure. This model starts with clarification and identification of the aims and goals of the activities together with the strategy to be applied in order to reach these goals. Based on these overriding strategy and goals, the operative goals were formulated and different operative consequences for the organisation (management, staff members, etc.) presented using a traditional PDCA-cycle. The vision and the operative goals were determined focusing on the satisfaction of customer expectations. See figure 2.

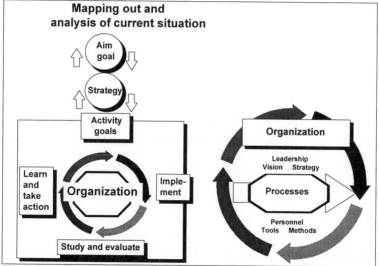

Figure 2. Outline of a work model for the project.

The practical structuring of the project was organised into four phases. All phases were determined in terms of time, the employees concerned identified, and different activities and expected results estimated. See figure 3 below.

Participants

Management group	Management group	Management group	Management group
Key persons	(Steering group)	Whole organisation	Project group
Trade union	Project groups	Vhole organisation	
Student union			

Phase 1	**Phase 2**	**Phase 3**	**Phase 4**
Initiation	Preliminary study	Main phase	Consolidation
- frameworks	- identification	-implementation	- evaluation
- goals	- testing	- continuity	
1-2 months	4-5 months	5-6 months	4-5 months ff

Measures/results

- Identification	- Mapping out processes	- Education	- Credibility and security
- Ambition	- Measurements, analyses	- Testing the process	in the organisation
level, goals	- Specifying and		- Final cost/utility
and vision	concretising the		analysis and
- Project definition	ambition level		implementation
	- quantifying the result		
	measurements		

Figure 3. The different phases of the project: participants, measures and expected results.

In addition, a financial budget for the project was prepared and the frameworks set at approx. SEK 1 million for the first year's work.

3. APPLYING SCIENTIFIC PERSPECTIVES ON THE WORK

On initiation of the quality project, it was decided that the work should be documented from a scientific perspective, allowing systematic evaluation and analysis.

The overriding method approach adopted for evaluation of the quality project was to map out the progress of the project based on a longitudinal and action-oriented perspective, mainly using participant observations. Different complementary evaluation instruments have been used, for example, open and closed interviews as well as different types of questionnaires.

4. RESULTS AND KNOWLEDGE GAINED

In the opening discussions regarding the quality project, three customer groups were identified concerning the activities focusing on basic education:
- the students
- the future employers of the graduate engineers (in most cases industry)
- society.

It was further considered that, as the actual quality outcome cannot be measured until the former student has been working for some time as an engineer, this picture needs to be complemented. Seen from this perspective, it could also be established that the proper goal of the basic education and the students' expectations from it was to be given the opportunity to attain "professional success in life". Therefore, on the 'market' where Chalmers operates, it is not only other universities of technology but also other educational alternatives perceived to lead to success that are competing for the customers.

One of the more demanding phases of the project in terms of work effort has been the mapping out of processes. Initially, a study programme (often covering three years) was defined as a main process, a year as a part process, a study period as a mini process and a course as a micro process. In addition, owners were defined for each process. After this, internal suppliers and customers were made part of the processes. Also, a number of different support processes were identified. The mapping out was then performed by the persons participating in the respective process. So far, examinations, laboratory experiments and course starts have been mapped out.

To facilitate a positive start, it was decided to begin with a number of tasks considered to be simple, which could produce concrete results quickly. For this reason, it was decided to standardise a number of the documents that are frequently used, e.g. examination covers, course descriptions and course memoranda. For this purpose, different work groups were formed. The group dealing with the examination covers arrived at the conclusion that such a cover ought to contain approx. 14 different items. It was primarily the administration office who were responsible for different demands on the covers, as they were required to differentiate and identify different tests during examination periods.

The proposed new examination covers met, however, with some scepticism. One of the arguments put forward was that this type of work seemed unnecessary, as the principles proposed were already believed to be practised. It was then decided to examine a sample of ten randomly selected examination covers. This done, it could be established that all the covers were different and that they contained only 66% of the information considered necessary for the proper use of them.

Additionally, the project has included a number of systematic mappings out: a preliminary study of the students' conception of the university and why they have chosen to study there (this round of interviews forms the basis for the design of a measuring instrument to be used in a future broad survey), a study focusing on the introduction of students to the university as well as a rough mapping out of the quality level among the personnel (based on a number of factors contained in the Swedish Quality Award). Furthermore, as a part of the in-house education programme, a mapping out was made of the issues which the university staff considered important to include within the framework of the project. After the completion of three such courses, approx. 50 different proposals have been presented.

At the present stage of the project, we are experiencing the same difficulties as predicted by earlier investigations. For example, we had received clear indications that providing information about the project was crucial. Despite this knowledge, the project has up until today been criticised on grounds of poor information. However, when it comes to information, there exists an awkward dichotomy. On the one hand, it is desirable to provide the personnel with as much information as possible in order to secure their involvement and commitment. On the other, it is difficult to know at an early stage what the present position is as well as the desired direction. For this reason, in order not to raise expectations which might later be difficult to satisfy, the information should not be too widely spread.

In line with this reasoning, we have opted for a middle course. At a very early stage, information about the project was given at a meeting attended by the School's approximately 100 staff members. Thereafter, the President of the School made a visit to each department personally presenting the project to them. On these occasions, time was allowed for question raising. At about the same time, an information leaflet in A4 format was produced describing the findings of the project so far. Moreover, six months after the start of the project, half a day of in-house education including all personnel was undertaken.

Despite this extensive programme to spread information, the project has been criticised on account of poor information. Many of the members who have perceived the information as poor have come to the conclusion that the project has been managed from the top down and that it has been propelled forward exclusively by the management. However, due to the in-house education programme, this criticism has tapered off. It can be concluded retrospectively that the observations made earlier regarding the difficulties involved in handling information were correct and that this problem has also affected this project.

5. CONCLUDING REMARKS

The quality work has been started at Chalmers amidst varying degrees of enthusiasm from its personnel. Some have adopted a wait-and-see policy while others have shown apparent enthusiasm. In retrospect, it can be said that a couple of mistakes have been made; however, at the time they were made it was difficult to foresee the problems they would create. The success of the project so far can in large be attributed to the management's commitment. As has been established previously by many people, "unless the management is totally committed, it is absolutely useless to even consider starting this type of project". The quality work at Chalmers has only just started; according to the quality philosophies it will never end.

6. REFERENCES

Carlsson, M., Development and empirical evaluation of a conceptual TQM-model for the forest industry, *39th EOQ '95 World Quality Congress*, Lausanne, Switzerland, 12-16 June, 1995.

Carlsson, D and Carlsson, M., 1996: Implementation of ISO 9000 in Swedish industry, paper forthcoming in *International Journal of Quality and Reliability Management.*

Howard, N., Implementing TQM at Oregon State University, in Chan, J. (ed.), *Quality and its applications*, Penshaw Press, Newcastle, 1993.

James, L., Using the criteria and process of the MENQA for improving educational institutions, in Kanji, G (ed.) *Total Quality Management*, Chapman and Hall, Sheffield, 1995.

Kanslersämbetet, Universitetskanslern, *Nytt från universitetskanslern*, Mars, 1995.

Autobiographical note.

Matts Carlsson (MSc. MBA, Lic. Eng., PhD) is associate professor of Quality and Reliability Management at the Department of Mechanical Engineeing at the division of Applied Engineering and Maritime Studies at Chalmers University of Technology, Gothenburg, Sweden. He is a member of the Faculty Senate at Chalmers. Member of AME, ASME, ASEM, IEEE, POMS and affiliate member of SAE International. He has been working as a senior consultant with most of the large Swedish multinational companies (e.g. ABB, Electrolux, Ericsson, Hägglunds, Pharmacia, SAAB, Volvo) as well as with the public sector. Hes research work has been focused on different aspects in the areas of management of product development and quality management, e.g. integration of technical functions, management of product development processeses and implementation of "total quality management" concepts. The results have been presented internationally in several conferences, reviewed and published as articles, in i.e. **European Journal on Engineering Education, International Journal of Production Research, International Journal on Quality and Reliability Management, International Journal on World Class Design for Manufacture, Journal of Quality and Reliability Engineering International, Journal of Product Innovation Management, Managing Changes in Production and Operations, R&D Management, Strategic Direction, Technology Strategies** and as research articles in books from **Chapman&Hall, Elsevier, Penshaw Press** and **Springler-Verlag**. In Sweden the results has reulted in several artikles and media apperance. Co-writer in the Swedish national encyclopedia. Member of Marquis 1996 edition of Who´s who in the world. He is a former member of the MIT project "International Motor Vehicle Program and EG/Comett program "World class manufacturing" ", is currently working in the EG/Leonardo project "Quality Management and Qualification Need Analysis" and with research in the area of quality management and management of product development as project manager at Gothenburg Research Institute. He can be contacted at the Department of Mechanical Engineering, Division of Applied Engineering and Maritime Studies, Chalmers University of Technology, Box 8873, S-402 73 Gothenburg, Sweden. Tel + 46 31 772 5025, Fax + 46 31 772 2689

17

An evaluation of the introduction of TQM in Castle junior school

P. Murgatroyd.
Murgatroyd and Hilsum,
27, Castle Road, Newport, Isle of Wight. PO30 1DT.
Telephone: 01983 523702

Abstract

This paper is a digest of an enquiry submitted as part requirement of an MA(Ed) degree. The study is an evaluation carried out over approximately two years of the introduction and implementation of TQM in a Junior School in the South of England. The TQM model adopted by the school was that described in 'Total Quality Management and the School' by Murgatroyd and Morgan, OUP 1993. The paper briefly addresses methods used to conduct the study, the data that emerged from the enquiry and some of the main findings. It concludes with some comments based on more wide ranging work in many other schools.

INTRODUCTION

At the start of the research period in 1993 the school was a Middle School with 415 pupils aged from 8 to 12 years on roll, and 17 teaching staff. The school was scheduled for reorganisation to a 7 to 11 (Years 3-6) Junior school in September 1994.

The Headteacher and a senior member of staff attended a day workshop on TQM and the school organised and run by Professor Stephen Murgatroyd, John Hilsum and myself in March 1993. Subsequently the school adopted TQM as a management process which it was hoped would assist in the major changes envisaged in the school. The Headteacher commissioned consultancy and support time from me which involved keeping records of observations, discussions, meetings and interviews with school personnel, governors and students.The Headteacher agreed that the findings would be used for an academic study.

METHODOLOGY

It seemed appropriate to adopt a qualitative approach since the investigation would focus on opinions and feelings, on impressions rather than empirical facts. This necessitated considerations of validity and reliability and constant reflection on the dual role of myself as consultant and researcher. The methods employed were: nonparticipant observation, participant observation, interviews, and analysis of documentation.

LITERATURE REVIEW

Reflections on the definition of quality and the nature of TQM informed the study. The literature review sought to trace the main features of TQM from the post war industrial setting (Deming 1982. Ishikawa 1986), through the various contributors to that movement (Crosby 1987. Juran 1989). It was argued that management development was largely ignored by education until relatively recently. The focus on management issues in education in the UK is set against the growing realisation that costs and demands for educational provision by the public purse are outstripping the available revenue. Furthermore, statistics show that examination results in the Pacific rim are considerably higher than those in the UK. The UK government increasingly expects schools to play their part in national economic competitiveness (DES 1988). Pressure is on to raise pupil achievement. The vocabulary of education management has changed (Sallis 1993. Murgatroyd and Morgan 1993). Commitment to quality is seen as essential for survival.

GATHERING DATA

The various stages of development in the school can be summarised as follows:
~ Development Day Closure Oct.1993.
Preliminary work on school Vision.Task teams established in four areas:
Communication; Standards; Parental Involvemen; Planning for Change.

~ Half a day spent with each Task Team to produce action plans.
Teams continue work in school reporting back progress at staff meetings.
Vision talk, vision imaging in progress.Interviews with Headteacher.

~ Development Day Closure Feb 1994.
Reviewing the School Development Plan. Signing up to the Vision.
THINKING, LEARNING, CARING.

~ Teams continue to work and report back.
Involving the children in the Vision.

~ School opens as a Junior School Sept 1994.

~ Review of progress through Interviews with staff, governors, children.
Observation of management meeting. Interviews with the Headteacher.

~ Written report to whole school Oct 1994.

CONCLUSIONS

I suggest that consensus is virtually impossible amongst a whole school community. However, I was witness to the attempt that Castle School made to give everyone a voice in the decision making process. The whole school community appeared to give its approval to the introduction of TQM. The data suggests some mixed views in the early stages:
* Caution as well as enthusiasm.
* Cynicism expressed by a small but powerful faction.
* Lack of understanding of TQM as a system.
* Widely expressed wish for improved communication.
* Willingness to join task teams.
* Early adoption of the language of TQM e.g. Vision, customers, goals.

Following the introductory stage a number of opportunities for observation and interview were built into the development plan. Members of the school were also recording their own reflections of the process in a number of ways, including a promotional video.

Taking into account the observations, interviews, analysis of documentation, and discussions there was evidence at the eighteen month review stage to suggest that the school's vision was known and understood by staff and pupils. The values of the school had been widely discussed and were evidenced in everyday processes in the school. The School Development Plan had stated goals, known to senior staff and many others. Communication, the priority of one of the Task teams, was thought to be more effective with evidence of improvements in the systems in the school. Strategy was only a vague concept for many. This is possibly because it was not considered to be contentious and little discussion had taken place about it. TQM tools, or ways of working, were making themselves felt particularly in management meetings. There was evidence of data being generated and used to inform decision making. Teams considered themselves to be more effective and once a team had done its job it could be disbanded. The culture of the school was something that people found difficult to define except in very general terms. The views expressed by the pupils confirmed the views of the teachers that the vision and values had been well communicated and were a part of everyday experience in school. All the evidence suggested a smooth transition from Middle School to Junior. Pupils spoke of a happy and caring learning environment. Even the youngest (7 year olds) were able to articulate what the vision meant in terms of their experience in school.

The data appear to suggest that the following factors contributed in some part :-
* Imposed external change (including reorganisation of the school).
* Commitment of the Headteacher.
* Time and resource dedicated to the preparation and introduction stages.
* Time and resource dedicated to support of implementation stage.
* Involvement of ancillary staff, parents, governors and children.
* Early identification of factors that would help/hinder the process.

However, there was also evidence to suggest that a high level of cynicism, albeit among only a few, can make a difference to the long term sustainability of a management system. Contrapreneurial activity can undermine positive attitudes and autocratic measures can work against a TQM culture. Good, hardworking classroom practitioners naturally have their focus on the children in front of them every day. Management was still seen by some as something that goes on elsewhere. Perhaps most telling was the lack of respondent perception, even after eighteen months of implementation, that TQM is a systematic way of working, and not just another initiative. Several respondents talked of TQM as something that had been "done" along with other things and was now over.

COMMENTS

I do not wish to make any claims about the generalisability of the findings in Castle School. But from the experiences of this school and others that I have worked with I can make a few observations. TQM is not a "quick fix". Any institution thinking of adopting it must be clear that it will throw up some contentious issues. It will bring to light some problems that people have allowed to remain undisturbed! It is about nothing less than changing the culture of an organisation. It takes a long time. I believe, and this has been confirmed by colleagues in schools all over the world, that the assistance of an external agent, whether it be LEA adviser, colleague from HE, or consultant , is a key factor in sustaining momentum over a period of time. Many schools are on a learning journey. I consider it a privilege to be travelling along with some of them.

REFERENCES

Crosby, P. (1979) Quality is Free. New York, Mentor Books.
Deming, W.E. (1986) Out of the Crisis.Cambridge, Cambridge University Press.
DES (1988) Education Reform Act. London, HMSO
Ishikawa, Kaoru (1985) What is Total Quality Control? New Jersey, Prentice-Hall.
Juran, J.M. (1989) Leadership for Quality. New York, Macmillan.
Murgatroyd, S. and Morgan, C. (1993) Total Quality Management and the School. OUP.
Sallis, E. (1993) Total Quality Management in Education. London, Kogan Page.

BIOGRAPHY

Patricia Murgatroyd is a partner in a freelance educational consultancy.She began her professional life as a teacher, worked for many years as Head of the IW Teachers' Centre and as an LEA projects manager. She currently divides her time between lecturing at the University of Portsmouth, consultancy work on management development in schools, and work overseas. She has run seminars and workshops on TQM in Hong Kong, Singapore, Hungary, Germany and Holland.She continues to write and work with Professor Stephen Murgatroyd when he visits the UK from his base in Athabasca University, Canada.

18

Assessing service quality in charity and voluntary organisations

Vaughan, E.   *Department of Management, Glasgow Caledonian*
                   University Glasgow G4 0BA Tel: 0141 331 3265
Shiu, E   *Glasgow Caledonian University*
Donnelly, M   *University of Strathclyde*

Abstract

This paper gives the first report of a survey of Scottish charities and voluntary organisations conducted in November 1995. The overall aim of the survey was to ascertain how these organisations currently articulate, assess and monitor the quality of service they provide. From analysis of 199 usable questionnaires it would appear that many are marketing research oriented and have an upward communication system in place which allows frequent face-to-face interactions between client-contact personnel and management. They state that they have a strong commitment to service quality and possess internal programmes for improving it. These findings require to be further investigated in terms of the nature and extent of the systems and procedures in place to support continuous improvement in this increasingly important sector of the service economy.

Keywords

Voluntary, charity, service quality, SERVQUAL

1   INTRODUCTION

The last two decades have seen considerable growth in the number of charities in Britain and the scope of their activities. There are now over 190,000 registered charities in Britain with a combined annual income of around £18bn; representing over 3% of GDP. With so many charities competing for a limited and reducing pool of funds and with the increasing needs of society in a prolonged recession, there is added urgency for the establishment of clear, meaningful performance criteria and means by which service quality can be measured, monitored and ultimately improved.

Many charity and voluntary organisations have found difficulty with the assessment of service quality even though they recognise the importance of understanding 'customer' needs (Bruce and Raymer 1992). These organisations increasingly make priority and resource decisions which directly impact on service quality and, perhaps surprisingly, is an area that has attracted little academic attention. Recent research has provided a rigorous method (the SERVQUAL Scale) for measuring service quality based on extensive theoretical and applied research in the US commercial sector (Parasuraman et al. 1988, Zeithaml et al. 1990). Essentially the SERVQUAL approach can be used to investigate the size and underlying reasons for five possible gaps in the process of service delivery in meeting customer expectations across the dimensions of Tangibles, Reliability, Responsiveness, Assurance and Empathy (Figure 1).

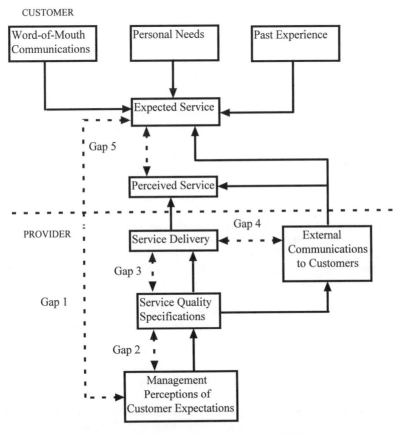

Figure 1 (Conceptual Model of Service Quality Zeithaml et al. 1990)

The SERVQUAL model has subsequently been refined as a general method for measuring service quality in both private and public sector organisations. Its application to the voluntary sector is the focus of this paper.

2   CASE STUDY

Investigations into gaps 1-5 were conducted in collaboration with a national umbrella organisation providing training and other support for Scottish voluntary and charitable groups. The outcomes from this study is reported elsewhere (Shiu E et al. 1996). In parallel a postal survey of managers of Scottish charities was administered in November 1995 to measure the extent to which the antecedents to gaps 1 and 2 were present within their organisations.

The charities were drawn from the SCVO[1] database (Vaughan E, Shiu E, Kelt R 1995). 404 charities were selected from the 22,500 plus on the database (by excluding organisations which are solely grantmaking, which have annual income less than £50,000, or whose addresses are not in either Glasgow or Edinburgh). The response rate was 50% with 199 usable returns. These were representative of the 404 contacted charities in terms of profiles according to 'annual income size' and 'source of financial resourcing'. The results from the analysis of these 199 questionnaires are summarised below:

2.1   Antecedents to gap 1 *'Not knowing what customers expect'*

- *Marketing research orientation.* Conducting marketing research and using the findings effectively is vital for management and empowered employees to obtain an understanding of clients in terms of their needs, wants, attitudes, expectations and perceptions. The survey results indicated that many of the charities who responded are 'active' in conducting marketing research, though charities with smaller income make less use of the information gathered.
- *Interaction between management and clients.* To truly understand the clients, management should have first hand knowledge of the clients. Most charities who responded believe that their managers do interact with clients regularly.
- *Upward communication.* Client-contact personnel are in regular contact with clients and as a result gain much insight and deep understanding of the clients' expectations and perceptions. This information needs to be communicated upwards to top management to help them understand the clients better. Most charities who responded believe that this is achieved within their organisations.
- *Levels of management.* Gap 1 can be reduced through upward communication, but the quality of the information can be greatly reduced if there are too many levels of management between top management and client-contact personnel. Almost all charities who responded perceive that this is not a problem.

2.2   Antecedents to gap 2 *'The wrong service quality standards'*

- *Management commitment to service quality.* Management commitment to service quality is essential in closing Gap 2. This commitment must be shared by both top and middle management in terms of establishing internal programmes for improving service quality,

---

[1] Scottish Council for Voluntary Organisations 18/19 Claremont Crescent Edinburgh EH7 4QD

supporting and rewarding staff in the drive towards better service quality. Many charities who responded believe that this is present within their organisations.

- *Perception of feasibility.* Management's perception of the feasibility of meeting clients' expectations affects the size of Gap 2, particularly if the perception of infeasibility is the result of an inaccurate view of clients' expectations. This is compounded by pressures most organisations face when operating at the limits of their capacity. In this respect, charities gave a mixed response.
- *Task standardisation and goal setting.* Standardisation helps the process of converting management perceptions into service quality standards and the setting of service quality goals. Most larger charities reported the use of computer systems and internal programmes to provide consistency in service to clients.

3   CONCLUSIONS

The responses overall indicated that at least one out of four charities collect little information on clients' needs and expectations and that further, half make little use of the information collected. As a consequence, even with commitment to service quality from top level management, specification of appropriate service quality standards are difficult if not impossible. Without standards and goals which are aligned with clients' needs and expectations, organisations have little success in delivering consistently high service quality. The survey results also indicated a lack of internal processes for setting specific service quality goals in support of continuously improving service quality. Furthermore, with many organisations operating at or near capacity, it is particularly important for them to focus on what is required by and expected from their clients.

The study provides a base line for the charities sector in terms of the management's view of Gaps 1 and 2 in the SERVQUAL model. Ongoing research will involve a qualitative follow-up study of the issues raised and the measurement of gaps 1 to 5 for particular charities.

4   REFERENCES

Bruce, I., and Raymer, A. (1992) Managing and staffing Britain's largest charities. *VOLPROF*, Centre for voluntary sector and not-for profit management, City University

Parasuraman, A., Zeithaml, V.A., and Berry, L.L. (1985) A conceptual model of service quality and its implications for future research. *Journal of Marketing*, **49**, 41-50

Parasuraman, A., Zeithaml, V.A., and Berry, L.L. (1988) SERVQUAL: a multiple-item scale measuring customer perceptions of service quality. *Journal of Retailing*, **64**, 12-40

Shiu, E., Vaughan, E., Donnelly, M. (1996) Measuring Service Quality in the Voluntary and Local Government Sectors. *Proceedings of the International Research Symposium on Public Services Management.* Aston Business School

Vaughan, E., Shiu, E., and Kelt, R. (1995) Charities Register in Scotland. Glasgow Caledonian University/SCVO technical report

Zeithaml, V.A., Parasuraman, A., and Berry, L.L. (1990) *Delivering Quality Service*, The Free Press, Maxwell Macmillan

PART THREE

The Role of Self Assessment

19

Converting an internal audit into a positive process

G.D. Beecroft
Institute for Improvement in Quality and Productivity
University of Waterloo, Waterloo, Ontario, Canada N2L 3G1
tel. 519-888-4593, fax 519-746-5524
dbeecroft@watdragon.uwaterloo.ca

Auditing is not new. Audits have been conducted for many years and consist of several different types – financial audits, tax audits, Total Quality audits and quality system audits, for example. Recent emphasis on both ISO 9000 and its automotive counterpart QS-9000 has generated a frenzy of quality system audit experiences. Each of the three types of audits associated with quality system auditing – customer audits, third party audits and internal audits – serves a different purpose. A *customer audit* is conducted by a customer on a supplier or potential supplier to assess the supplier's quality system in order to evaluate the supplier's ability to meet the product quality requirements of the customer. A *third party audit* is conducted by an independent auditor licensed as a Registrar by a national accreditation body (such as the Standards Council of Canada or the UKAS). The purpose of a third party audit is to evaluate a supplier and then grant a certificate to the supplier to demonstrate that the supplier's quality system meets a particular Quality System Standard such as ISO 9000 or QS-9000. An *internal audit* is conducted by a company on itself to determine if its quality system is in place and is effective. Opportunities for improvement should be identified during this process and then plans put in place to implement these changes. Documented internal audits are required of both ISO 9000 and QS-9000 quality systems.

THE TYPICAL NEGATIVE AUDIT

Historically audits have been viewed as a negative process (summarized in Figure 1). This viewpoint is the result of how the audit was conducted, who conducted it and how audit findings were implemented. Audits typically imposed from outside the organization – usually governments, customers or corporations – only result in problems, things that the organization must respond to and fix. Many companies prepare employees for an audit in an effort to minimize this negative impact. They coach them on how to respond to the auditor's questions so that the company does not "fail" the audit. During the many lectures I present on looking for?" Yet processes and procedures should be put in place to address the issues of product quality or service, costs and/or customer satisfaction – not to satisfy some "perceived" auditor requirement. Such preparation and rehearsal only increases the stress level caused by the audit and drives fear through the organization. Auditors are escorted through the plant to ensure that they talk to only the "right" people. Often real problems or weaknesses remain hidden from the auditors. Such an audit process focuses on people – many audit findings are attributed to an employee failing to follow a specific procedure. The audit tends to be seen as destructive due to the lack of any positive feedback. There is minimum opportunity to change the external audit process as guidelines are strict and the process tightly controlled by standards themselves, such as in ISO 10011 *Guidelines for Auditing Quality Systems*.

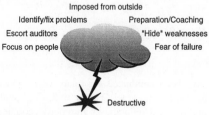

Figure 1   The usual audit process

DEVELOPING A MORE POSITIVE APPROACH

Given this history, and the fact that most of us have years of such auditing experiences to overcome, an internal audit will likely be viewed with similar negativity. The process will not add any real value to the organization – problems will still be hidden from the auditors and the cost of auditing will simply increase customer product or service costs. Many of the external audit practices are duplicated in the internal audit, but the internal audit process is not controlled to the same degree by external standards – there is sufficient flexibility to convert it into a positive process. While this is not a simple task, and much has yet to be learned, it has been found that by addressing several key points (shown in Figure 2) internal audits can be much more constructive.

1. Change process, change name
2. Share responsibility
3. Identify strengths
4. Focus on process
5. Make recommendations
6. Solve "real" problems
7. Prioritize findings
8. Drive improvement

Figure 2   Converting the audit into a positive process

In order for the internal audit process to be *seen* as different from the external audit process it must *be* different. If the process is different it should also be called by a different name. Organizations that have tried to make the internal audit process more constructive but have retained the same name have been less successful because of all the "baggage" the old name brings with it. I used to like to call the internal process an "assessment"; however, now external auditors are also calling their process an "assessment" in order to minimize the negative impact that they have historically had on organizations. Therefore it is necessary to come up with another new name, possibly "review".

Usually companies set up an internal audit department or function, which tends to limit the ownership of the quality system to the audit department. But by sharing the "review" between different departments each time, perhaps even with different individuals, ownership of the quality system is transferred back to the various departments – the only restriction is that a department can not review their own area. The downside of this role sharing is that training is required prior to each review. Training should include an understanding of the quality system requirements plus information on the audit process itself. However, this disadvantage then becomes an advantage as the workforce becomes more knowledgeable about all requirements and thus more likely to consistently meet requirements.

DRIVING IMPROVEMENT

It is important to identify strengths of the organization during an internal review. Positive feedback can increase morale throughout the workforce and will stimulate improvements built upon the strengths of the organization. Strengths identified in one area can be transferred to other departments.

Auditing is often practiced as a punitive process. The internal review should focus solely on the processes and *not* the people. If it is discovered that a particular process is not being implemented, assume that there is something wrong with the process and change *it* rather than try to force employees to conform to the process. While employees do occasionally neglect to follow a required process, all too frequently there is insufficient effort taken to learn the root cause of such a mistake. It is much easier to simply "reinstruct" or "retrain" the employee on the "correct procedure". If deficiencies or opportunities for improvement are discovered, involve the review team in identifying solutions and their implementation. This participation will increase the positive value of the internal review process by making life easier and by solving real problems for the workforce. An internal review is successful when the people performing the processes under review feel the internal review team has made their job easier or better.

One of the biggest challenges of the internal review process is to prioritize the findings of the review team. It is very easy to bury the organization with review findings. As the number of deficiencies or opportunities for improvement increase, the probability of implementing solutions decreases. Therefore a key role of the review team is to prioritize their findings and select those which have the biggest impact on driving improvement.

The internal audit process – the internal review – is the key to an effective quality system implementation. Until organizations successfully transform their internal audits into a positive experience the process will be viewed as a tool for compliance verses a tool for continuous improvement, and add minimal or negative value to the business.

20

Integrating quality and business planning using a self assessment matrix

A. Brown and T. Van der Wiele
Department of Management, Edith Cowan University, Pearson St,
Churchlands, 6018, Australia, 61 9 2738278, 61 9 2738754,
a.brown@cowan.edu.au
Strategic Quality Management Institute, Erasmus University, PO Box
1738, 3000 DR, Rotterdam, Netherlands, 31 10 4081354, 31 10
4526094, wiele@intorg.few.eu.nl

Abstract

This paper explores how quality award criteria (quality management principles) can be integrated into the business planning process in organisations to provide an effective means of self-assessment for the entire organisation.

The experience of several large Australian public and private sector organisations is examined. Various issues are explored including the link between quality and the organisational mission, vision and values, the use of a self-assessment matrix as a guide for quality and how the matrix is used as an operational tool at all levels in the organisation on the quality journey.

Keywords
Quality management, self-assessment matrix, planning

Introduction

Many TQM efforts have floundered because organisations have only given attention to teams and tools. They remain what Lascelles and Dale (1991) term drifters and tool pushers rather than moving to improvers and winners in business excellence. This is largely because quality principles have not been integrated into the business planning process, quality has not been viewed as a strategic variable, something which permeates all business processes, activities and functions.

The challenge for organisations who pursue quality is, therefore, how to incorporate quality management principles into the organisation's planning process and to ensure that all organisational functions adopt them. This paper draws upon some case study research to show how large organisations are using a self-assessment matrix to facilitate this process.

Quality and Strategy

Organisations may take various steps in order to integrate quality into their business strategy and include;

• incorporating it into the mission, vision and values;
• formulating quality based performance targets and goals;
• communicating the quality strategy throughout the organisation;
• making quality an essential part of all review processes;
• having all organisational sections adopt quality in their operational planning.

Many organisations have found that a quality development (or self-assessment) matrix assists all sections of the organisation in building quality into their strategic planning activities. The matrix identifies the elements of quality which are important in the organisation (horizontal axis) by various levels of achievement on these (vertical axis). Cells within the matrix usually contain descriptions which assist in locating the position of an organisation or part of it. In many respects it is an adaptation of Crosby's (1979) quality maturity grid.

In a recent Australian survey of self-assessment (Brown and Van der Wiele, in press), twenty seven percent of respondents indicated that a quality matrix was used in their organisation. Most often the criteria of the Australian Quality Award (AQA) model or a slightly modified version was used.

Applications of the Matrix

The experience of three large Western Australian organisation's in using a self-assessment matrix is outlined below. They are representative of a number of Australian organisations who use such a matrix. The two public sector organisations are, the BMA, which is responsible for managing public sector building and maintenance projects in the state of Western Australia and secondly, the WAWA, responsible for the overall water management in Western Australia including water supply, waste water treatment and drainage. The third, Alcoa, is a large, fully integrated aluminium producer. Before developing a self-assessment matrix, all three had been involved in quality management activities for several years and all have quality built into their vision and mission statements.

The BMA strategic plan incorporates nine specific directions as a focus for all activities (BMA, 1993). These directions include; delighted customers, continuous improvement, private sector partnerships, strategic asset management and motivated and productive employees. Specific business strategies are defined for each of these directions, measures are developed and targets are set. One example is shown below.

Direction	Measures and Targets
Delighted customers	Customer satisfaction by service - 80% by June 1995 Customer focus of employees - Index of 5.5 by Dec. 1995

As a tool to facilitate continuous improvement and progress on the strategic directions, the BMA "quality ladder" (self-assessment matrix) is used. The matrix is built on seven categories of the AQA, with the addition of one extra, private sector partnerships. It has maturity levels extending from 0 to 10 reflecting a state of ignorance [level 0] through to excellence [level 9 and 10]. Each cell in the matrix identifies operational indicators and strategies for implementing a quality management approach and incorporates the approach, deployment and results of the quality awards.

The ladder plays a central role in business planning, particularly at the divisional level, and is used to monitor progress and to define actions for improvement on a regular basis. Specifically, the ladder is used for;
• measuring how well the BMA is achieving quality;

• identifying areas for improvement;
• providing improvement targets;
• enabling comparisons with other quality organisations, which measures themselves against the model and criteria of the AQA;
• preparing the BMA for applying for the AQA.

Organisational divisions use the ladder to address questions such as; Where are we?, What targets can we define for the next 12 months?, and, What are the key quality initiatives to take in order to reach that goal? Quality mentors and workshops are used to assist each division to develop an action plan which improvement teams then use as a guide for their activities. The Planning and Quality department in the BMA has intentionally been kept small (4 persons) and acts as a facilitator for the departments and business units.

Methods used for self-assessment of positioning on the matrix include; benchmarking, employee opinion surveys and customer surveys. These all provide input into the strategic plan for the next period. Applying for the AQA in 1994 provided an external measure of progress.

Quality has now become a monthly agenda item for the management executive board related to the monthly review of the business and the progress in improving the organisation. The significance of quality is reflected in the BMA annual report which makes reference to quality indicators.

Benefits claimed from this approach by the BMA include; more effective communication of how the different elements of quality fit together, a universal understanding of quality, a united direction, a means of self-assessment and it is based on best practice which offers a credible measure of quality.

At the WAWA, the Strategic Direction Plan 1994-2004 contains five main elements which are: mission, objectives and culture; guiding principles and activities; vision; corporate strategic initiatives; and performance indicators.

Quality is included in all of these. For example, the culture includes five primary values, namely; satisfying customers, continuous improvement, integrity, respect for people and concern for the environment. Corporate strategic initiatives outlined in the long term strategic plan include; to implement quality improvement, to implement new business planning and management processes and to foster a more commercial orientation as a public agency.

The guiding (quality) principles are placed in a matrix similar to that of the BMA which serves as a planning tool for all business units. These principles include; customer perceptions determine quality, planning drives improvement, treat suppliers as partners and include everyone creatively in continuous improvement. Managers in each division use it to identify their current status and to set improvement themes and targets for the next twelve months. Bi-annual employee surveys and annual customer surveys are conducted to assist in an assessment of status. The CEO of the WAWA also has a performance agreement with the relevant state government minister which is based on these seven principles.

At the branch level (eg engineering, finance, etc) the matrix is used to identify key organisational processes and improvement priorities and this has proven to be the more challenging part of the process. A small team has been assembled to act as internal consultants and self-help guides have been prepared to assist in using the matrix. Training is directed at operational units and includes instructions on how the matrix is used to provide overall direction and provides various tools and processes which can be used for moving up the matrix.

The adoption of a more strategic approach to quality has helped the WAWA revive quality management by providing direction and a framework which has universal application throughout the organisation. It has helped define what quality means and allows each organisational unit to develop their own operational plans within the broader quality framework.

At Alcoa, a cross functional team has developed a matrix referred to as the "Alcoa improvement roadmap". The aim is to link all quality activities within Alcoa to a comprehensive strategic quality approach. The "roadmap" is based very much on the European Quality Award structure of enablers and results and is now being piloted throughout the organisation.

Categories in the matrix include; leadership, people management, information management and process management. For each category, two or three themes are defined which are essential elements in relation to Alcoa's vision, policy and values. An example of a theme is shown below.

Category:	Theme:
Process Management	Process identification and standardisation Process control Process improvement

The matrix is linked to the business planning process which defines a small number of issues which are considered as important for the organisation for the next planning period. These focal points [major improvement milestones, and continuous improvement milestones] are than deployed to the different levels in the organisations and to the several sites of the company. At lower levels of the organisation the quality matrix is used to define what has to be done related to specific criteria in order to be able to reach the specific goal.

For each theme, concrete and measurable maturity levels are defined (seven levels). These statements make the matrix an operational tool whereby it is possible for every group within the organisation to define where they are on the maturity ladder and provide direction to the improvement activities to move to higher levels. It is intended that groups will be able to score where they are on the matrix.

Benefits which Alcoa expects include; a common language within the organisation, a checklist for defining improvement goals in different parts of the organisation, the provision of benchmarks and that it forces people to think and act on quality issues in a more holistic way.

Summary

These cases provide an insight into how quality can provide a strategic focus in organisations and how self-assessment matrices help to facilitate this. The matrix provides a strategic focus by linking the vision to action strategies based on quality. All sections of the organisation can use these to identify where they are and where they need to be. They are able to identify specific actions/measures of quality within each cell of the matrix to give meaning to quality progress. The responsibility for quality management is then placed throughout the organisation from senior executive level to "front-line" operational levels.

According to Raynor (1992:8), "none of the benefits of strategic quality are possible unless quality becomes the measure to which all company initiatives are compared". The cases above suggest that these companies are attempting to create a culture in which this is possible.

References

Brown, A. and Van der Wiele, T. (in press) Quality Management Self-Assessment in Australia, *Total Quality Management.*.

Building Management Authority, (1993) Annual Report.

Crosby, P.B. (1979) *Quality is Free; The Art of Making Quality Certain*, New American Library, New York.

Lascelles, D.M. and Dale, B.G. (1991) Levelling Out the Future, *Total Quality Management*, **3**, 6, 325-30.

Raynor, M.E. (1992) Quality as a Strategic Weapon, *Journal of Business Strategy*, **13**, 5, 3-9.

Water Authority of Western Australia, (1993) Strategic Direction Plan (Long Term Plan) 1994-2004.

Biography

Alan Brown is Associate Professor in Management at Edith Cowan University and also Director of the Small and Medium Enterprise Research Centre. He has published and presented many papers in the area of quality management and human resource management.

Ton van der Wiele is Director of the Strategic Quality Management Institute at Erasmus University in the Netherlands. He has published widely in the area of quality management including self-assessment. He was a Visiting Fellow at Edith Cowan University in 1994.

21

Driving commitment to business excellence through self-assessment

Dr S.A. Black
Organisation and Quality Development Manager
Empire Stores Ltd
Canal Road
Bradford
West Yorkshire
United Kingdom
BD99 4XB
Tel: 00 44 1274 763707
Fax: 00 44 1274 763819

Abstract

Top management commitment is commonly recognised as a prerequisite for driving long-term improvement. The launch of many improvement programmes is usually supported by training and educating managers in improvement concepts and techniques. Where organisations have failed with TQM the causes are often a lack of commitment from top management, or a failure to integrate improvement into organisational objectives. Empire Stores Ltd is using the European Model for TQM and the self-assessment process to launch a company-wide Business Excellence Programme. This paper examines how Empire has used self-assessment as a vehicle for providing senior management with a practical education in Business Excellence, for establishing their commitment to a long term process of improvement and for building company improvement objectives into business plans.

Keywords

European Model for TQM, Self-Assessment, Business Planning, TQM implementation.

1 INTRODUCTION

Empire is an established player in the UK home shopping market. Whilst in a loss making position in 1991 the company was acquired by the French retailer Redoute Catalogue SA. Significant investment in technology and an emphasis on improved customer service enabled a return to profit in 1993. In addition, a number of teamworking initiatives introduced within the warehousing and distribution centres in 1993 have proven successful. It is recognised, however, that further progress requires an organisation-wide approach to improvement.

Recent research has identified management commitment, active leadership, education, planning and prioritisation as significantly important elements in the development of a successful TQM system (Black and Porter, 1995). Self-assessment using the European Model for TQM (EFQM, 1995) is commonly viewed as a diagnostic tool to support progress reviews and improvement planning (van der Wiele, 1995). It is the author's view that there is also potential for using the European model to achieve a common understanding of TQM and for self-assessment to provide managers with practical experience of TQM thereby driving their commitment to Business Excellence. For all these reasons, the model has been introduced in Empire to support the implementation of a company-wide improvement process.

2 PRACTICAL EDUCATION AND A COMMON UNDERSTANDING

Until 1995 the general understanding of the TQM philosophy amongst Empire management was rather mixed and no formal quality awareness training had been conducted outside the operations departments. A number of departments within the business had, however, adopted teamworking approaches for improving performance during 1993, so a number of improvement concepts were being introduced into the business. For many departments, however, the diversification of approaches was proving to be a complicating factor and those involved recognised the need for a consistent company-wide approach for improving the business. A series of senior management forums during 1995 debated this issue, during which the European Model was introduced and agreed as the basis for a commonly understood language and approach to improving the business. 'Business Excellence' was adopted as the preferred term for labelling the TQM concepts described by the model.

As a first encounter with Business Excellence, all directors, senior managers and key departmental managers were introduced to self-assessment through externally approved EFQM assessor training courses. Further experience was gained from participation in data collection and assessments within Empire itself. As part of the learning process it was felt that practical use of the self-assessment approach would expose managers to the whole range of TQM issues and concepts to allow an understanding of their relevance in the business. Empire has since started to use the model to underpin and reinforce training, development and change initiatives during 1996.

3 GAINING COMMITMENT

Developing an understanding of the logical approach suggested by the European model is not difficult. A more critical success factor is the tangible commitment of managers to the Business Excellence approach. It was recognised that the visible involvement of Board members would encourage the commitment of others (Wall and Zeynel, 1991), so Board members and managers are collectively involved in the self-assessment process. Secondly, managers see how their contribution through the assessments shape future company improvement plans.

In the early stages of the programme, Empire's approach to introducing Business Excellence focused on gaining the support and involvement of the senior management team. The involvement of middle management in self-assessment has been relatively limited although their role in the pursuit and implementation of improvement action is critical.

4 A DIAGNOSTIC TOOL

The self-assessment process is primarily a diagnostic tool for identifying improvement priorities. As Empire was effectively starting out on the Business excellence route it was felt that an in-depth review of the current situation across the business was required. In the autumn of 1995 Empire ran a pilot assessment using the Customer Satisfaction criterion of the European Model. The project involved a cross-functional team of senior managers that had been externally trained on self-assessment techniques. This pilot proved that the self-assessment approach was a suitable method for providing a common and practical understanding and commitment to Business Excellence.

It was recognised, however, that the improvement actions resulting from this pilot project were confined largely to specific departments represented by the individuals involved. This suggested that:-

1. The most meaningful assessment would require an examination of all 9 criteria from the European model, covering all departments within the business.

2. The Board must be involved in the decision making process following the assessments in order to drive departmental and cross-functional improvement activity.

5 INPUT INTO BUSINESS PLANNING

The experience of many organisations embarking on this process is that the assessment reveals a huge list of improvement issues (Mason, 1996; Porter and Tanner, 1995; Shacklady, 1995). The Board's role in prioritising improvements in the light of resource requirements and business plans is viewed, therefore, as critical. The findings of self-assessment should provide an informed input into planning future business improvements, defining business and departmental objectives and supporting the financial planning process.

The Empire process is designed so that assessment findings from a number of project groups examining different criteria are pooled. Improvement opportunities are defined at Board level based on the outputs of the assessments. The Board's priorities are cascaded into departmental objectives, against which progress is regularly reviewed. The on-going objective of the process is to build Business Excellence into the way that Empire works.

6 REVIEWING PROGRESS

The structured self-assessment exercise commonly allows periodic reviews of progress against the model (Bowden, 1995; Porter and Tanner, 1995, van der Wiele, 1995). Empire's process is designed to fit in with the annual planning and budgeting cycle. It is expected that the same in-depth learning exercise will not be required at each review and that an alternative methodology can be applied. Fortunately self-assessment is an approach that can be readily customised to suit organisational needs, from questionnaires and focus or discussion groups through to "audit" teams and more sophisticated review systems (EFQM, 1995; Hakes, 1995).

7 CONCLUSIONS

The self-assessment process has proved to be a useful tool for educating directors, senior and middle managers on the issues of Business Excellence. It has also been effective in making individuals aware of the need for improvements within the business thereby forging commitment to the company's improvement process. In particular, experience of the European model highlights the need for managers to appreciate the interdependencies between departmental activities rather than merely their own functional responsibilities.

For most businesses, constraints on resources are a significant factor when planning improvement activities. It is critical for initiatives to be aligned with business needs and for time, effort and resources to be directed effectively. This requires an approach that can reliably inform business planning by identifying improvement opportunities across a wide range of fronts including people, process and resource issues. Self-assessment is a tool that can be used by to provide the improvement agenda for an organisation's planning processes.

8 REFERENCES

Bowden, P. (1995) A Practical Implementation of Business Management Assessment, in *Proceedings of the 1995 Learning Edge Conference*, EFQM, Vienna.

Black, S.A. and Porter, L.J. (1995) An empirical model for total quality management. *Total Quality Management*, **6**, 149-164.

E.F.Q.M. (1995) Self Assessment. *1995 Guidelines*, European Foundation for Quality Management, Brussels.

Hakes, C. (1995) The Corporate Self-Assessment Handbook. *Second Edition*, Chapman & Hall, London.

Mason, J. (1996) World-class water. *Self-Assessment: The Magazine of Continuous Quality Improvement*, **1**, 19-21.

Porter, L.J. and Tanner, S.I. (1995) Business improvement through self-assessment - a case study from financial services, in *Total Quality Management Proceedings of the First World Congress* (ed. G.K. Kanji), Chapman & Hall, London.

Shacklady, G (1995) A refined programme at Gulf Oil, *Self Assessment: The Magazine of Continuous Quality Improvement*, **4**, 13-16.

van der Wiele, T. (1995) Pan European Survey on Self-Assessment, in *Proceedings of the 1995 Learning Edge Conference*, EFQM, Vienna.

Wall, S.J. and Zeynel, S.C. (1991) The Senior Manager's Role in Quality Improvement, *Quality Progress*, 24, 1, 66-68.

9 BIOGRAPHY

Simon Black is Organisation and Quality Development Manager for Empire Stores Ltd. He holds a PhD in Management from the University of Bradford Management Centre, UK. His doctoral research won the EFQM's 1994 European Quality Award for Doctoral Theses in TQM and his continuing research interests include the assessment of TQM systems and the development of scientific research methods. His current role is one of driving a corporate improvement programme and includes the design, introduction and management of a self-assessment process that integrates continuous improvement into business planning.

22

The use of the European business excellence model as a business planning tool by an NHS trust

H. Walshaw
Director of Corporate Development
Wakefield and Pontefract Community Health NHS Trust
Fernbank
3-5 St John's North
Wakefield
West Yorkshire
WF1 3QD
Tel: 01924 814814
Fax: 01924 814987

Abstract

This paper describes how one NHS Trust identified the European Business Excellence Model as the most appropriate tool for use in supporting it on its continued journey towards TQM. The model will enable the integration of various quality initiatives into the main business planning cycle of the Trust, building upon the Trust's previous achievement of 'Investor in People' status and a Charter Mark for its full range of services.

INTRODUCTION

Wakefield and Pontefract Community Health NHS Trust was established on 1st April 1993 to provide community health and mental health services principally to the 319 000 people who live in the Wakefield Metropolitan District. The Trust employs approximately 2000 staff, its services are purchased by 35 GP fundholding practices (80% of the population) and 10 District Health Authorities.

From the beginning of the Trust there has been a strong focus on developing a culture of Continuous Quality Improvement led by the Chief Executive and the Trust Board. In April 1995 senior managers self-assessed the Trust against the organisation's own Quality Strategy, an NHS Executive letter *'Achieving an organisation wide approach to quality'*, (NHSE,1993*)* and a framework developed as part of an NHS benchmark initiative. This process identified major achievements by the Trust in developing a CQI culture, areas were also identified where further improvements were required. The Trust analysed the suitability of known quality frameworks to take the Trust forward into its next phase of quality improvement. From this work the European Business Excellence Model was chosen.

The Trust achieved 'Investor in People' status in March 1995 and received the Prime Minister's prestigious award of a Charter Mark for the whole of its services in December 1995.

WHAT IS THE EUROPEAN BUSINESS EXCELLENCE MODEL?

The model is aimed ultimately at achieving excellence in business results and is based on the premise that customer satisfaction, employee satisfaction and impact on society are achieved through leadership, driving policy and strategy, people management, resources and processes and leading ultimately to excellence in business results.

The model identifies five enabler criteria which deliver the four result criteria as identified in the diagram below

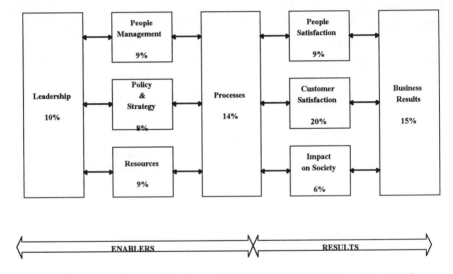

Figure 1 The European Business Excellence Model (The British Quality Foundation, 1995).

The model is coherent and comprehensive encompassing all the aspects necessary for an organisation to operate successfully. The model is designed to enable the organisation to assess current performance and to identify opportunities for improvement in development. It provides a basis for comparison both internally and externally and shows the progress which has been made over time.

To enable self-assessment each of the criteria in the model is broken down into a number of criterion parts. Different scoring systems are used for the enabler and result areas. The enabler criteria are concerned with how the organisation approaches each of the criterion parts. Information is required on the excellence of approach used and the extent of deployment of the approach vertically through all levels of the organisation and horizontally to all areas and activities.

The result criteria are concerned with what the organisation has achieved and is achieving. The organisation's results and trends for all criteria are addressed in terms of the organisations actual performance, performance against its own targets and wherever possible, the performance of competitors or similar organisations and the performance of 'best in class' organisations.

WHY THE EUROPEAN BUSINESS EXCELLENCE MODEL?

The model was identified for the following reasons:

- Its common sense approach was easy to understand.
- It provides a systematic approach to the quality journey already begun.
- It builds upon the achievements of a Charter Mark and 'Investor in People' status.
- It provides a framework for the development of annual Trust Business Plan and the Strategic Direction.
- It enables the full integration of quality improvement into business planning.
- It provides a systematic self-assessment process by which to identify areas for improvement and monitor improvements made.
- It enables benchmarking both within and out of the Health Service.
- It is fully applicable within the Health Service environment.
- It enables communication within the organisation with customers of the Trust and other service providers.

WHERE NOW?

Six internal assessors have been trained to use the European Business Excellence Model by a trainer licensed by the British Quality Foundation. They are undertaking a systematic assessment of the organisation, by assessing documentary evidence, staff focus groups, a staff questionnaire and individual interviews with senior Directors and Managers within the organisation. This will provide a baseline assessment against which an annual re-assessment will take place. Action planned in the light of these assessments will then be fed into the following year's Business Plan and corporate objectives. The Business Plan and Strategic Direction themselves use the model as a framework. Following the initial assessment the Trust plans to develop a benchmarking club, initially with other Health Service organisations utilising the European Business Excellence Model.

During 1998 the Trust is due to re-submit itself for assessment for a Charter Mark and 'Investor in People'. During the same year it is proposed that the Trust will use the British Quality Foundation to externally validate its score using external assessors. The organisation plans to be in a position by this time to reach a score of 500 plus. If it achieves this then it will then consider applying for the United Kingdom Quality Award in 1999.

REFERENCES

British Quality Foundation. (1995) Guide to Self Assessment (Health).
NHSE. (1993) Achieving an organisation wide approach to quality, EL(93)116.

BIBLIOGRAPHY

Hazel Walshaw a qualified nurse has worked in the Health Service since leaving school, working as a Health Visitor in Barnsley, Doncaster and the Shetland Islands. She gained a BA(Hons) degree, Social Dimensions of Health at Sheffield Hallam University in 1988 after studying part time. Hazel has held various general management positions within the Health Service before gaining her present post of Executive Director of Nursing and Corporate Development.

22a

Is the business excellence model applicable in the UK public sector?

Deborah M. Reed
University of the West of England
Faculty of Engineering, Coldharbour Lane, Bristol, BS16 1QY,
England, Tel. 0171 963 8013, Fax. 0171 963 8001.

Abstract

The UK Quality Award was opened to the "not-for-profit" sector in late 1994. Six months earlier a research programme began to test the assumption that the Business Excellence Model and self assessment processes are applicable and of value to public sector organisations (PSOs).

This paper describes the history and development of the Business Excellence Model and self assessment in the West, the use of pilot sites to test the applicability and value-add of the model and self assessment techniques within UK PSOs, some results from the first eighteen months and the ongoing development of guidance in the use of the model and self assessment.

Key words

Model of Business Excellence, Self Assessment, public sector.

1   THE DEVELOPMENT OF THE BUSINESS EXCELLENCE MODEL

Total Quality Management (TQM) is not a single concept but a convergence of ideas initially developed with the post-war renaissance of Japanese industry, supported by Deming (1982) and Juran (1992), which gradually moved from an emphasis on quality control, to a deeper concept based on organisation-wide principles of the ideal organisational culture. Later the commercial significance of quality was supported by anecdotal evidence put forward by writers such as Thomas L. Peters and Robert H. Waterman Jr. (Peters, 1982) and the concept that "quality is free" as developed by Phillip B. Crosby (Crosby, 1980).

By the early 1980's governmental and industrial leaders in the West were concerned by a lack of productivity leading to a failure to compete in world markets. In America a national productivity study was legislated in October 1982 which lead to the recognition of the need for a national quality and productivity award. The process to legislate the award led to the development of a bill which stated, inter alia, that it would help to improve quality and productivity by "establishing guidelines and criteria that [could] be used by business, industrial, governmental and other enterprises in evaluating their own quality improvement efforts" (DeCarlo,1990). The Malcolm Baldrige National Quality Award (MBNQA) was established on August 20 1987 with a basic structure of seven categories for self appraisal. The concept of self assessment had been born!

In early 1992 , the UK Quality Award (UKQA) Committee was established "to consider and report ... on the feasibility of developing a new prestige award for British business ... ." (Henderson, 1992). The proposals were to be in a form suitable for self assessment, in harmony with the European Quality Award (EQA), launched by the European Foundation for Quality Management (E.F.Q.M.) in 1992, and incorporate the lessons learnt from MBNQA.

The EQA model had been developed from the MBNQA, with the active involvement of UK organisations, and to develop an alternative for a UKQA could have undermined the world-wide TQM development process. The EQA model with its emphasis on self assessment and improvement planning was accepted . The European process was not seen as a catalyst to inspire nationally-focussed businesses, small and medium sized organisations, regional or locally based businesses, and the public and voluntary sectors and that therefore there was a need for a new UKQA. This model is now known as the Business Excellence Model.

2.   THE BUSINESS EXCELLENCE MODEL

The Business Excellence Model states that **Customer Satisfaction, People** (employee) **Satisfaction** and **Impact on Society** are achieved through **Leadership** driving **Policy and Strategy, People Management, Resources** and **Processes,** leading ultimately to excellence in **Business Results**. Each of the nine elements of the model can be used to assess an organisation's progress towards excellence. Full details of the model can be found in the Guide to Self Assessment (British Quality Foundation, 1995).   The model is shown graphically in Figure 1.

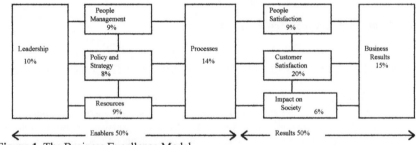

Figure 1. The Business Excellence Model.

3.   PUBLIC SECTOR PILOT SITES PROGRAMME

This research is based on a network of PSOs piloting self assessment, with the objective of creating improvement plans towards organisational excellence. The pilots are the Benefits Agency, the Employment Service, the Inland Revenue, a faculty of a University, a regional health authority, an Army maintenance and distribution workshop, three local authority units, a city council, a hospital trust, a county constabulary and a small "not for profit" membership organisation. The examination of the use of the model and self assessment in the pilot PSOs is based on regular, structured reviews.

3.1 Model applicability

The lessons learned fall into two major categories - Organisational Influences and Model 'Fit'.

The influences assumed in the model can be categorised into five basic areas, the *Internal Influencers*, the *People* of the Organisation, the *Customers* of the Organisation , the *External Influencers* and the *Suppliers* to the Organisation. Analysis of the model shows that these influences are assumed to be approximately 50%, 20%, 20%, 5% and 5% respectively. Figure 2 below shows the equivalent levels ascribed by the pilot PSOs. It is apparent that the 'influence' assumptions of the model, although not exactly matching with the influences on and within PSOs, are sufficiently similar to facilitate the use of the model in this sector.

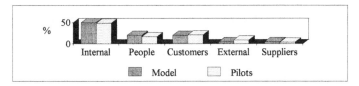

Figure 2 Comparison of the influences assumed in the model and perceived by PSOs

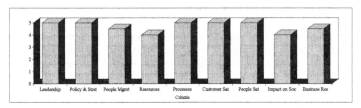

Figure 3 Perceived 'Fit' of the model criteria to PSOs.

When reviewing the model 'fit' - assuming that 'no fit' is one and a 'perfect fit' is five - the results suggest that there is generally a good 'fit', see Figure 3. Similar testing of the weightings of the model suggests that the proportions are accurate for PSOs, see Figure 4.

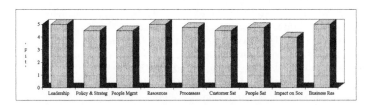

Figure 4 Perceived 'Fit' of the model criteria weightings to PSOs.

3.2 Self Assessment

A common concern to emerge, as the pilot programmes developed, was which method of self assessment to use. Consequently, the pilot representatives, jointly, carried out an analysis of the six methods described in the Guide to Self Assessment (British Quality Foundation, 1995) and the "pros and cons" associated with them. The analysis identified that the choice should be based on nine variables, the culture and style of the organisation, the level of resources available, the objectives of the organisation and the self assessment, the level to which TQM is understood within the organisation, the amount of time available, the potential threats and benefits of each approach, as perceived by the staff, the size and geographical dispersal of the organisation.

3.3   Guidance Development

The Guide to Self Assessment available in the 1993/4 was specifically devised for use in the private sector. The guidelines for 1994/5 were influenced by the lessons learned from the early research; a brief introduction specifically for PSOs and two additional sections of guidance were incorporated. For the 1995/6 Guide to Self Assessment various enhancements were incorporated. In addition to the UK research, the E.F.Q.M. was developing ideas in readiness to open the EQA to PSOs and in America preparations were being made, through pilot applications, to potentially open the MBNQA to PSOs. The result was that five versions of the Guide to Self Assessment were developed, recognising the various sectors within the UK economy. These publications are the subject of an evaluation exercise, across Europe..

3.4   Conclusions

The research suggests that the model is generally applicable in PSOs however it requires a level of interpretation and clarification to facilitate its use. The development of guidance is an iterative process and the current Guides to Self Assessment will be further refined in the 1996/7 Guides.

4.   REFERENCES

British Quality Foundation (1995) The Guide to Self Assessment. London
Crosby, Phillip B. (1980) Quality is Free. *The art of making quality certain.* Penguin, Middlesex.
DeCarlo Neil J. and Sterett W. Kent (March 1990) History of the Malcolm Baldrige National Quality Award. *Quality Progress*, 21-27.
Deming, W. Edwards (1982 & 1986) Out of the Crisis. *Quality, productivity and competitive position.* Cambridge University Press, Cambridge
Henderson (August 1992) The Henderson Report. DTI, London
Juran, J. M. (1992) Juran on Quality by Design. *The new steps for planning quality into goods and services.* Maxwell Macmillan International, Oxford.
Peters, Thomas J. and Waterman Jr, Robert H. (1982) In Search of Excellence. *Lessons from America's best-run companies.* Harper Collins, Chatham.

5.   BIOGRAPHY

Debbie Reed is a Research Associate with the University of the West of England. She is seconded to the British Quality Foundation with a brief to research, develop and coordinate a programme to promote and enhance excellence through self assessment, in relation to the Excellence Model in UK public and voluntary service organisations.

International Comparisons

23

Material and scheme for continuous quality improvement in Catalonia

X. Tort-Martorell*, P. Grima*, A. Robert⁺
*Universitat Politècnica de Catalunya
Av. Diagonal, 647 - 08028 Barcelona   SPAIN
Ph: +34-3-4016628   Fax: +34-3-4016575
e-mail: tort@eio.upc.es

⁺*Centre Català de la Qualitat*
Ronda Can Fatjó, 23-A   -   08290 Cerdanyola   SPAIN
Ph: +34-3-5802767   Fax: +34-3-5809202

Abstract

This paper briefly describes the general activities of the "Centre Català de la Qualitat (CCQ)" (created by the Catalan Government) to promote quality and productivity in the local industry. It focuses on the scheme and materials developed together with the "Universitat Politècnica de Catalunya (UPC)" to promote and implement continuous quality improvement.

Keywords

Catalan Quality Centre, Collaboration Government-University-Industry, Continuous quality improvement, Quality promotion schemes.

1   THE "CENTRE CATALÀ DE LA QUALITAT"

The "Centre Català de la Qualitat" (Catalan Centre for Quality) was created in 1990 by the Catalan Government, to promote quality and productivity in the Catalan area. The systematic implementation of quality and productivity methods and technologies, and encouraging the cultural change needed to carry it out successfully are its main objectives.

CCQ activities are targeted towards the SME's. They are carried out in collaboration with professional bodies and sector associations, universities and big companies in order to facilitate technology transfer and experience exchange.

The main activities can be grouped as :

- **Motivation:** Publication of a quarterly magazine, well-publicised seminars with recognised international experts (eg Juran, Crosby, Yamashina, Goldratt, ...), an annual prize for industrial quality, etc.
- **Training and experience exchange**: Organisation of open seminars and workshops for the exchange of experiences.
- **Information**: Publish and circulate information about specific techniques and methodologies for quality and productivity improvement.
- **Implementation**: More than 1000 companies have so far participated in the programs.

The general scheme of the program is:

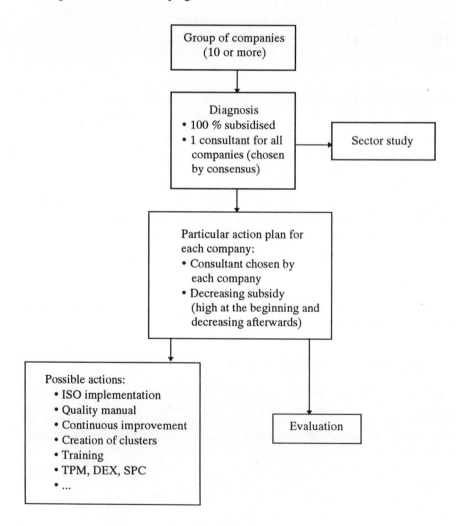

This scheme has proved to be very effective, since it takes advantage of working in groups in several ways: Increasing effect of the promotion and marketing activities, obtaining of sector studies, sharing of resources and the consultants become experts in the sector.

2 SUPPORT MATERIALS

To obtain better results with less expenditure on resources (i.e. less consultant time) the CCQ has developed tools and material, in collaboration with UPC and consultants specialized in the different areas. Among them, it is worth mentioning:
- DEX: An expert system that guides and helps companies using Design of Experiments to improve their processes.
- ISOPLA: Software and material to help SME's to prepare themselves (with a little help from a consultant and a student assistant) for ISO 9000 registration.
- PMC: A set of material designed to help implement quality improvement teams. They are described in more detail below.

3 PMC (Plan for Continuous Quality Improvement)

The Plan for Continuous Quality Improvement is oriented towards enabling the company to develop an organised procedure to improve its activities. It would be carried out by it's own personnel working as a team and has the following characteristics:
- Has been designed so that definite actions are undertaken.
- Is oriented towards improving practical problems.
- Maintain all efforts focussed in the same direction
- Produces results that can be quantified.
- Encourage the participation and interest in learning
- Is oriented towards maintaining continuity.

Structure
PMC is structured in three phases, each one pursuing definite goals:
- **Planning**: This has to be done by the board of directors of the company. It involves the initial selection of the projects for improvement and deciding on the persons who will be part of the teams that will be working on each one of them. Additionally, objectives have to be established, responsibilities have to be assigned, resources have to be allocated and dates of completion have to be fixed.
- **Training**: The successful start of a PMC requires that the persons involved be trained previously. As a first step, the CCQ will train a co-ordinator who in turn will be responsible for training the other members of the team.

- **Action**: This involves putting into practice the Plan for Continuous Quality Improvement (PMC) so that the objectives that were established for each team are achieved. It is intended that the duration of any one project does not exceed 6 months

Material

PMC is supported by an abundance of educational material and instructions consisting of:

- Instructions and guidance on **Planning** written for the management.
- A collection of **5 case studies** have been compiled with the objective of clearly illustrating the basic features of how to use the PMC and the results that can be expected from it.
- The **Co-ordinator's Manual**, includes detailed information on all aspects of the PMC and instructions on how to train the participants of a team..
- The **Participant's Manual**, contains information relating to general aspects of the PMC, it's characteristics, methodologies used and the tools available. It also has exercises, questionnaires and other helpful information.
- **Practice Cases** , are presented that simulate real situations and have to be solved by the teams during their training period.
- A **Video** that depicts situations that one may encounter when starting the PMC is also included. It has been made with the idea of encouraging discussion.

4. CONCLUSIONS

The Catalan Government through the CCQ has devised a scheme to promote Quality and Productivity that has proved to be highly effective in terms of the amount of money invested and the results accomplished. The results are excellent both in the number of companies participating in the program - over 1600, and in terms of their achievements. More than 30 % of the Catalan ISO registered companies are participants in the programme and the average cost reduction per company is estimated at 5 % of sales in the particular areas.

The success is based on several factors:

- Working with groups of companies.
- The relationship with UPC (Politechnic University of Catalonia). It has produced important mutual benefits among them the development of high quality advanced materials at reasonable costs and the use of student assistants working in companies.
- The use of especially designed support materials.
- The decreasing support given to companies. It allows them to start the program with small initial costs and assume full responsibility once they see that it is a good investment.

The materials and the application scheme of the PMC described above, are an example of the type of support materials and collaboration offered by the CCQ. So far over 120 companies are using the PMC program and the benefits are estimated at an average of 3.000.000 ptas per project. In November of 96 the CCQ will organize a congress where the participating companies will have the opportunity to exchange experiences.

24

Quality problems in Libyan industry

Mr T.M.S. Tarbaghia
Al-Tawaan General Service Company
P.O. Box 21, Benghazi, Libya,
Phone: ++218 61 90992223, Fax ++218 61 9099616

Dr J. Betts
Department of Industrial Technology
University of Bradford, Bradford, West Yorkshire, UK,
Phone:++44 1274 384252, Fax: ++44 1274 391333, email:
j.betts@bradford.ac.uk

Abstract

This paper briefly describes the historical development of Libyan industry, which was made possible through the exploitation of its oil resources. Oil extraction started in 1969, and the first industrial development plan was drawn up shortly afterwards. Development was driven from the centre and suffered the usual problems associated with this type of regime. Along the development chain from industry through to the company level many problems have been identified, which could be resolved if the philosophy of Total Quality Management (TQM) could be applied within every link in the development chain. This would be ambitious even by western country standards. Since quality at the company level is so dependent on links with other institutions within Libyan society, especially public sector companies, applying TQM at the company level only would not have any significant effect. The paper makes recommendations for changes that have to be made along the development chain to facilitate the effective exploitation of TQM in Libyan industry.

Keywords

TQM, Libya, development chain, quality chain

HISTORICAL BACKGROUND

Before 1970, the Libyan Government was not convinced of the importance of establishing national industry. This was due to a shortage of the necessary basic elements. Those resources that were available were fully employed in keeping the existing economic infrastructure intact. These elements were the shortage of investment resources coupled with the existence of more persistent demands on development expenditure consuming national income and lack of properly qualified technical and managerial manpower capable of dealing with industrial development projects (Tarbaghia, 1995). However, the discovery and exploitation of Libya's oil resources from the late 1960's overcame the capital problem and so industrialisation was at least possible. They would have to be allocated in a way that not only made the technological hardware available, but educated and developed the human resources necessary to manage and maintain the developing industrial base.

An indication of the changes that occurred within the Libyan economy between 1970 and 1990 is given in Table (1). This indicates both changes in industrial output, and resources, especially human, that could facilitate future industrial development.

Table 1:   Libyan Economic Statistics for years 1970 and 1990.

	1970	1990
Total National Income	1288 M.L.D.	7577 M.L.D.
Population Income (per capita)	642 L.D.	1582 L.D.
Population	2,000,000	4,800,000
Students in basic schools	340,000	1,780,000
Students in polytechnics	1,450	51,000
Students in universities	3,663	53,127
Total investments	22.5 M.L.D.	575.1 M.L.D.
Total income	15.6 M.L.D.	5615 M.L.D.

(Source: political, economic and social developments 1994. N.B. 1L.D. = 3$ US)

The industrial companies in 1970 were mostly small, either owned by the private sector or built on loans to the private sector (Haftari and Betts, 1994). These companies were of the type characterised by high revenue, guaranteed income and lower investment costs using imported semi-finished materials, such as Food, Textile and Paper works, handicraft industries for production of carpets and shoes, hand tools and carpentry workshops. Because of the dirth in development of the industrial sector, the national income was mostly generated by oil sales. Since 1970, the Secretary of Industry established successive industrial plans, starting with a three year plan for 1972-1975. Data on industrial investment and industrial output during the period 1970-1990 are given in Table (2). During this period more than four billion Libyan Dinars were spent on more than 400 industrial projects.

Table 2:   Libyan Industrial Investment and Output During 1970 - 1993 (in millions of Libyan Dinars

Year	Industrial Investment	Industrial Production Value	Av. Annual Industrial Investment	Av. Annual Production Value
1970	15	17.5	15	17.5
1971-75	363.6	139.8	52.72	27.96
1976-80	1276.7	455.3	255.34	91.06
1981-85	1723.4	1886.6	344.68	377.72
1986-90	683.3	3198.6	136.66	639.72
1991-93	54.2	2732.2	18.07	910.73

Industries' contribution to the value of output of the various industrial sectors in percentage terms during 1993 is depicted in table (3) below.

Table 3: Distribution of the Value of Libyan Industrial Output by Sector in 1993

Sector	%
Food Industries	27.2
Textile and Leather	9.8
Furniture and Paper	2.8
Chemicals	11.3
Cement and Construction Materials	12.2
Basic Metals	19.8
Metallic & Electrical Technology	18.9

There were considerable difficulties experienced during the construction stage, and later in the operation stage. The main difficulties during the operation stage were weak management in the industrial plants and companies. This was due to the continuous change in management's' philosophies creating instability and the absence of a continuous improvement philosophy in companies. Tarbaghia (1995) in his research on private and public sector Libyan companies found that Libyan industry suffered from lack of research and poor management. His research established that almost all quality problems experienced by Libyan industry were caused by a combination of the following:-

1. Lack of sufficient knowledge of quality control methods and techniques.
2. Lack of strong and direct incentives for good quality work.
3. Poor materials, poor specification and poor equipment as well as other technical causes that require further study and development.

To overcome these problems it is proposed that each Libyan manufacturing company:-

1. Establishes a quality measuring body within the company to measure and report on quality.
2. Start a comprehensive technical training and upgrading program for staff.
3. Grade the quality based on company's weekly measuring reports.
4. Encourage all personnel to be actively involved in the quality development program.
5. Quality improvement or otherwise should be disseminated to all personnel at regular intervals.

The problems listed above, together with recommendations for change, are all at the company level. In reality both problems and solutions are not totally under individual company's control. The relationship that companies have with funding institutions and with the Secretary for Industry are crucial to the establishment of high quality at the company level.

The successful implementation of TQM in western companies is possible when companies are not highly dependent on the behaviour of institutions external to the companies, or when the behaviour of external influential institutions is in line with TQM aspirations at the company level.

CONCLUSION

To start to apply TQM in Libyan industry it requires full and total commitment of the company organization, especially the top management.   Implementation success depends on coordinating the system's five ingredients of measurement, reward, punishment, technical upgrading program and active involvement of all company staff.

These ingredients are required of all companies aspiring to establish high quality, irrespective of the economic environment in which they exist.   The behaviour of external bodies which can effect quality at the company level is also essential to the establishment of high quality.   In such circumstances these institutions, which are usually to do with finance or government, need also to be convinced of the quality message and persuaded to behave in a manner that will facilitate quality development at the company level.

This is again true for all companies in all economic environments, but is especially true for companies in developing countries like Libya.   Developments of this type are analogous to extending quality performance to whole supply chains, giving rise to "quality chains".   In developing countries financial institutions and government agencies usually comprise extremely important and possibly weak links in quality chains.

REFERENCES

Basha, I & Gab Allah, A., *"An implementation of TQM for a Highway Contractor"*, Inter Build Conference, Cairo, Egypt, 1995.
Betts, J. & Tarbaghia, T.M.S., paper to be published in 1996.
Haftari, A., Betts, J. & Tarbaghia, T.M.S., *"Partnership the Key to Successful Management"*, Arab Management Conference, Bradford, 5-7 July, 1994.
Tarbaghia, T.M.S., *"Key Factors Influencing the Success of Industrial Companies in Libya"*, Ph.D. Thesis, Bradford University, December 1995.

BIOGRAPHY

Mr. Tarbaghia is a Mechanical Engineer working for an engineering consultancy in Benghazi, Libya. He has recently completed his Ph.D. on the performance of Libyan industrial companies at the Department of Industrial Technology of the University of Bradford.

Dr Betts is a lecturer in Industrial Technology at the University of Bradford. He initially qualified and worked as an engineer in the British gas industry, but later qualified and practiced in Operations Research in the same industry. He subsequently became an academic, initially in the area of Operations Research, but in recent years he has concentrated on Operations Management problems in manufacturing industry. He has retained an interest in economic development in developing countries since his initial academic appointment which was in Tanzania.

25

The origins of European quality

J.G. Roche, Ph.D.,
Quality Assurance Research Unit,
Department of Industrial Engineering,
University College, Galway, Ireland.
Tel : +353.91.524411, Fax : +353.91.524913.

Abstract

This paper describes the key role of American experts in the events leading to the foundation of EOQC in 1957. Its subsequent development and further European initiatives since 1987 are briefly outlined.

Keywords

European Productivity Agency, European quality organisations, origins, development.

1   INTRODUCTION

Japan's quality revolution is well documented and Drs W.E. Deming and J.M. Juran are rightly honoured for their contribution to this revolution. But while Deming and Juran were continuing their involvement in Japan's quality developments, other American experts were active in Europe.

There were similarities between the situation in Japan and in Europe after World War II. Much of Europe and parts of Japan were devastated; economic recovery was a priority in both areas; external assistance was available only from the USA; there was a nucleus of quality experts in both areas. But Japan was a unified country whereas Europe had diverse nationalities, cultures, languages and political structures.

2   THE EUROPEAN PRODUCTIVITY AGENCY (EPA)

The journey to a European quality movement began in 1953 with the establishment of the

European Productivity Agency (EPA) by the 17 Member countries of the OEEC (Organisation for European Economic Co-operation).   EPA's task was to stimulate productivity and thus raise European living standards by influencing public and private organisations.   One of its primary aims was to convince both management and workers of the benefits of productivity and to enlist their co-operation.

3   STATISTICAL QUALITY CONTROL (SQC)

Statistical Quality Control was identified by EPA as a factor in higher productivity.   This led to a series of visits, seminars and conferences conducted by American experts in Europe during 1954-5.   Professor S.B. Littauer and Dr. A.N. Benson led seminars and discussions in different countries between June and August 1954.   The work initiated by Littauer and Benson was considerably extended by Professor Paul C. Clifford who arrived in Paris in September 1954 on a one-year's assignment to EPA.   Clifford was Professor of Mathematics at Montclaire State College, New Jersey, a founding member of ASQC and in 1950 had served on a technical assistance mission to India. His longer European assignment enabled him to evaluate in depth the status of quality control in each country he visited and to build a network of experts in each one.

Reporting in 1955, the three American experts identified problems common to all countries :

•   Inadequate training facilities for senior staff, engineers and production supervisors.
•   A serious shortage of qualified teachers/trainers.

They warned of American quality failures which were due 'to over-emphasis on statistical techniques and under-emphasis on other management techniques'.

The absence of an organisation resembling ASQC in Europe or in any one of the countries visited was noted.   But there were small groups in each country interested in forming a quality control association (EPA, 1956).

At a Paris conference in July 1955, delegates from ten countries presented reports on the quality situation in each country.   Responding to the problems identified by them and by the delegates, the American experts recommended that :

•   A body of instructors should be established.
•   An intra-European system of co-operation and exchange of information should be organised.

Clifford was a strong advocate of the need for a European association for quality control, but the 1955 conference participants failed to agree on its form and structure.   Despite this failure, it was decided to set up a working party with delegates from each OEEC country. EPA agreed to provide funds for a secretariat.

At the ASQC Annual Technical Conference in Montreal in 1956, Clifford presented an overview of quality developments in Europe and listed the following needs :

- There is a need for management education as to the objectives and functions of Quality Control.
- There is a need for training of production personnel.
- There is need for co-operation between the statistician and the engineer.
- There is shortage of competent trainers in the field.
- Both within and between countries there is need for channels of communication (Clifford, 1956).

4   THE EUROPEAN ORGANISATION FOR QUALITY CONTROL (EOQC)

While his EPA assignment had ended, Clifford was active at a second Paris conference in 1956 to assist in assessing the work of the EPA-sponsored experts and to encourage 'a closer co-operation between the many national organisations in this way or another in order to make optimal use of the methods outlined in the reports'. Dr. Walter Masing, EOQC's founding President, commented, 'that seemed reasonable'.

An informal meeting of delegates form France, Germany, Italy, the Netherlands, the United Kingdom and four other countries followed. It led to the decision to form a European umbrella organisation with the delegates from the five named countries taking the founding roles. As Dr. Masing recalls, 'So, with a handshake of five men, the cornerstone of EOQC was laid' (Masing, 1987). 'It can be said without exaggeration that this (the founding of EOQC) would not have happened when it did in the way that it did without Clifford' (Masing, 1994).

The national quality organisations in France, the Federal Republic of Germany, Italy, the Netherlands and the United Kingdom formally joined EOQC in 1957, followed by Denmark and Sweden in 1961. By the end of the 60's, EOQC had 17 Full Member Organisations (FMO); by 1980, there were 24 FMOs. Ireland became the 25th Member in 1980 and in 1993-94 there were 29 FMOs.

From its inception, EOQC emphasised its trans-European focus by welcoming members form both Western and Eastern Europe. This policy was adopted despite East-West tensions and the rejection of Marshall Aid by the USSR and East European countries. Of the 29 FMOs, 18 are from the West, 11 from the former 'Eastern' bloc (EOQ, 1994).

In 1988, the Council of EOQC decided to adopt the name 'European Organisation for Quality' (EOQ). The new title reflected the development and expansion of the quality sciences and EOQ's aim to be recognised as the major representative quality body in Europe.

5   THE FULL MEMBER ORGANISATIONS OF EOQ

In his Montreal paper, Clifford noted 'the tremendous differences in industrial development that exist between different (European) countries.... Organisations devoted to Quality Control are in the embryo stage in each country'. In the intervening years, national quality organisations developed in most European countries but the pattern of development in uneven. The stronger industrial countries provide more and better services for members while the weaker countries have to contend with apathy and a shortage of resources.

The national quality organisations in EOQ are private organisations in most Western countries and government or semi-government bodies in Eastern Europe, Greece and Turkey. Most make provision for individual and corporate members. In Belgium, Iceland and the Netherlands there are only corporate members; in Russia and Slovenia, there are only individual members.

Membership numbers vary from a high of 13,000 (mainly individuals) in the United Kingdom to a low of 86 (74 individual) in Estonia. The majority (19) operate national quality award schemes; all provide some form of education and training and organise national conferences (EOQ, 1994).

6   30 YEARS OF EOQC

When EOQC marked its 30th anniversary in 1987, Professor Hans Dieter Seghezzi, President EOQC, expressed his unease about EOQC's readiness for the future. He noted that committees were unable to give detailed consideration to developing problems; new sections were needed to deal with quality in services. Where national activities like quality campaigns and awards were introduced, EOQC had little, if any, role in these activities. There was a need to shift the emphasis from quality specialist to management (Seghezzi, 1987).

Later in 1987, Seghezzi's views were accepted by EOQC's Executive. As noted earlier, it was decided to adopt the title 'European Organisation for Quality' to reflect its changed strategy and aim.

The New Strategy had three strands :

•   Broader Target Group - Managers, not just quality professionals.
•   Methodology - improved information flow.
•   Expansion - into new areas, e.g. services.

7   RECENT DEVELOPMENTS

1988 marks a turning point in European quality. EOQC became EOQ; reflecting increased management awareness of quality issues, the European Foundation for Quality Management

(EFQM) was established. In 1991, the European Quality Award (EQA) was introduced by EFQM with the support of EOQ and the European Commission.

In the education and training area, both EOQ and EFQM have been active. The European Masters Programme in Total Quality Management (EMPTQM) was established by academics from seven different countries with support from EFQM in 1992. EOQ's Harmonised Scheme for quality professionals, systems managers and auditors became effective in 1994.

In July 1994, the European Quality Platform was created by EOQ and EFQM to reflect their common goal to make Europe a leading force in the world market through quality. The European Commission is expected to finalise its 'European Quality Promotion Policy' later this year.

Europe has been slow in developing the enthusiasm for quality which Paul Clifford advocated. But it now seems that the breakthrough has been made to ensure a more quality-conscious and competitive Europe in the 21st century.

8   REFERENCES

Clifford, P.C. (1956) Quality Control in Europe - Past, Present and Future.   ASQC Technical Conference Transactions 565-573.

European Organisation for Quality (1994) EOQ Annual Report 1993-94, European Quality I (3) 57-92.

European Productivity Agency (1956) Statistical Quality Control, Paris OEEC.

Masing W. (1987) Success from a Modest Start, EOQC Quality 31, 2, 4-5.

Masing W (1994) Tribute, Professor Paul C. Clifford (1901-1993), European Quality, I, (3), 95.

Seghezzi H.D. (1987) EOQC Today after 30 Years, EOQC Quality, 31, 2, 1-2.

9 BIOGRAPHY

Dr. John Roche, FASQC, FIQA, has retired from his full-time position but continues his quality promotion and research activities at University College, Galway.   After some years in industry, he began his teaching career in Dublin and moved to University College, Galway in 1969. He developed a number of quality programmes for undergraduate and postgraduate students and in 1992, proposed the establishment of the European Masters Programme in Total Quality Management (EMPTQM).   His book on Product Liability was published in 1989.

His current activities focus on quality improvement in SMEs quality and improvement and innovation, product liability and safety.

26

QC circle activities - Japanese and European way

H. Yui[1] & G. K. Kanji[2]
[1] Ryukoku University, Fukakusa, Fushimi-ku, Kyoto 612, Japan
[2] Sheffield Hallam University, 100 Napier Street, Sheffield S11 8HD,
UK. Tel: +44 0114 2533137, Fax: +44 0114 2533161, email:
g.k.kanji@shu.ac.uk

1   INTRODUCTION

QC circles are organised in almost all Japanese big manufacturing companies. They have not only saved enormous sums of money and offered high quality, but also improved the morale and skills of workers. Since the end of the 1970s, the QC circle movement was followed by the rest of the world including the UK and the US with considerable interest. It was felt that they have found a reason why Japan is successful in QC circles for achieving high quality and productivity. Therefore, in various discussions of QC circles the premise that they were a part of Company-Wide Quality Control (CWQC) or TQM was neglected. We believe that this was one of the real reasons of misunderstanding of QC circle activities. Recently, the concept and practice of TQM have been diffused to western companies [1] and QC circles were recognised as part of TQM by many companies.

  In this paper the following areas are looked at in order to identify the critical features and problems of QC circle activities. They are:

(i)   **actual state of QC circle activities:** diffusion, objectives and appraisal
(ii)   **comparison between Japan and Europe:** history of QC circle, employee's involvement, activity themes, definition and way of activity, effects, etc.
(iii)   **direction that QC circle should take**

2   ACTUAL SITUATION OF QC CIRCLES

Recently there were some comparisons of QC circles between Japan and Europe. Some critical features of QC are presented in Table 1 and circle activities are discussed as follows:

2.1 Diffusion and Objectives of QC circles

In Japan, the beginning of QC circles was before 1962 and in Europe it started after the late 1970s. In general the number of companies and the participation rate of employees in Japanese companies were always higher than in Europe. It is clear to us that the major objectives of introducing QC circles in Japan was the quality improvement, cost reduction and productivity improvement whereas in Europe it was job satisfaction, quality improvement and communication (see Dahlgaard et.al. 1990).

2.2. Appraisal of QC circles

(i) general evaluation
- It seems that results of QC circles both in Japan and UK are reasonably good.
- It is not so good in Denmark in terms of the number of proposals received.
- Cost reduction and efficiency are not shown as the objectives of QC circle activities.
- Cost/benefit criterion for justification of QC circles has been adopted by UK industries.

(ii) detail evaluation
According to the survey which examines the effects of QC circles both labour union and management in Japan indicates that the most important items are improvement of work method, improvement of communication, cost reduction and improvement of morale. Another survey indicates that QC circles activity in many countries is the most important aspect of quality motivations e.g. bonus for high quality, quality campaigns, economic rewards and job rotation.

2.3. A cause and effect model

From the above consideration, we will propose a cause and effect model of QC circles as shown in Figure 1.

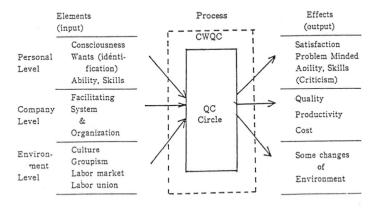

Figure 1 Cause and effect model of QC circle activity

Table 1 Comparison of QC circles

Items	Japan	Europe
beginning	before 1962	1977 BL, 1978 Rolls Royce 1979 Ford, 1981 Wedgewood
the number of QCCs firms	1968, 40%+(3000+employees) 1970, 56.3%(3000+emplyees) 1984, 60%(100+employees) 84%(5000+employees)	1981 100+companies 1982 200+companies 1985 400+companies about 10-20% of big UK manufacturing companies [3] 12% (Denmark) [4]
employee's participation	more than 90%	less than 20% (average:2.9-4.9%) [3] about 1% (Denmark)
objectives	quality improvement 31.5% cost reduction 24.9% productivity 23.5%	job satisfaction 78.8% quality improvement 70.5% communication 68.2% [2]
theme	efficiency 31.6% cost reduction 18.3% quality 15.7%	quality 24.1% productivity 12.0% cost reduction 10.7%
results	very good 22.0% good 70.4% not so good 5.5% [5] number of recommendations per employee 4.7/year [4] increasing job satisfaction	benefit/cost = £4+/£1 (51%+companies) average:£3.60[2] 0.02/year (Denmark)[4] increasing job satisfaction
facilitating organisation	well organised and working effectively	a small number of firms having formal organisations for QCCs
definition	Table 2	Table 2
differences and reasons	not voluntary working time and overtime meeting is part of activity cooperative union	voluntary working time meeting is main activity hostile union
success or failure	working well 1/3 not working 1/3 borderline 1/3 [7]	average failure rate per company 20.5% [8]

Table 2 Definition of QC circles

QC circle is a small group, implementing quality control activities voluntarily in the same workshop. This small group make self and mutual development, and implements management and improvement for their tasks continuously, using the QC tools with everybody's participation basis. QC circles are an integrated part of CWQC (JUSE).

The quality circle may be defined as a group of workers doing similar work who meet:
   Voluntarily. Regularly. In normal working time. Under the leadership of their **supervisor**. To identify, analyse, and solve work related problems. To recommend solutions to management (J.Oakland).

3 SOME COMPARISONS

Some definitions of QC circles are given in Table 2. On the basis of Tables 1 and 2 we will find the similarities and differences as follows:

3.1. Similarities

- activity of worker's group in the same workplace
- activity of solving problems and proposing recommendations
- theme

3.2 Differences

- quality control circle Vs quality circle
- not voluntary in practice Vs voluntary
- both working and overtime Vs working time
- meeting is only part of the activity Vs it is the major part of the activity
- group concepts Vs individualism (cultural difference)
- cooperative unions Vs hostile ones

3.3 Problems

In Japan QC circle activity is another additional work to main work. Therefore this approach provides worker's satisfaction partly, but it might not basically improve employee's morale and satisfaction in their primary job.
- In Europe it seems difficult to gain support from both workforce and management, because they feel that quality circles are not part of their activities and they have very little commitment on the after work of Quality Control circle activities.

4 CONCLUSION

There are three levels of elements which effect the general activities of QC circles as shown in Figure 1. In 2.2 we have already indicated the advantages and disadvantages in each level. These disadvantages need to be eliminated. However, disadvantages and problems in 3.3 need to be addressed in order to create interest in the QC circle in Europe.

REFERENCES

Cole, R. (1989) Quality Progress July.

Dahlgaard, J.J. et.al. (1990) Total Quality Management 1(1).

Dale, B. (1984) *Quality Circles in UK Manufacturing Industry- A State of the Art Picture and Respective Trends.* Occasional Paper No. 8402, UMIST.

Dale, B. (1994) *Managing Quality.* Prentice Hall.

Hayward, S.G. et.al. (1985) European Management Journal 3(2).

Kanji, G.K. and Asher, M. (1993) *Total Quality Management Process: A Systematic Approach.* Carfax.

Kristensen, K. et.al. (1993) Total Quality Management 4(1).

Mishima, R. (1992) *Small Group Activities in UK Industries* (in Japanese).

Oakland, J.S. (1993) *Total Quality Management* Butterworth Heinemann.

Rosei-Jiho. (1983) No.2666 (in Japanese).

Yasui, T. (1991) Journal of Southern Osaka University 26(3) (in Japanese).

PART FIVE

Enterprise and Industry

27

Self assessment in the small company environment

G. Wilson
Shorts Quality Unit
Centre for Executive Development
Ulster Business School
University of Ulster at Jordanstown
Newtownabbey BT37 0QB
Tel: 01232 368145 Fax: 01232 366831

INTRODUCTION

This paper focuses on the development of the continuous improvement activities of a small family owned engineering company, through the self-assessment using the criteria of the European Model for Self-Appraisal. The Company was formed in 1970 and is the leading manufacturer and supplier of electrical switchgear and factory built assemblies in Northern Ireland. The main market for these products is local, although several major projects have been undertaken for export markets.

The Company firmly believes that its market position is directly attributable to its commitment to meeting the needs and expectations of its customers through Total Quality Management (TQM).

RATIONALE FOR THE QUALITY PROGRAMME

The Northern Ireland manufacturing sector began to experience an increasingly competitive marketplace and rising customer expectations in the 1980's. The Managing Director of the organisation realised that if it was to survive, a new, more proactive way of managing the business was required. This led to an investigation of TQM and, in recognition of the potential benefits of this approach, the completion of a TQ audit in April 1990.

The audit indicated that the Company had a positive perception in the marketplace but that the management structure was insufficiently developed and no formal and systematic quality system existed. Furthermore, although the Company was profitable, it was recognised that significant improvements could be achieved through better planning and increased employee involvement and motivation.

The diversity of problems revealed by the audit convinced the Managing Director that a management approach that embraced all aspects of the Company's activities would be required. So in 1990 a TQM programme was formally launched.

GETTING STARTED

The Company began by forming a steering group and establishing 34 quality objectives, embodied in 6 policy statements. These policies reflected the need to develop a quality culture within the Company and focused on business/strategic planning, customer, supplier and employee relationships, and performance monitoring.

Based on the actions needed to implement the policies, and on the problems exposed during employee training sessions, three joint management and employee teams were formed. Over the next two years many teams were formed to address specific problems, strengthening relationships within the Company by increasing cross-functional working and improving communications. This approach also created a work environment where ability and initiative are encouraged, recognised and rewarded.

The importance of effective process management is well understood and process improvements have been sought since TQ was introduced. This emphasis on processes, combined with the recognition that the market would eventually demand evidence of quality capability, prompted the Company to seek ISO 9002 certification in 1992. It is interesting that this was just one of the 34 objectives identified during the planning phase of the programme and was not seen as the main objective, or as an end in itself. Furthermore, it emphasises that the quality system is only a part of their TQM approach.

The introduction of Total Quality Management has had an enormous effect on the organisation, and impressive results have been achieved in many areas:

-       on-time pricing of enquiries and subsequent confirmation has increased from 25% to 98%
-       value output per employee has doubled
-       new inventory policies and improved stock valuations have resulted in stock reductions of over 30%
-       improved profitability ratios
-       winning of the NI Quality Award (1992).

ORGANISING FOR SELF-ASSESSMENT

To conduct an effective and efficient assessment, using the European Model for Self-Appraisal, trained assessors are essential. The organisation needs guidance on the information to be collected and on how to score in a consistent manner.

If the process that is followed is based upon that used to assess applications for the European Quality Award, the Company can compare its operations against best practice as set out in the Model, and can identify where to place additional effort.

One of the main challenges for the small organisation wishing to conduct a self-assessment on a regular basis is a lack of appropriate resources. Having identified the need for an objective assessment of current status, the Company could neither afford the time or expense of having a member of staff trained as an assessor. In addition, they did not believe they had the knowledge and experience needed to formulate action plans based on the "areas for improvement" identified through the assessment process. The solution in this case was to enlist the support of Shorts Quality Unit at the Ulster Business School who suggested that the initial assessment could be facilitated through a research project conducted by two of their EFQM trained assessors. It was agreed that the assessors would be supported by a new member of staff who would take responsibility for information gathering.

The experience would serve as a development opportunity for the person concerned in that they would gain a broad understanding of the business whilst becoming conversant with the self-assessment process. The Company would then be able to conduct future assessments without external assistance.

In determining how to gather and present the information necessary for the assessment, further issues arose. For example, detailed information relevant to the "enablers" criteria of the European Model was not readily available. Indeed much of the organisation's approach and how this was being deployed has not been documented. In addition, the scope of performance measurement was limited to "business results", meaning that measures of customer satisfaction and people satisfaction did not exist. Furthermore, little comparative data existed.

The first step in the assessment process was therefore to gather and document information on current status and the results achieved. The lack of formal measurement systems based upon the "results" criteria of the Model was an immediate area for improvement.

DISCUSSION OF FINDINGS

A number of issues arose during the assessment process that impinge on the ability of the small organisation to conduct self-assessments using a business excellence model such as the European Model. These are discussed below.

Small organisations do not require the same degree of formality and sophistication often found in larger organisations. However, this lack of formality proved to be a problem because it was allowed to extend to the measurement and review of the company results and the approach that caused them. Irrespective of the type and size of an organisation, it is essential that the company conducts a regular and systematic assessment of its operations, and that it documents the findings, including resulting action plans.

The scope of the European Model, which is much broader than that of the National Quality Award, has implications for the small organisation. In some respects the Model was considered to be more relevant to larger organisations. For example, a company's involvement with its suppliers in improvement activities features in the "Leadership" criterion of the European Model yet this is an area that cause the Company particular problems. A number of unsuccessful attempts have been made to encourage suppliers to become involved in joint improvement activities. Indeed the Company has attempted to persuade its suppliers to embrace TQ themselves.

Unfortunately, the small size of the Company, in relation to its suppliers, has resulted in it being unable to "influence" its suppliers.

The reference to career progression in the "People Management" criterion of the Model also caused concern. The promotion opportunities in a small company may be limited, so career progression is likely to consist of increasing the level of accountability and responsibility through job enlargement and enrichment, and through increased empowerment in the organisation.

Perhaps the greatest concern for the small company considering self-assessment using the European Model is one of resource limitations. A lack of resources can limit the ability of a company to address each criterion of the Model eg the promotion of Total Quality outside the organisation, and the exploitation of its technology. Indeed the resource implications of introducing techniques such as benchmarking resulted in it never being seriously considered by the Company. In the latter example, it has since been agreed that benchmarking studies should focus on organisations that are considered to be best-in-class locally, rather than on attempting to benchmark against "world-class" organisations in other countries. The formation of best practice "clubs" at a local level would also facilitate benchmarking.

The cost associated with assessor training may discourage small organisations from developing suitable expertise. Indeed the availability of suitable staff can also be a problem. Small organisations must be prepared to invest in training and to develop in-house self-assessment expertise so that they do not have to rely on outside assistance. There may be a case for reducing the assessor training fee for small organisations, or for the provision of such training locally as the national awards align themselves with the European Quality Award. Indeed this option will probably result in a substantial increase in the number of small organisations conducting self-assessments.

Despite the above concerns, self-assessment was found to be of immense benefit and can be considered to be applicable to a company of any size. Indeed the monitoring of progress, and formulation of policies and associated action plans based on the areas for improvement identified, are essential in the drive towards Total Quality.

FUTURE PLANS

In the short-term, a series of action plans have been generated by the company based on the feedback from the self-assessment process. Their efficacy will be reviewed as part of the next assessment.

A medium to long-term strategic plan is to be formulated. In addition a strategic quality plan is to be introduced to ensure the TQ programme is focused on the needs of the business. In addition, the Human Resource plan will be developed in parallel with the strategic plan.

Formal mechanisms for measuring customer and employee perceptions of the organisation are to be introduced. Company targets will be specified during the policy and strategy formulation process.

A structured approach to the identification and management of the Company's key processes is to be introduced. Benchmarking and process based performance measurement is to be introduced to identify process improvement opportunities.

CONCLUSIONS AND LESSONS LEARNED

The general principles of Quality Management apply equally across all sectors of business, and to companies of any size. The European Model has been developed with such principles in mind and has proved to be an effective framework against which a small organisation can appraise its operations. Self-assessment has enabled this Company to quantify how well its Total Quality programme is progressing and to identify where to focus future effort. It is intended that regular assessment will be used to ensure the continued development of their award winning approach to TQM.

It must be recognised that small organisations do not have, and do not require, management systems and approaches as sophisticated as those found in larger organisations. The assessor must be conscious of this issue when conducting the assessment.

Any small organisation wishing to introduce self-assessment must recognise the cost implications. This cost can only be justified where self-assessment is to become an integral part of their TQ process. The experience of this organisation suggests that it is a worthwhile and necessary investment when a company is genuinely interested in achieving world-class performance standards.

BIOGRAPHICAL DETAILS

George Wilson is Management Development Advisor at the Ulster Business School. He is responsible for the promotion and development of quality related activities on the University curriculum, and the provision of training and consultancy support to the local business community. This encompasses providing training in quality related management in both the public and private sectors. George is also involved in a PhD research project which is assessing the value of total quality management systems as a mechanism for organisational self assessment. He has been trained as an Assessor for the European Quality Award and is a Senior Assessor for the NI Quality Award. George is also the co-author of a text on quality.

28
Achieving culture change in an integrated steel works rolling mill

P.C. Dobson
Plant Manager
Lackenby Beam Mill - British Steel, Teesside Works, England
(Tel No. 44 1642 406262, Fax 44 1642 465310)

Abstract

The structural sections market is currently one of the most competitive sectors in world steel. Lackenby Beam Mill, a major supplier of heavy sections, invested in a high technology mill in 1991 to satisfy ever more demanding product quality and customer service requirements. One key aspect of the new mill operation was to reduce roll build-up times from 18 hours to 3 hours in order to offer more frequent rolling and a wider product range.

This paper highlights the strategy and training process devised and implemented to produce multi-skilled personnel, working successfully in self-managed teams and the associated key development of working team leaders to exploit capabilities of the new technology in the roll preparation area. Using both in-house and external modules, with continuous assessment, review and modification at each stage, the 3 hour roll build up has been achieved.

1 BACKGROUND

The process

The process of forming structural sections involves passing heated slabs through sets specifically profiled work rolls until the desired shape is achieved. Every serial size requires its own sets of rolls which are built up off-line into three stacks and, prior to commencement of rolling, transferred into fixed mill stands. To introduce greater flexibility into mill scheduling and provide shorter lead times, the development of the new Universal Beam Mill included the requirement to be able to strip and build these roll stacks in three hours. Reduced roll build and roll change times allow the mill to accept customer orders in smaller quantities and with shorter lead times with minimal down-time costs. Thus, as a supplier, the mill can synchronise its rolling schedules with the customers delivery requirements.

Performance

Following the mill installation in the summer of 1991, attention was turned upon the part of the mill where the stacks are built, the roll preparation area, where the length of time taken to strip and build the roll stacks which although down to 6 hours, was still running at double the design time. The roll preparation task involved employees of mixed disciplines i.e. production operatives (roll changers) and mechanical craftsmen. With two separate groups of employees working with limited flexibility, it was impossible to achieve the required standard strip and build time.

Agreement

Successful negotiations between management, production (ISTC) and craft (AEEU) unions, an agreement was reached in July 1994 to create a self sufficient and fully integrated team. This paved the way to fully integrate mixed discipline team working in the roll preparation area. A key element of the agreement was the creation of a leader or controller, responsible for engineering standards, organisation and control of the group in the roll preparation area.

Harmonising conditions was the final element of the agreement where the two groups prior to this had different working conditions such as starting and finishing times, earnings and bonuses. All of these were barriers to achieving the move towards a single working group which was self managed, self sufficient for all activities and fully utilised..

2   TRAINING STRATEGY

The introduction of team working does not happen by itself but requires real commitment to move away from traditional working methods. Thus, to achieve the objectives set, training was given top priority, not only to enhance employees skill levels but to also change their culture and thinking into becoming a leader or member of a team. In this context the team leader has had an important role to play. The roll preparation controllers and deputies have risen to the challenges placed upon them and have developed successfully into their new roles.

An analysis of skills indicated that a major training programme was required to fully integrate the two work groups in this area. A strategy or culture change model as it is known was developed, based on four distinct phases of training scheduled to take place over a period of time. See Figure 1. This model was tested, then improved and fully implemented.

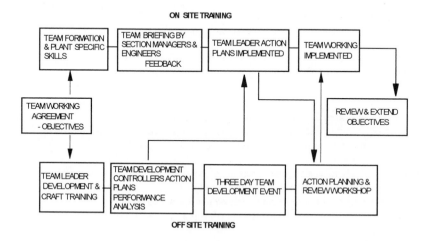

Figure 1   Strategy / Culture change model.

Dedicated roll preparation centre

To enhance the process of team bonding, it was essential that all the members of the roll preparation team were based together. Previously, the groups had separate amenity areas.

Following discussions with the groups involved, a location within the mill and central to the roll preparation area was agreed. Facilities at the new roll preparation centre include wash areas, a locker room, mess area, controllers office, workshop, conference room and storage area. This was a focal point in bringing together two separate groups of employees.

Training phase one - Task specifics

In this foundation phase, training was essentially a matter of providing elements which would support the formation of the teams and included:

i.   All members of the teams attending short modules carried out on the job by unit trainers which allowed individuals to move away from their traditional roles and become fully flexible across all the roll preparation area.
ii. Mill operatives receiving 'off the job' mechanical skills training at an external education facility. This included developing a basic knowledge in the use of hand tools and gaining an appreciation of hydraulic systems. Fault diagnosis of Farval dual line lubrication systems was also covered.
iii. Initial training for group controllers in team leadership and team development at Rushpool Hall, Saltburn.

Training phase two - Team working

This phase involved two workshops. The first, a half day workshop concentrated on devising action plans for the controllers and their deputies. The second workshop which ran for a full day at the Training Advice & Development Centre in Middlesbrough brought together the full shift team and included:

- Concepts of team working.
- Developing and implementing group controllers action plans.
- Analysing team performances and operational problems.

This was approached through a series of presentations, team exercises and open discussion sessions.

Training phase three - Team development

Phase three was a three day team development course at Brookfield Manor in Sheffield which was designed to bring the teams closer together and break down the functional barriers between mechanical craftsmen and operators. Specific training included:

- Recognising individual strengths in teams and barriers which hinder performance.
- Raising the profile of the controllers role as leader.
- Recognising the importance of communication in all aspects of the work.
- Enabling team members to understand the concepts and practice of team working.
- Practising key skills in a problem solving environment.
- Exploring real issues and problems caused by the introduction of team working, then designing solutions and action plans to be implemented on return to the work place.

Training phase four - Team Leadership
This training is currently ongoing and involves a series of reviews and problem solving workshops for the individual shift teams and management. More emphasis is to be placed on the controllers with formal supervisory training to give them more managerial responsibilities within their role, especially planning and co-ordinating future activities as well as their current workload.

In this phase the aim is also to extend the teams responsibilities by training them in maintenance activities within a defined area of the mill. This will provide a further stimulus for the team members to develop new skills and bring increased benefits to the business.

3   OUTCOME

The benefits of the teamworking agreement and the training programme outlined earlier have been :

- Stack strip and build times have reduced from six hours to three hours. See Figure 2.
- Increased mill availability in circumstances of short rollings.
- Reduction in unplanned mill delays due to improved quality of workmanship.
- Major improvement in morale.
- Teams are now accepting both ownership and responsibility for their actions.
- Significant increase in flexibilities between mechanical and production personnel.
- Individual team members have personal training plans.
- Improved relationships between team members.
- Effective leadership by the controllers and deputies.

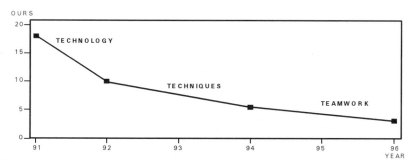

Figure 2   Improvement of strip and build sequence times.

4   LESSONS LEARNT

In leading this strategy over the last 18 months significantly more time has been devoted to this project than first envisaged. It has meant a big commitment by all levels of personnel but the reward is the satisfaction of seeing real change develop. It is important that individuals in a team are given the opportunity to discuss their problems and reach consensus. Experience has shown that initial leadership by management is necessary to set the framework and provide encouragement. This is then overtaken by enthusiasm within the team itself.

29

Best practice implementation of Total Quality Management: multiple cross-case analysis of manufacturing and service organisations

M.Terziovski and A. Sohal, Department of Business Management, Monash University, PO Box 197, Caulfield, Victoria 3145, Australia, Phone (61)(3)99032674, Fax (61)(3)9902718, e-mail: mile.terziovski @ buseco.monash.edu.au

D. Samson, Melbourne Business School, University of Melbourne, 200 Leicester Street, Melbourne, Victoria 3053, Australia, Phone (61)(3)93498183, Fax (61)(3)93498188, e-mail: Samson.GSMStaff is@ muwaye.unimelb.edu.au

Abstract

The paper examines 'best practice' implementation of Total Quality Management (TQM) in eight Australian manufacturing and service organizations. Multiple cross-case analysis is used to synthesize the information obtained from the case studies. The insights gained from the case studies are used to discuss the critical success factors that characterise Australian quality organisations and the essential steps in implementing TQM. Leadership and quality-based vision of world class performance have emerged as major factors that underpin best practice in TQM implementation. Participation by employees and unions in the development of an organization's vision was seen as critical in gaining high level commitment to the organization's goals.

Keywords

Best practice, Total Quality Management, implementation, leadership, quality

1. INTRODUCTION

Although the connection between Total Quality Management (TQM) and its benefits is beginning to be understood by managers at different levels of the organisation, the processes associated with the implementation of the TQM philosophy and methods are not well understood. This weakness is highlighted by Gupta and Ash (1994) who point out that there are many success stories about the implementation of TQM in the literature and the popular press. However, very few of these stories discuss the best practice in TQM implementation in any detail. Furthermore, quantitative studies that have been based on a few variables across large samples generally fail to capture process and multiple stakeholder considerations. Using longitudinal and multisource data makes the case study approach well suited for management inquiry into unique situations. Therefore, this paper examines, using a case study approach, eight Australian companies that have adopted the TQM philosophy and methods. The five manufacturing companies are: South Pacific Tyres; Van Leer Australia Pacific Dunlop Bedding; Varian Australia; Exicom; Safeway Australia; Smorgon ARC; Don Smallgoods (Terziovski and Samson 1995; Lu and Sohal, 1993).

The insights gained from multiple cross-case analysis of these organisations provide useful lessons concerning the introduction of a TQM process into an organization and the factors that contribute to success. The critical success factors (best TQM practices) are identified and implications for managers are discussed. The multiple cross-case analysis was facilitated by addressing the following questions for each case study:

. What is the reason for introducing a TQM based management philosophy?
. How did the organisation proceed down the path of culture change?
. What difficulties were encountered and how were these difficulties overcome?
. What lessons can be learned from the implementation process?
. What benefits have been achieved?

2. MULTIPLE CROSS-CASE ANALYSIS

The general approach in implementing the TQM philosophy and methods amongst the five manufacturing and three service companies has been to use a particular implementation methodology that is suited to the particular culture. As part of this methodology, companies generally create an "awareness" at all levels of the organisation and then later modify their approach to suit the organisation's specific requirements. The public display of commitment from senior management is absolutely critical in launching the quality initiative. This was very much the case at Safeway Australia where the General Manager played an active role in the implementation process; also at Smorgon ARC where the new CEO was the "Quality Champion;" This was also the case at South Pacific Tyres where the CEO was the main driving force behind the implementation of the new technology within an evolving Total Quality Culture. Another key feature of successful implementation of TQM is the simplicity of the improvement initiative. At Safeway Australia, the subject of TQM had been simplified to a level where all employees can identify with the key principles. Only the simplest and most relevant problem-solving tools were selected and taught to employees in a simple and straightforward manner. In a number of cases initial attempts did not fully satisfy the expectations of management and employees because the TQM concepts being implemented were off-the-shelf packages which did not contain business specific information. These programs were strong on training but weak on facilitating change - ie., ignoring the cultural and attitudinal issues in the organisation.

The results of our TQM case study research as well as research into other manufacturing improvement initiatives in Australian organisations (Samson et al, 1993) show that the employee input and participation is centrally important to the potential success of any improvement strategy being implemented. The human resource and cultural issues within an organisation require careful attention. Consultation, training, involvement, reward systems and recognition are vital elements of a successful people management strategy. This was found to be the case in all of the eight case study examples discussed in this paper. Overall, a number of key factors are recognised as critical to the successful adoption of TQM. Based on the qualitative analysis of the eight case examples, the following profile is developed of what a quality organisation should look like after several years of practicing best practice in Total Quality Management. In contrasting organizational situations such as unionised and non-unionised firms, large corporations versus small to medium producers and old technology firms versus new technology firms, certain TQM characteristics recur:

Customer Focus, both internal and external: Staying close to the customer. All of the eight organisations in our analysis are making a concerted effort to develop closer ties to their customers. These ties, in most cases, increased the likelihood of rapid response to shifts in the market. Companies were able to pick up more differentiated signals from the market and thus to respond to different segments of demand.

Strategic alliances with suppliers: Coordination with external firms was found to be crucial in cutting inventories (hence costs), in speeding up the flow of products, and in reducing defects.

Leadership: A commitment to change throughout the organisation, driven by the full and public support of the CEO where management encourages trust and involvement. Leadership throughout the organisation pursues continuous improvement in accordance with a shared vision which aims for world class performance in quality, productivity, timeliness, innovation and cost.

Innovative Human Resource Practices: The pursuit of a learning quality-based organisation and a commitment to occupational health and safety (OH&S). In all of the cases, there was a departure from conventional job classifications, career paths, training and compensation. Best Practice firms recognised that improvements in quality and flexibility require levels of commitment, from individual employees at all levels of the organization and not simply by changing and enforcing the human resource policy.

Competitive benchmarking and performance measurement system: Five out of the eight firms pursued the practice of benchmarking and had implemented a performance measurement system based on key performance indicators (KPIs). Firms attempted international benchmarking but later realised that the value for the resources invested did not compare favourably with domestic benchmarking. Best Practice firms applied benchmarking as part of the planning and vision setting phase of the TQM implementation process and not as an individual program that would change the profitability situation of the firm.

Union commitment: The relevant unions contribute to the process of change through effective consultation throughout the organisation.

Flatter organizational structure: Supported by empowerment of the employees at all levels of the organisation and improved communication. This involved a team-based organisation in all of the eight cases analysed.

The pursuit of new technology for strategic advantage: A trait common to the best practice firms was the technology transfer into production and the marketplace. These firms have integrated technology into the rest of their business planning, including strategies for human resources, marketing, manufacturing and all other related functional strategies.

3. CONCLUSION

The discussion in this paper has been based on the experiences of companies which have successfully adopted TQM. However, there are many thousands of companies which are struggling to introduce TQM into the workplace and have not progressed beyond the "awareness" stage. The main cause is that senior management in these companies is only paying lip service to implementing TQM without any real commitment to making changes. Lower level managers are frustrated because they cannot convince senior management of the benefits of TQM. What is required is more understanding at senior management level and empirical evidence of the value of TQM.

(NB:THE FULL LENGTH PAPER, INCLUDING REFERENCES, IS AVAILABLE FROM THE AUTHORS OR Vol. 7 No.5, 1996 of the TOTAL QUALITY MANAGEMENT JOURNAL).

30

Cultural change for survival

P.J. Hogg
British Steel Plc, Sections, Plates & Commercial Steels, Scunthorpe Works.
PO Box 1, Brigg Road, Scunthorpe, South Humberside, DN16 1BP, UK.
Tel: (01724) 404040 Fax: (01724) 402191
E-mail: gbbs27t2@ibmmail.com

Abstract

The Heavy Section Mill at British Steel's Scunthorpe Works, largely dating from 1948 was under the threat of closure during the late 1980's. Now in 1996, after an initial capital investment of over £10m, and a further £28m currently being invested, it has become a leading global producer of steel sheet piling products. This turnaround was only possible by changing the culture of the employees from one of despondency at the thought of closure to one of commitment to the mill's future in the 21st century. This has been achieved despite further planned manning reductions of 100 people due to new technology.

This paper illustrates how this transformation has been achieved. Building on earlier steps in the TQ process, an open book philosophy has been used, with all employees involved in workshops with senior managers in which the forward market development strategy and the quality requirements of these new markets were discussed. Product quality has improved to match these requirements and levels of customer satisfaction are even higher. The culture is changing, the mill has survived and as a result, is now well placed for the future.

1. BACKGROUND

During the late 1980's the Heavy Section Mill at British Steel's Scunthorpe Works appeared to have only a limited future. A lack of capital investment had left the mill with much old, outdated equipment which was difficult to maintain. Some of the steel sheet piling products which the mill rolled were approaching obsolescence and many of the mill's other products; structural sections, could be rolled more efficiently at other locations within British Steel. At that time the workforce, which numbered approximately 450, were often seen as the most cynical and least receptive to the Total Quality process spread in Works-wide Total Quality Performance (TQP) workshops. These workshops were the Works' first step in taking TQP to the shopfloor and first line supervisors. Although virtually all who attended the sessions would agree that the concepts of satisfying customers, right first time and good teamwork made extremely good common sense, many perceived that implementing change back in the workplace would be near impossible. The perception that Management was not interested in employee's ideas or opinions was often cited as a major reason for this. In 1996 the Heavy Section Mill workforce and management are working together to ensure the future of the mill into the next century with a competitive product range and global sales position.

2. NEW PRODUCT RANGE

Steel sheet piling is a specialist civil engineering steel product used mainly for retaining walls in foundations, road, railway and marine applications. The Heavy Section Mill is the sole producer in the UK and one of a relatively small number in the World. Such a specialist product is more difficult and costly to produce than standard structural steel sections. Faced with a near obsolete product range, British Steel was in danger of being forced to withdraw from steel sheet piling manufacture altogether. The option of installing a modern facility to produce more competitive piles was prohibitively expensive, therefore the option selected was a relatively small capital investment (approximately £10m) in the Heavy Section Mill in order to support the development of a new range of piles. The more efficient and competitive piles would allow British Steel to compete more effectively on a world stage, with less reliance on the domestic market.

It was known that the new range would test the mill's capability. New equipment in itself, however, would not ensure the success of the development. The workforce would need to have a large involvement supported by a significant training programme. Many operators were involved in the design stage, developing the operator interfaces for the new control systems. Involvement was also vital during the installation and commissioning phases, and some employees broke their Christmas week holidays to come to work and receive training on new equipment.

New equipment allowed the new piles to be rolled; the development of the rolling processes for these new sections proved to be the biggest challenge. Finite Element modelling and lead rolling trials on scale test rigs were precursors to full mill rolling trials. It was obvious at the early stages that blending the knowledge and experience of the rolling operators with research theory would be the most successful strategy. The operators were heavily involved in pre-trial planning and trial debriefs, and now have ownership in the established rolling processes - the 'white-coats' are long departed.

The new steel sheet piling range has been well received both within the UK and export markets. Sales have increased and currently around 80% of piling production is exported, with much of this currently going into Far Eastern markets.

3. ORGANISATIONAL CHANGES

The capital investments (in a mill previously thought to have a limited future) can be cited as a change agent which has allowed for fundamental changes to the organisation of work at all levels within the mill. Predominantly these changes have focused on teamworking, or at least the removal of functional barriers, which help facilitate the cultural change required for the Mill to survive and prosper.

Amongst the changes made has been the creation of teams organised around work activities; this has led to the term "Natural Working Groups". Pay grades have been rationalised to remove any barriers within the team; there has been a reduction in shift supervision to allow responsibility to be driven down the organisation; shift craft personnel have been placed on a common rota system with process operators to aid the development of the wider shift team, and allow the further development of the craft/process interface.

Attention has also been focused on traditional management structures. An integrated management structure has been established with an emphasis on a common manufacturing focus, encouraging TQP principles of ownership and accountability for geographic areas of plant, thus moving away from the functional organisation based around discrete production or engineering bias - i.e. multi functional supervision.

Although still in its first year, the new structure is demonstrating a more focused approach, with plant being engineered for the quality of the product, and processes being refined to be less demanding of equipment.

4. FURTHER CAPITAL INVESTMENT

Having developed the new range of piling and begun to exploit it commercially it became clear that in order to significantly advance British Steel's position in the World markets, fundamental improvements in production capability would be required. Other European competitors were investing in plant to enhance product range and quality. The decision was taken to invest a further £30m in the Heavy Section Mill. The mill and its workforce had obviously gained the confidence of the company with the success of the initial development.

The workforce are again heavily involved with this second development, which includes significant modification to product flows, bottlenecks and replaces large amounts of old equipment. Ensuring the correct equipment specification is vital; it must be fit for purpose yet not overspecified as this would jeopardise the project budget. The people who use the existing equipment are quite obviously those best placed to review proposals for the replacements. This second phase of capital investment brings with it a reduction in the required workforce of 100, with a firm management objective of avoiding compulsory redundancy. The Trade Unions are currently involved in assisting management manage the manpower programme and the development of more modern working practices aimed at maximising the contribution of the remaining employees. The workforce have remained positive despite these job losses, recognising they are necessary for the future of the Heavy Section Mill.

5. QUALITY SEMINARS

The cornerstone of the effectiveness of the enhanced quality process route needed to be explained to the whole workforce. Unless everyone in the Mill was aware of the market strategy it would be impossible for them to be fully committed to it. Communication was achieved through Market Development Workshops.

Senior Commercial Managers explained the current market position of both British Steel and major piling competitors including the effect of the capital investments. An open book philosophy was used in these sessions which enabled the true picture of the business position to be explained, including the threats and opportunities for the future of the mill . The specific requirements of different markets were discussed and members of the workshops encouraged to translate these into improved practices and procedures at their workplace, with the ultimate goal being complete customer satisfaction.

With a clear vision of the way forward for British Steel's piling business, Heavy Section Mill's employees went back to the workplace with a different perspective. More than ever they recognise they are stakeholders in the piling business, and subsequently real and lasting improvements have been seen in the operation. Operators are more prepared to stop the process and put things right even if the improvements are slight. Personal standards of workmanship have improved, and levels of customer satisfaction have risen, as employees have become more tuned into these requirements.

6. CULTURE CHANGE FOR SURVIVAL

The Heavy Section Mill and its employees have come a long way. The mill faced closure in the late 1980's and is now well placed to begin the next century as one of the World's leading producers of steel sheet piling. This can only be accomplished with a workforce committed to this aim. The progress of the market development strategy will be fed back regularly to the mill personnel, enabling product process routes and requirements to be customer driven. Challenges ahead include the commissioning and full utilisation of the new equipment, when two-thirds of the current workforce will be doing different jobs.

What has been achieved to date is only the beginning. With a modernised mill and a better motivated workforce, there will be an increasing emphasis placed upon developing even more innovative products and new markets. The culture change is only just starting!

PART SIX

Quality Methods

31

The investors in people and total quality Venn diagram

H M Solomon
Chrysalid Consultants
Transformation House, 10 Meadowlands, Scholes, Cleckheaton, W. Yorkshire, UK, tel/fax 01274 869524

Abstract

The plethora of approaches advertised and received by mailshot and the often heard complaints of initiative fatigue have motivated the author to seek to clarify that which Investors in People and Total Quality have to offer and whether these approaches can be used in isolation or combination to continuously improve organisations.

The paper will define the approaches and the benefits to be gained from IiP and TQ. It will compare the IiP model and a TQ model considering their advantages and disadvantages. By considering the process of implementation and the outcomes to be gained the audience will be assisted in determining the most appropriate approach for them and their organisations.

Keywords

Investors in People, Total Quality, goals, measurement, customer, people, processes.

1   INTRODUCTION

What will improve your organisation? Only you know the answer to that. However, before you can know the answer you need to understand your organisation, its structure, culture, people, markets and stakeholders. In addition if you are a member of the top team you will also need to know what drives your behaviour and the behaviour of the other members of the team. Based on this knowledge you can determine which of a myriad of approaches will help your organisation to continuously improve. You should also decide to tailor these models and approaches to fit your own organisation and its needs at any given point in time.

2   THE INVESTORS IN PEOPLE STANDARD

This standard approaches organisational improvement through planning and training and development. It complements well the process and systems approach of ISO 9000. The standard consists of 24 Indicators which need to be met in order to achieve the standard. The Indicators can be split into four categories.

An Investor in People:

1. makes a public commitment from the top to develop all employees to achieve its business objectives
2. regularly reviews the training and development needs of all employees
3. takes action to train and develop individuals on recruitment and throughout their employment
4. evaluates the investment in training and development to assess achievement and improve future effectiveness

The process to achieve this follows the quality principle of plan, do, check, act. It necessitates that an organisation must identify its goals and objectives and translate these into departmental, team and individual objectives. It then requires the company to determine whether the employees have the right skills and abilities to achieve the goals. This results in organisations setting up means, if they do not already exist to achieve these requirements. Any training and development interventions must then be evaluated against the criteria set. The focus therefore is on knowing what your organisation is trying to achieve and appropriately gearing the human resources to be able to deliver it. Implicit in the requirements is the need for effective organisational communication and managerial competence.

3   A TQ MODEL

The first difficulty with TQ is how to define it. Mike Robson defines it as ' the development of a total organisational way of life which puts quality first in order to satisfy customer needs and expectations.' What seems more important is how do we use TQ to help our organisations improve?

Total Quality is about taking a look at your business as a whole and the context in which it operates and after diagnosis determining priority areas for improvement. There are some absolutes of a quality organisation which would include:

- a clear vision owned by everyone
- customer focused
- utilising the potential of employees and treating them with respect
- doing the right things right
- continuous improvement

However much of what would form your definition of TQ would depend on what was appropriate for your organisation to achieve its vision.

Diagnosis and understanding of 'total organisational way of life' in terms of structures and processes, market and environment and people and culture will help the organisation to determine the capability of the organisation and its management. Armed with this knowledge, realistic goals can be set to move towards the vision. All progress needs to be measured and monitored and approaches modified to respond to internal and external changes. Since TQ is ' a journey not a destination' as the organisation improves it will continue to strive for higher goals.

The TQ Model which I have developed from my work with organisations and Lombardy Consulting Group is shown in Fig.1 below.

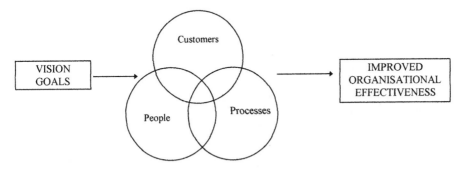

Coherent and successful organisations focus on all of these areas over time, balancing and selecting the appropriate interventions according to the needs of their organisation.

4   IMPLEMENTATION AND BENEFITS

The process of implementation for both IiP and TQ is very similar and consists of a diagnostic phase, identifying areas for action, planning how to address these, making interventions, ongoing measurement, evaluation and corrective action. In the case of IiP there is a framework provided by the 24 Indicators whereas for the TQ model the organisation would need to determine its own standards of performance. An external award also has additional strengths which are as follows:
- a tried and tested formula
- a benchmark and guidance for action
- a goal to unite people
- external recognition

Both TQ and IiP require an organisational vision or mission. Both result in improvements to 'organisational way of life.'

way of life and the culture becomes one of openness, co-operation and self development with everyone seeing themselves as a customer of each other.

5   CONCLUSIONS

To return to the question in the title what would the Venn diagram look like? This paper has shown that both IiP and TQ are approaches that can help organisations to continuously improve. TQ is a holistic approach which has the potential to bring about quite radical benefits in changing the culture of the organisation although it is much less tangible and more complex to advance. It is externally focused and by placing the emphasis on delighting customers major business benefits can be achieved. IiP is internally focused and approaches the improvement process through the people circle as shown in Fig.1. In developing plans and systems to achieve the standard it will also have a positive impact on the process circle. As an externally awarded standard, IiP has a set of principles to guide action planning and provide an independent judgement of performance.

The Venn diagram therefore should portray IiP as a subset of TQ. This is not to say that IiP is not a very useful stepping stone towards TQ but it order to realise the full potential of your organisation it is necessary to embrace TQ.

6   REFERENCES

Robson, M (1988) The Journey to Excellence. MRA International Ltd, England.
HEQC The Higher Education Quality Council and UCoSDA The Universities' and Colleges'
    Staff Development Agency (1995) Investors in People in Higher Education Progress
    Report Including Background Directory of HEIs Case Studies.
Investors in People UK (1994) Investors in People The Benefits of Being an Investor in
    People.
Whittle, S. Total Quality Management: Redundant Approaches to Culture Change ACAS
    Review Spring 1992.

7   BIOGRAPHY

Since graduating as a social scientist in 1977 Hazel Solomon has spent 18 years creating and developing ways to support the improvement of people and processes within organisations. Her work experience includes management services in the steel industry, lecturing in human resource management, managing the total quality function within manufacturing and education and management consultancy with an international consultancy firm, where she specialised in change management. She now manages Chrysalid Consultants.

32

Are quality plans necessary in a total quality organisation?

Martin Gibson
Company Statistician
Leamington Spa, Warwickshire, CV32 6PX, UK.
Tel. +44 (0)1203 216361 Fax. +44 (0)1203 216912

Abstract

In this paper we question the necessity of quality plans in a Total Quality Organisation. We suggest that a plan for process improvement is required but that separate quality plans for distinctive products or services are not. Gibson (1995) demonstrated the importance of quality improvement through statistical thinking which may have been interpreted as a quality plan. Deming's suggestion for the organisation for improvement for quality and productivity is endorsed.

Keywords

Quality plans, Total Quality Organisation, culture, guru, dominant factor, road map, process improvement, facilitator.

1 INTRODUCTION

In this paper we pose the question "Are Quality Plans necessary in a Total Quality Organisation?" We propose that for an organisation to prosper separate quality plans are unnecessary **if** a Total Quality Management **culture** exists. The management of quality improvement processes will produce the necessary quality and productivity improvements.

Gibson (1995), demonstrated the importance of quality improvement through statistical thinking so that the appropriate measurable quality and reliability characteristics (QRCs) were determined in all stages of the product (service) development cycle.

These QRCs are essential, but the management of them should not necessarily be interpreted as a product (service) quality plan.

Western management does ask for plans which would include quality plans. This we believe demonstrates a fundamental lack of understanding of TQM.

2 THE QUALITY GURUS

None of the quality gurus or their followers provide a quality planning process with the exception of Juran (1988) and Feigenbaum (1991). Juran gives a 'Quality Planning Road Map' for products or services. This road map involves flow diagrams, suppliers, processes, customers and multi-functional teams based on the financial processing trilogy of planning, control and improvement. Juran & Gryna (1993) then reference this road map plus many other technical disciplines so that quality goals can be set, planned and evaluated for in the resultant product or service, again from a financial analogy. They recommend application in 'breakthrough projects' so that a gradual pace of change can be achieved within the organisation. In a project chosen for model implementation, all people, processes, suppliers and customers inside the project will have interfaces with other systems, people, processes, suppliers and customers in the organisation which may not be using the same quality planning process. Hence barriers both visible and invisible will prevent the model succeeding.

Feigenbaum (1991) offers a brief outline of a quality plan supported by a technology triangle of test, inspection and control which we do not believe is valid for today.

What the quality gurus do offer is a general scope of application (Ghoboadian & Speller, 1994) which can vary from an holistic approach to quality e.g. Deming, Feigenbaum, and Ishikawa to a comprehensive programme for product life span (Juran), implicitly functional (Crosby), all processes (Groocock) or off-line in design and on-line in production (Taguchi). There is general agreement between them on a **culture** which emphasises people, processes and performance from a focus which can be through customers, suppliers or value. This resultant culture will have a guru dependent dominant factor which may be any one of the following: control of variation, fitness for purpose/use, conformance requirements/zero defects, total quality control, chain of conformance, company wide quality control/quality circles or quality loss function.

Clearly the choice of the dominant factor and ultimately which guru to follow could be influenced by which product (service) the organisation provides. We believe this should not happen. The organisation should adopt a quality strategy which is suited for its own **people and processes** and not focus on the products (services).

Given the organisation has chosen its guru and respective dominant factor, we pose the question an executive may ask, "Where is the quality plan?" as if this were a discrete entity which should be evident for the product (service). We believe this question should be "What plan do I need to improve my quality processes?"

3 THE QUALITY PROCESS

If this question is asked then we believe that **all** products and services will be affected, not merely the ones chosen for implementation. The next question is "How will this be achieved?"

For an organisation to realise quality improvement, it is essential that they have a TQM strategy for process improvement that 'recognises all work occurs in a system of interconnected processes each of which has customers; variation exists in all processes; causes of variation can be loosely segregated into "common" and "special causes"; understanding the unique nature of both common and special causes is the key to reducing variation, and reducing variation is the key to improving quality, productivity and profitability' (Hoerl et. al., 1993).

This strategy must embrace all systems, processes, internal customers and suppliers and most importantly be applied equally to **all employees** whether they be executives or part-time workers. External customer and supplier wants also need to be understood. To achieve the improvement in quality, productivity and profitability a complete change of culture within the organisation will have to be created from an empowered group with authority to achieve that change.

Clearly it would be misleading to employ the organisation's quality department to implement a change of culture as this would merely help to alienate that department with it's internal processes from the rest of the organisation. The ownership of quality would still be perceived to be in the hands of the quality department and create barriers opposed to process improvement. To be successful a separate cross-functional group reporting directly to a chairman who can champion the new wave of process changes is essential. This group would produce a **long-term** process improvement strategic plan involving identified individuals within departments across the organisation to act as key facilitators. These identified facilitators would have in-depth knowledge of the all the systems, constraints and opportunities in their respective areas, plus expert knowledge in specific subjects, e.g. statistical methods, reliability, FMEA, timing, QFD.

A preliminary strategy for the group could be to:

1. identify;
- all affected systems, processes and internal customers and suppliers in the organisation,
- quality improvement processes which are being used, (e.g. QFD, FMEA)
- statistical which are being used, (e.g. DoE, SPC),

2. create;
- an initial training package for the empowered group and it's facilitators in quality improvement and statistical methods, human skills, psychology and team building,
- a training package for the total workforce which recognizes their individual skills and strengths which would include business and non-business interests,

3. implement;
- the necessary tools and techniques through the facilitators,
- cross functional approaches to innovative process quality improvement, including financial and timing planning,
- continual self development in the total workforce.

4 CONCLUSIONS

We suggest that if such a group exists, then;
- a symbiotic relationship for the total organisation will be evident as all processes will be linked,
- all necessary quality actions that are required for the organisation to prosper will be evident,
- separate quality plans will not be necessary, and,
- a Total Quality Organisation will be created,

In conclusion we endorse Deming's (1986) suggestion for improvement of quality as the only viable proposal. Until that happens, quality plans will be a necessity and Total Quality Organisations will not exist.

5 REFERENCES

Gibson, M.G., (1995) Quality improvement through statistical thinking, or 'What has a Statistician got to do with TQM?' in *Total Quality Management, Proceedings of the First World Congress,* (ed. by G.K. Kanji), Chapman & Hall.

Deming, W.Edwards (1986) *Out of the crisis.* M.I.T. Centre for Advanced Engineering Study.

Juran, J.M., (1988) *Juran on Planning for Quality.* Collier Macmillan

Feigenbaum, A.V. (1991, 40th Anniversary Edition) *Total Quality Control.* McGraw-Hill International.

Juran, J.M. & Gryna, F.M., (1993, 3rd edition) *Quality Planning and Analysis.* McGraw-Hill International.

Ghoboadian, A. & Speller, S. (1994) Gurus of Quality: a framework for comparison. *Total Quality Management,* **5**, 53-69.

Hoerl, R.W., Hooper, J.H., Jacobs, P J. & Lucas, J.M. (1993) Skills for Industrial Statisticians to Survive and Prosper in the Emerging Quality Environment. *The American Statistician,* **47**, 280-292.

6 BIOGRAPHY

Martin Gibson is a Company Statistician and Quality Improvement Specialist in the automotive industry. He is interested in the application of statistical thinking for quality improvement across all processes within companies. His background includes engineering, medicine, physiology, oceanography, marketing, paper making, oil exploration and lecturing in higher education. He is a Chartered Statistician of The Royal Statistical Society and is active in it's Business and Industrial Section, Professional Affairs Committee and Council.

33
Business process re-engineering: a retrospective case study

L.R.P.Reavill
Engineering Management Centre, Systems Science Department, City University.
Northampton Square, London EC1V 0HB, UK, Telephone: 0171 477 8375; Fax: 0171 477 8579; EMail: L.R.P.Reavill@city.ac.uk

Abstract
Some critics of Business Process Re-engineering, (BPR), claim that the concept is not new, and that the activities now compiled as BPR have been part of the managerial tool kit for some decades. This paper discusses a series of major changes instituted around 1980 by a company in the precious metals refining business, and argues that the actions of the company replicate BPR, at a period before BPR was promoted as a major new managerial concept.

Keywords
Business Process Re-engineering, change management, innovation, precious metal refining

1   INTRODUCTION

Business Process Re-engineering has been adopted in the USA as a major new management concept, and has generated great interest in the UK without achieving the evangelical fervour of the USA. The enthusiasm is perhaps due to the missionary zeal of its initial proponents, Hammer and Champy (1993), or perhaps to the speed with which it has been adopted by both management consultants and the vendors of process modelling software. Grint (1993) attributes the popularity of BPR to 'sympathetic resonances' from the market, and challenges both the internal coherence and the novelty of BPR. It is this latter element that will be addressed by this paper. The author re-examines some major changes undertaken by a company in the precious metals business some 15 - 20 years ago, and suggests that these replicate the basics of the then unknown BPR.

2   BACKGROUND OF THE CASE STUDY

The Case Study concerns a major company in business in the precious metals industry, and in particular with a partly owned subsidiary of that business providing a refining service for materials containing precious metals. The business activity is normally termed "toll refining". Customers have materials containing precious metals such as gold, silver and platinum, of which they wish to realise the value. To do so, the precious metal must be separated from a very much larger quantity of non-precious material, and refined to individual metals of high purity which can be sold in the market. There are four principal stages of the business process:

1.   Sampling, evaluation, and agreement of the precious metal content of the material.
2.   Negotiation of the % recovery of the precious metal, the product purity, the time for the delivery of the pure metal, and the fee (toll) for the refining service.
3.   The refining process, performed by chemical, electrochemical and/or metallurgical procedures.
4.   The delivery of the metal to the customer; or its sale on the metals market with the proceeds credited to the customer's account.

The refining process is quite long, weeks or months rather than hours or days. The cost of the process varies according to the concentration and species of the precious metals, and the type of non-precious metal content of the material. The expertise of the toll refining company rests in its ability to provide a speedy evaluation of the customer's material by means of an accurate sampling and analysis service, and a refining process which gives the best recovery of the customer's precious metal in the shortest time. The customer must agree the analysis, and therefore the precious metal content, before the material goes into process. Since the refining process is long, and additional delay may occur while agreement is reached on content, regular customers often adopt procedures involving duplicate sampling which will allow for re-analysis, with or without the help of third-party evaluation. This affords an early entry to the refining process, and an earlier recovery and sale of the metal.

There are two major types of customer for this service, and these relate to the source of the input material, which can be designated "primary" or "secondary". The largest quantity of precious metal containing concentrate is termed "primary" material, in that it is derived directly from mined ore. Concentrates are obtained from companies which mine for precious metals; or which mine for base metals such as copper and nickel on a large scale, and which produce precious metal concentrates as a small but valuable by-product. This material tends to be regular in supply, and consistent in content, and is therefore relatively easy for the toll refiner to process. Evaluation procedures, recoveries, processing times and product purities can be the subject of ongoing long term contracts. Secondary material is derived from a wide variety of sources, and is the result of the recovery of the precious metal content of waste products and scrap materials. It is termed "secondary" as it is about to have a second working life in the cycle of raw material to product to discard. With more attention being paid to conservation of resources, and the re-use, recovery, and recycling of useful materials, such material has changed from being a minor component of throughput to becoming rather more significant. Its disadvantage, from the viewpoint of the toll refiner, is its high variability, both in quantity and in content.

3   REVIEW OF THE BUSINESS PROCESS

In the 1970s, the company reviewed its toll refining business in the light of current developments and anticipated trends, and identified a number of areas for attention. There was a need to improve the purity of the final product, not for all uses, but for a number of known and anticipated new products. To address the needs of the customers for the toll refining service, there was a need for a reduction in evaluation time, processing time, and % recovery. With the long process time, the value of the materials, and the high interest rates of the period, the financial driver of these changes towards higher performance standards is clear.

The company then set some quantified goals in the areas requiring improvement, and investigated how these might be achieved by incremental improvement of the existing systems. The outcome of this preliminary investigation was not encouraging, indeed it exposed a serious problem. It was highly unlikely, even with substantial expenditure of time and resources, that improvements to the current systems would deliver the required new performance standards.

The situation was one which is addressed by Kirton (1984) in his differentiation between 'adaptors' and 'innovators': "adaptors do it better; innovators do it differently". Since the required standards were unlikely to be achieved by improvements to existing methods, only new and different methods might be viable, and the company embarked on a major programme of research and development work to devise new and superior evaluation and processing systems. These involved quicker and more reproducible sampling techniques of high accuracy; rapid but reliable and accurate chemical analysis procedures; and processing methods which reduced substantially the time to finished product while improving the % precious metal recovery. Means of accommodating a more variable input was also considered, but this was not given the high priority accorded to the other goals.

It is not within the remit of this paper, which seeks to indicate the adoption of BPR procedures in the pre-BPR era, to go into the technical details of this work, some aspects of which are covered in some ancient writings (Reavill 1984; Reichart and Reavill 1977). Suffice to say that the research and development processes were successful, and the new systems achieved the required higher standards.

4   COMPARISON WITH BPR

Thus we have a case history of a company in a very specialised area of industry reviewing its future business needs, and identifying some major potential problems. This accords with, and to some extent develops the view of Holtham (1996):

> 'If it was possible to identify such a key [to BPR], it would undoubtedly be the combination of:
>
> A.   A weak or disastrous level of current performance.
>
> and   B.   A charismatic, hard driving newly appointed chief executive, who can articulate the new vision, and then successfully set in train the whole range of practical implementation steps necessary.'

Though the performance was not disastrous, it was perceived as weak, and potentially inadequate for a more competitive future. The chief executive (General Manager) of this area of the company's activities was indeed newly appointed and hard driving, but the massive development programme was also motivated, and to a large extent financed, by the largest of the primary material suppliers, which had a part interest in the refining company and could see considerable advantages for their business in savings in both processing cost and inventory.

Holtham (1996) also expresses some views on 'what BPR is not': those aspects of change management incorrectly assumed to be BPR. Holtham identifies three elements of change management which are peripheral or unconnected to BPR: software re-engineering led change; technology initiated change; and computer based tools led change. Of these exceptions, only that of technology initiated change need be considered, and it is apparent that in this case, the technology changes were initiated by the business needs.   The technology was not available at the outset, and had to be generated to fulfil the perceived business need.   At the start, it was not certain that suitable technology could be created.

The definition of BPR given by Hammer and Champy (1993) is:

> 'the fundamental rethinking and radical redesign of business processes to achieve dramatic improvements in critical contemporary measures of performance, such as cost, quality, service and speed'

More automated sampling was introduced where possible, and advanced instrumental chemical analysis techniques were adopted and further developed, both saving time and cost. More use was made of duplicate sampling and contractual third party referral, which reduced delay in starting processing, and thereby saved time and opportunity cost.   The new refining processes gave higher stage efficiencies of separation which reduced recycling, and provided more rapid treatment.   In combination, these gave a substantial reduction in refining time, and process and inventory cost.   The purity of the final products was improved, giving enhanced product quality.   Thus, it could be argued that dramatic improvements were obtained in all four of Hammer and Champy's critical measures of performance.

5   CONCLUSION

It is concluded that the situation described in the case study shows in retrospect the use of BPR more than a decade prior to its promulgation as a 'new' managerial concept.

6   REFERENCES

Grint, K. (1993) Reengineering history: An analysis of business process reengineering. *Templeton College, The Oxford Centre for Management Studies Management Research Paper*, 93/20.

Hammer, M. and Champy, J. (1993) *Reengineering the corporation: a manifesto for business revolution.* Nicholas Brealey, London.

Holtham, C. *Business Process Reengineering - contrasting what it is with what it is not* (1996) To be published.

Kirton, M.J. (1984) Adaptors and innovators - why new initiatives get blocked. *Long Range Planning* 17 2 137-143.

Reavill, L.R.P. (1984) A New Platinum Metals Refinery. *Platinum Metals Review*, 28 1, 2-6

Reichart, B.J. and Reavill, L.R.P.   (1977) Statistical Analysis for Input and Output Control in the Precious Metals Refining Industry. *Proceedings of IChemE Symposium*, Manchester.

7   BIOGRAPHY

Dr. Lawrie Reavill is a senior lecturer in the Department of Systems Science at City University, London, and is Director of the Engineering Management Centre. His main area of research is management of change.   Previously, he worked in technology and innovation management in the metallurgical and chemical industries.

34

Implementation of total productive maintenance in support of an established total quality programme

Dr Rodney McAdam and Anne-Marie Duffner, MBA
Ulster Business School
Newtownabbey, BT37 0QB, Northern Ireland
Tel : +44 (0) 1232 368148   Fax : +44 (0) 1232 365117

ABSTRACT

Total Productive Maintenance (TPM) is increasingly being seen as a suitable initiative/technique for effectively involving the workforce in manufacturing based organisations to produce increased productivity and add new impetus to Total Quality efforts.

This paper discusses how Total Productive Maintenance can be implemented within an organisation that has an established Total Quality programme in place. The relationship between TQM and TPM is investigated with regard to improving the synergy between the initiatives and the effectiveness of each respectively.

Case study data on Harris Ireland Ltd (part of the Harris Corporation) is discussed. The data includes questionnaire and interview data. The paper also shows how TPM implementation in Harris has been driven by the results of Baldrige based audits.

INTRODUCTION

Total Productive Maintenance (TPM) is increasingly being seen as a suitable initiative initiative/technique for effectively involving the workforce in manufacturing based organisations to produce increased productivity and add new impetus to Total Quality efforts.

Harris Ireland Ltd (part of the Harris Corporation) has an established Total Quality (TQ) Programme in place and is now in the process of implementing TPM as part of the overall TQ programme. This process has highlighted many points in regard to improving the synergy between TQM and TPM and the effectiveness of each respectively.

HARRIS IRELAND LTD

Harris Corporation headquartered on the east coast of Florida, is an international company based on 4 major Divisions - Electronic Systems, Semiconductors, Government Information Systems and Lanier Office Equipment, and employing 28,000 people world-wide.

Harris Ireland, a manufacturing, design and development facility based in Dundalk, is part of the multinational Harris Corporation. It was founded in 1966 as a wholly owned subsidiary of the Semiconductor Product Division of General Electric.

The company currently manufactures a wide range of Metal Oxide Varistors (MOV) - transient voltage suppressors made of sintered metal oxides, primarily zinc oxide with other additives. Output is 154 million units per year. The total business represents sales of $30 million and employs 275 people with a temporary pool used to cater for short term swings in demand.

TOTAL QUALITY MANAGEMENT IN HARRIS IRELAND

Since 1991 the Harris Semiconductor sector has introduced the Total Quality concept to their locations world-wide, with major emphasis on empowerment, employee involvement and development.

In order to ensure TQM and its associated methodologies were aligned with the company's goals, the management team took on the role of "Steering Committee" for the TQM process. This ensured that the TQM goals would be focused on company's business interests. Since then a process of devolution has led to a devolved system of TQM involving Operational Steering Committees (OCSs).

The Steering Committee's role is to advise, recommend and develop further the process of TQM throughout the organisation with a major focus on the so called "soft issues".

The focus is on longer term issues as opposed to the OSC's who are focused on operational continuous improvement.

Since 1991, TQM as implemented in Harris Ireland has helped in achieving substantial business improvement. At the end of the financial year on June 30, 1993, the business had turned around from one of loss making to profitability.

THE NEED FOR FURTHER IMPROVEMENT

The adoption of the TQM initiative is primarily responsible for the recent success in Harris Ireland. The initiative will continue to evolve in search of further competitive advantage. Key to this continuing success is the increase of manufacturing capacity and the reduction of the total Cost Base required to make the product.

Obviously investment will play a key role in achieving these objectives. However, any further development of TQM which will achieve increased throughput while reducing production costs would be a major benefit. This has resulted in Harris applying the principles of TPM. (Nakajina, 1989; Hartman, 1992).

STRUCTURAL CASE STUDY - DATA ANALYSIS AND RESULTS

To achieve the deserved business improvement using TPM the following objectives were defined.

Objective 1:

To benchmark the current quality culture in Harris Ireland by analysing the results of Harris Ireland's Total Quality Systems Review (TQSR) held in May 1995.

Objective 2:

To examine the attitude and role of employees in the implementation of TPM. This includes an organisational survey of Harris Ireland employees.

Objective 3:

To determine a basic structure for implementing a TPM programme within an organisation. This includes: literature review, organisation survey results and structured interviews with the TPM Facilitators of NEC Semiconductors Ireland, Ltd., Ballivor, and Short Brothers Plc.

BENCHMARKING THE CURRENT QUALITY CULTURE IN HARRIS IRELAND

Harris have as a corporate goal, the winning of the Malcolm Baldbridge National Quality Award (MBNQA) by 1999. This goal is seen not as an end to a journey but as the beginning of a new stage which is consistent with the conclusion of Zink et al (1994). To achieve this goal they have set up a team and a measurement system to monitor progress towards Total Quality throughout the Corporation. The system is called Total Quality Systems Review (TQSR).

Structured interviews were held with a cross section of the workforce.
The interviews are conducted by a four man team from Corporate headquarters, including the Director of Quality. The duration of each interview is approximately one to two hours and consists of structured questions with scores assigned for each standard. The interviewing process takes three days. When this is complete the TQSR team collate their scores for each standard of excellence making observations and recommendations regarding each standard. The audit process ends with the team presenting the results and findings to all the interviewees collectively.

By referring to Figure 1 and Table 1 it can be seen that Harris Ireland are moving along the path of continuous improvement. The 1993 results compared to 1990 shows a 46.5% increase with a further increase of 18.5% in the 1995 results.

Central to achieving this improvement were the gains in the elements that make-up quality culture. Within the TQM framework, the tool of TPM will be used to focus the company's manufacturing continuous improvement thrust. The TPM strategy will focus on how Harris Ireland can use its manufacturing equipment to maximise resources.

RESULTS AND DISCUSSION FROM THE TPM SURVEY

TQM Environment

The survey showed there is a widespread understanding of the TQM objectives within the organisation. The key to success in the electronics industry is producing high quality, cost competitive and innovative products. The TQM initiative is perceived to be the guiding philosophy to achieve this objective, thus making the company profitable. This was reflected in the results which showed increased employee involvement, increased market share and cost reduction as the perceived objectives of TQM. The majority of groups viewed its implementation as the way to survive, and no-one saw it as a means to reduce the workforce.

Employee Involvement

There is widespread belief among all groups that the contribution they made towards the company's objectives is high and 95% of these employees also feel that they participate in making decisions associated with their job. This data reveals that the levels of employee involvement are high within the organisation. However personal performance is not thought, by 55% of the groups, to be linked to positive recognition. This could lead to a weakening of the employee involvement and teamwork concept in the future.

Teamwork

The teamwork concept has been embraced by the organisation as the vehicle for driving the TQM initiative. All employees are presently members of PWGs and many are members of improvement teams. There is a dislike for imposed goals, a preference by the PWGs from both lines for goals to be set by the team. All groups, with the exception of the Radial PWG, who have only recently formed as a team for one month, feel they have been adequately trained to meet team task needs. This data reinforces the concept of teamwork within the organisation.

Skills and Training

Following on from this, more than 80% of all groups have sufficient training to do their jobs. However, training overall within the organisation is only rated between fair and good. With training being one of the twelve steps required for the successful implementation of TPM within an organisation, this issue will need to be addressed.

TPM Concept

TQM is seen as a management led initiative focusing on continuous improvement in all aspects of the business to increase the competitiveness of the organisation. The culture in which TPM is implemented has a large impact on whether or not it will be successful. It is perceived by all groups within the organisation that everybody is responsible for quality, and a majority of employees within the groups feel ownership for their jobs. All this data, which focuses on the empowerment and utilisation of the knowledge, skills and abilities of all the employees reveals the quality culture within the organisation and secures the continuing success of the TQM process. This is further substantiated by data which revealed a clear majority of all groups practised ongoing improvement as part of their job when asked about the 5'S' activities.

Key to this continuing success is the implementation of TPM. Which is seen as maximising the effectiveness of equipment currently in use through total employee involvement. The performance of the existing equipment within the organisation is rated as low leading to the belief that implementation of TPM is needed.

The majority of all groups feel that equipment is maintained only sometimes. Machine performance is rated as the most important criteria associated with reducing equipment downtime.

The majority of groups see machine performance as critical, yet perceive the maintenance of equipment as occurring only sometimes. This data reveals a gap that can be narrowed through the implementation of TPM.

TPM IMPLEMENTATION RECOMMENDATIONS

The task of implementing TPM can be daunting as the practical details and procedures for using TPM to maximise equipment effectiveness must be tailored to the individual company (Maggard, 1992). Each organisation is different, and TPM implementation should reflect these differences. This is substantiated in the responses from each of the TPM facilitators interviewed (the companies were Short Bros Plc and NEC Semiconductors Ltd).

Analysis of the data shows that each company must develop its own plan, depending on the needs and problems of that organisation, the type of industry, production methods, equipment types and conditions used.

While customising the implementation of TPM is essential, the overall implementation plan for each organisation should have certain similarities. Figure 2, based on the overall analysis conducted proposes a basic structure for the development of a TPM programme within an organisation.

Key to the continued success of the TQM initiative is the strategy to keep ahead of demand and grow sales cost with minimum investment. This can be achieved through the implementation of TPM. The strategy to maximise the effectiveness of equipment currently in use through total employee involvement is being pursued through employee involvement, teamwork and training.

Table 1: 1990, 1993 and 1995 Harris Ireland TQSR Results.

Standard of Excellence	Available Pts.	% Improvement 1993/1990	% Improvement 1995/1993
Quality Culture	475	+ 58.3	+ 13.9
Strategic Focus	275	+ 7.8	+ 42.7
Product/Process Leadership	200	+ 91.8	+ 2.6
Market Performance	50	+ 10.0	+ 36.4
Total	**1000**	**+ 46.5**	**+ 18.5**

REFERENCES

Nakajima, S.   **"TPM Development Programme"**,
                                    Productivity Press Inc., Cambridge, MA, 1989.

Hartman, E.H.   **"Successfully Installing TPM in a Non-Japanese Plant"**,
                                    TPM Press, Inc., Allison Park, PA., 1992.

Zink, K.J., Humer, R.,   **"Quality Assessment: instruments for the analysis of**
and Schmott, A.   **quality concepts based on EN 29 000, the Malcolm**
                                    Baldrige Award and the European Quality Award",
                                    Journal of Total Quality Management, Volume 5, 1994.

Maggard, B.N.   **" TPM Maintenance Operations that Works"**,
                                    TPM Press Inc., Allison Park, PA., 1992.

35

Achieving contractual requirements and a TQM approach

M. J. Cook
Foresterhill College, Westburn Road, Aberdeen, AB9 2XS, UK, 01224
681818 Ext 52541, Fax 01224 685249

Abstract

The majority of nursing and midwifery education is now provided through contracts. Quality is a vital factor in the award and satisfactory delivery of a contract. Drawing on personal experiences of introducing, sustaining and maintaining a TQM approach to achieving quality requirements within contracts', the author will identify the importance of quality to ensure the award and satisfactory delivery of a contract. As part of this approach new job descriptions that focus teachers' activity on customer (student) requirements have been introduced.

Keywords

Contracts, Total quality management, nurse and midwifery education, job descriptions.

INTRODUCTION

The majority of nursing and midwifery education is now provided through contracts. A contract usually has three main components; cost, volume and quality. Volume and cost are reasonably easy to determine, quality however is more complex, and is a vital factor in the award and satisfactory delivery of a contract. "...the old assumptions that local established colleges should be maintained are being replaced...by a realisation that quality...is the best determinant of who gets the business of education...." (Humphreys and Davis 1995, p537). Dahlgaard et al (1995) identify five cornerstones (key principles) of Total Quality Management. These are, leadership, focus on the customer and the employee, continuous improvements, everybody's participation and focus on facts. The approach adopted by Foresterhill College has reflected these key principles. This paper deals mainly with the principle of focusing on the customer and the employee. However it is important to note that the other principles are subsumed within the activity described.

ELICITING THE CRITICAL QUALITY ISSUES

To win and satisfactorily deliver contracts, the institution must have in place mechanisms for eliciting and delivering the purchasers critical issues with respect to quality. A review of quality factors for organisations that the College contracts with, identifies the critical issues. See Table 1.

Table 1 Quality factors required by organisations with which the College has contractual relationships

Health Boards	*Professional body*	*Higher education*	*Scotvec*
consumer influence /satisfaction	organisation of institution	aims and curricula	strategic management
access	teaching staff	curriculum design	quality management
environment	support staff	teaching and learning environment	marketing
efficiency	students		
effectiveness	teaching facilities	course organisation	staffing
suggestion and complaint procedures	course/programme information	teaching and learning practice	staff development
	programme aims	student support	equal opportunity
	objectives	assessment and monitoring	health and safety
	curriculum		premises and equipment
		student's work	
	practice based experience		communication and administration
		teaching and learning output and outcomes	
	committee structure		financial management
		quality control	
	examinations		guidance services
	disciplinary issues		programme design
	evaluation and monitoring		programme delivery
			assessment for certification

These factors coupled with an examination of the College's Mission Statement and Philosophy enabled the following factors to be identified: health and safety; college meetings; staffing; staff development; student recruitment and selection; courses/programmes (college-based); courses/programmes (clinical/practice-based); student support and strategic management.

These factors provide a basis on which to focus quality improvement initiatives, reflecting important areas both to the College and to those with which contractual relationships are formed. Using a range of indicators, standards have been developed for each of these key areas and an audit undertaken to determine the College's baseline in respect of the standards. Further work with respect to quality improvement has been focusing staff activity on students as customers. Chase and Hayes (1990 p.368) identified the following attributes as important to customers; reliability-ability to perform the promised service dependably and accurately; responsiveness- willingness to help customers solve individual problems and provide prompt service; assurance- employees' knowledge and courtesy and their ability to inspire trust and confidence; empathy- caring individual attention to customers; tangibles- physical facilities, equipment, and appearance of personnel.

Using these attributes academic staff job descriptions were redesigned using a student focused approach. This has helped to ensure that the focus of staff activity is on meeting both student needs whilst also meeting contractual requirements. An examination of the essential requirements of students led to the identification of key requirements to be included within the job descriptions of nurse and midwife teachers. These key requirements are: programme development, development of theme group content, teaching resources, delivery and evaluation of programmes, individual students, clinical link teacher role, personal development and research and development. Specific actions are identified to meet these requirements. For example, with respect to individual students the following key requirement is identified: 'Provide academic supervision and support to students so as to monitor individual progress, ensure regular feedback and facilitate remedial action when necessary'. To ensure that courses are managed to meet the students needs, job descriptions for the next level of staff (Course Leaders) were redesigned using the nurse/midwife teachers descriptions as a base, with the focus clearly relating to managing the resources to meet the requirements of students. Using the example of individual students the Course Leaders job description states, 'Ensure the availability and effectiveness of academic supervision and support to all students on the course/programme so that monitoring and feedback by academic staff/supervisors allows timely and relevant management and academic action to be taken.' This alignment of job descriptions with students needs has helped to focus teachers' activities more precisely.

To further reinforce the focus of job description's each member of staff devises annual objectives that form the basis for an appraisal interview. In this way, it is possible to monitor the achievement of the organisation against requirements of contractual agencies and students. Further to this activity each student has the opportunity to complete an evaluation form that is translated into a student satisfaction score. Areas can be directly linked to job descriptions of academic staff. In this way it is possible to focus on facts, in respect of what students identify as areas for improvement. This provides a basis for continual improvement, using the plan, do, check, action cycle (Deming,1986). Very few difficulties have been encountered in gaining acceptance for the new job descriptions. This is probably as a result of full consultation (staff participation) with staff using their experience and ideas to build and refine the initial ideas. The leadership for each of these activities is invested in the Vice Principal (Nursing Studies/Quality), who is a key member of the Senior Management Team with authority to recommend changes in working practices based on audit findings, student satisfaction scores and academic staff appraisal.

In conclusion clearly identifying the needs of contracting agencies and students focuses staff activity on ensuring that identified needs are met that helps to meet identified needs. Thereby, enhancing the organisations' reputation and increasing satisfaction of customers, staff and contractors.

REFERENCES

Dahlgaard, J. J., Kristensen, K. and Kanji G. K. (1995) Total quality management and education, *Total Quality Management*. **6 (5&6)** , 445-455.

Deming, W.E., (1986) *Out of the Crisis* MIT Center for Advanced Engineering Study, Cambridge, Mass.

Chase, R. B. and Hayes, R. H. (1990) Operations role in service firm competitiveness. Working Paper, Harvard Business School. in Sohal, A. S. Managing service quality: developing a vision and strategy. *Total Quality Management* **5 (6)**: 367-374.

Humphreys, J. and Davis, K. (1995) Quality assurance for contracting of education: A Delegated system involving consortia of British National Health Service Trusts. *Journal of Advanced Nursing.* **21 (3),** 537-543.

Peters, T. J. and Waterman, R. H. (1982) *In search of excellence*. Harper and Row, New York.

BIOGRAPHY

The author is a Vice Principal within a College providing nursing, midwifery and health care education in Aberdeen, Scotland. Has responsibility for all quality related matters. Recently completed a Post Graduate Diploma in Quality and Reliability Management at the University of Abertay, Dundee and continuing the studies towards the completion of an MSc in Quality and Reliability Management. Has been involved in the education of health care professionals for 10 years. Special interests include, quality in education, management of change in education and curriculum design. Prior to entering education worked in a wide range of nursing posts throughout the UK.

PART SEVEN

Continuous Improvement Process

36

Why is it sometimes so hard to implement process capability studies?

Mats Deleryd
Division of Quality Technology & Statistics
Luleå University, S - 971 87 Luleå, Sweden, phone: +46 920 917 28,
fax: +46 920 72160, e-mail: Mats.Deleryd@ies.luth.se

Abstract

In a recent survey, performed at the Division of Quality Technology & Statistics, Luleå University, Sweden, it has been studied how 100 Swedish organisations conduct process capability studies. As a result from the survey it was obvious that many theoretical aspects of how process capability studies should be conducted were not considered within the organisations where process capability studies actually were conducted. This fact led to a second survey, trying to explain this gap between theory and practice. This paper focuses on the result from this second survey. It has been found that the reason why the implementation of process capability studies sometimes fails is mainly due to management errors, but also due to some facts of reality, traditional personal attitudes and methodological issues. All identified reasons to failures in implementation of process capability studies are illustrated in an Ishikawa diagram. Most of the obstacles causing difficulties when implementing process capability studies can probably also be related to the implementation of other "hard" methods of TQM.

Keywords

Process capability studies, variation, implementation, obstacles, management

1 MASTERING VARIATION—AN IMPORTANT PART OF TQM

One of industry's major problems since the industrial revolution has been the presence of variation. Even if two identical processes are controlled in the same way, their output will not be identical. One part will never be an identical copy of the other. Traditionally, industry has tried to solve this problem by setting specification limits for important characteristics of a particular product. If the characteristics of a product are within these specification limits, then that particular product is claimed to be capable. As time has passed, focus has moved from claiming specific products to be capable to claiming the actual processes to be capable. Today, capable processes within an organisation can be viewed as a prerequisite to stay in business and capable processes can be achieved only when the organisation manages to master the inherent variation in all its processes. By this fact, the ability of mastering variation and conducting process capability studies becomes an important part of TQM.

2   ASPECTS OF IMPLEMENTATION

Since the 1980's a theoretical framework has been established in order to describe how to judge whether a process is capable or not. These studies are often called process capability studies or process capability analysis, see, e.g., Runger (1993). When conducting a process capability study, data is collected from the process and compared with the pre-set specification limits for the studied parameter.

In a recent survey, performed at the Division of Quality Technology & Statistics, Luleå University, Sweden, it has been investigated how 100 Swedish organisations conduct process capability studies, see Deleryd (1996). It has been found that the theoretical aspects of how to conduct process capability studies are often violated. This fact is in some way or another caused by different obstacles when implementing process capability studies. In order to investigate which obstacles that might occur, a second survey was initiated.

In the second survey, the respondents from the first survey were asked to present their view of what kind of obstacles there might be when implementing process capability studies. A total number of 60 respondents answered and their opinions have been categorised into 21 different obstacles. These obstacles have then been arranged in an Ishikawa diagram, presented in figure 1.

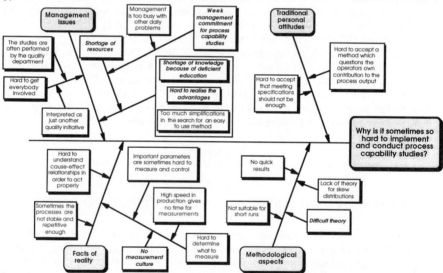

Figure 1 *This Ishikawa diagram shows different reasons why it sometimes can be hard to implement and conduct process capability studies. The obstacles most frequently mentioned by the respondents have been written in italics in the figure.*

In order to fully understand figure 1 all implementation obstacles are described in detail below. It has been found that the obstacles can be divided into the four categories Management issues, Facts of reality, Traditional personal attitudes and Methodological aspects.

2.1 Management issues

It is interesting to notice that one of the obstacles is that the management is too busy with other daily problems. This is perhaps one of the most common reasons why a TQM-programme fails. The fact that managers are often too busy with other daily problems directly leads to a weak commitment for process capability studies. Without knowing it, their weak commitment directly leads to the fact that insufficient resources, if at all any, are allocated to implement and conduct process capability studies. The lack of appropriate resources, directly results in a shortage of knowledge about how to conduct process capability studies among all co-workers. Even if all theoretical aspects of how process capability studies are to be conducted sometimes are known within the organisation, the final method used is often too simplified since the lack of resources forces the organisation to find the cheapest possible way to proceed, without reflecting on how these simplifications influence the results. The relatively poor knowledge about the theoretical concepts, necessary for process capability studies, among co-workers combined with managers occupation with solving daily problems, make it hard for everyone within the organisation to realise the advantages of conducting process capability studies properly.

Another obstacle which sometimes makes it hard to conduct process capability studies is that the studies sometimes are conducted by the quality department, which obviously leads to a modest interest in the concept among co-workers. Another aspect which also influences the interest when implementing process capability studies is that often, process capability studies is just another improvement method implemented. Since the implementation of all previous improvement methods more or less failed, the belief in the success of implementing process capability studies is almost immeasurable.

2.2 Facts of reality

Some of the obstacles which make it difficult to implement process capability studies mentioned by the respondents can be thought of as facts of reality. For instance, often it is not obvious which parameters are of interest to measure and control.

The basic principle of process capability studies is to measure parameters and compare the process output with the pre-set specifications. Obviously this method requires that members of the organisation are used to measure different parameters. However, in some organisations, there are no such things as gauges, and if they exist, they are often inadequately calibrated. Another obstacle when conducting process capability studies is the high speed of modern production techniques. In some operations there are simply no time left to perform measurements, which on the other hand enhances the importance of capable processes. Another aspect of this problem is that important parameters are sometimes hard to measure and control. This problem has special significance within process industries, where important parameters sometimes are almost impossible to measure due to practical reasons.

Even if the process output is monitored and the result indicates an obvious need to make changes in the process, it might be difficult to determine what parameters to change in order to make the process operate efficiently. It is also relatively common that processes are not stable and repetitive enough, in order to justify the use of process capability studies.

2.3 Traditional personal attitudes

The concept of process capability studies enhances the idea of achieving a process output with minimal variation centred at a target value. This concept is sometimes hard to accept by co-workers who are used to working under conditions where it always has been accepted to fully use the whole specification interval.

Another aspect is that it is hard to accept a method which questions the workers own contribution to the process output. When conducting process capability studies, the aim is to monitor all components of variation, influencing the process output. Since one of these components is contributed by the operators themselves, a rather intricate problem appears. It is extremely important to insure that the aim of using process capability studies is to reduce the total amount of variation in order to reach a higher level of customer satisfaction and not to check who are the best operators in order to fire the others.

2.4 Methodological aspects

Finally there are some methodological reasons to why the implementation of process capability studies can be difficult. For instance the concept of process capability studies is difficult to conceive due to the mathematical and statistical techniques used, it is not suitable for processes with short runs, the method gives no quick results and finally, since the theory of process capability studies is heavily based on the assumption that the process output is normally distributed, organisations do not know how to handle skew situations.

3 FINAL REMARKS

The most critical obstacles related to the implementation of process capability studies found in this survey are related to management issues. As much as 65% of all the respondents' comments concerned management issues. This fact clearly indicates the importance of actions taken by managers when implementing process capability studies. The implementation demands proper allocation of resources and education efforts due to its relatively difficult theory and the fact that the method is time consuming.

Many of the obstacles found in this survey can almost certainly be related to the implementation of other "hard" methods of TQM, since they too often are theoretically complicated and time consuming.

4 REFERENCES

Deleryd, M. (1996). Process Capability Studies—Theoretical and Practical Aspects. Licentiate Thesis. To be published in June 1996. Division of Quality Technology & Statistics, Luleå University, Sweden.

Runger, G. C. (1993). Designing Process Capability Studies. *Quality Progress*, vol. 26, no. 7, p. 31-32.

5 BIOGRAPHY

Mats Deleryd received his M. Sc. in Mechanical Engineering and Industrial Economics at Luleå University, Sweden, 1992. Since then he is employed as a Ph.D. student in Quality Technology at the Division of Quality Technology & Statistics, Luleå University. His main research interest is in the area of total quality management, with special focus on statistical process control, and process capability studies. He is expected to reach a licentiate degree in June 1996.

37

Has TQM really taken advantage of the IT revolution?

A.M.Pybus, MIQA
Altis Consulting Ltd.
Partners House, Crown House, Theale, Reading RG7 5BQ, UK.
Tel: (44) (0) 1734 302884
Fax: (44) (0) 1734 302885
E-Mail: altis@dial.pipex.com

Abstract

TQM offers a methodology of best management practices aimed specifically at meeting (or exceeding) customer requirements and expectations. To be widely accepted by the business community, TQM should be taking advantage of whatever Information Technology can offer in enabling its principles to be put into effect. This paper considers the areas where IT has played a major role within the TQM culture, but more significantly where it has been of far less influence.

1.   INTRODUCTION

In the last fifty years, the nature of business has evolved considerably. Three changes in particular are worthy of note:

1   The move from production-lead thinking to management focusing on its markets, where product cost was a prime driver.
2   The focus changed to the customer, who demanded quality and value for money.
3   As markets have globalized,. competition has become far more intense; survival a prime goal. Time is crucial.

The product life cycle from innovation to market to obsolescence has decreased significantly as a result of these changes.

During the last thirty years, there are few businesses which have not been affected by the phenomenal growth of the IT industry. It does not seem that long ago that it was considered that the world's requirement for computing could be satisfied by three or four "Super Computers"! (and this was many years after W.A. Shewhart's development of the use of statistics in the control of quality of manufactured products). Without IT, much of this progress would have been impossible. The ability to collect, process, and deliver information to management concerning not only their processes, but also customer intelligence and the performance of competitors, is now recognised as vital.

It is debatable as to whether the shape of business today has been driven by the development of the technology, or vice versa. What is reasonably certain is that is that the companies who will survive and prosper in future will be those that take maximum advantage of what IT can offer.

2   THE TQM MODEL

Those companies that apply the principles of TQM will have been affected by IT, in much the same way as any other business. IT has had its biggest impact in automating business processes. Examples are legion; within industry and commerce alike. But the TQM model demonstrates areas where IT has had far less impact. To identify these, the examination of the TQM model is very helpful.

The model splits the business into three component parts. Two of these are clear and generally well understood.

Firstly, the organisation, its culture, its structure, its management style.

The second part relates to the business processes; concentrating on those which are key to the business; "Mission-critical"; "Doing the right thing in the right way". It is in this area where business process re-engineering (BPR) plays a key role in increasing business efficiency and performance.

The third element is more difficult to label, and indeed its emphasis has changed over time. Various alternatives have been in vogue. Initially it was considered that it was the techniques, specifically Statistical Process Control (SPC) which has always been the bed-rock of its development; but there were many others. They all had one aim in common - to control and manage process.

Figure 1.   *The TQM model*

It is now generally understood that a Quality Management System (QMS) is fundamental to the achievement of Quality. The ISO9000 quality standard, which for a long period was considered as an alternative approach, has now become recognised as providing a basic framework for building a QMS within a TQM company.

That ISO9000 is the most widely recognised standard for Quality Assurance is not in any dispute, but it is certainly not the only one in use. What all such control mechanisms have in common, is providing the means by which the right information is sent to the right people at the right time.

People and Organisation
It is first worth examining the fundamental differences between tradition organisations and those that have committed to the TQM philosophy. The table below covers some of the more obvious variations.

Table 1 *Differences in management style between the traditional and TQM organisation*

Characteristic	Traditional	TQM
Work pattern	Individual performance, quantitative	Teamwork, collaboration
Power	Centralised	Distributed, delegated
Boundaries	Functional, departmental	Process
Management style	Command, control	Open, participative, consultant
Communication	Simple, down - (up)	Complex, lateral + down - up
Attitude to change	Resistant, dislike, inflexible	Acceptance, flexible
Management Structure	Hierarchical	Flat
Focus	Product, market	Customer

Although these characteristics can be associated with the TQM culture, there has nevertheless been amongst the business community at large, an undercurrent of change away from the traditional approach, more in line with the TQM philosophy. Further inspection shows that in many ways the development of IT has mirrored these changes, and is now much more aligned towards satisfying business needs. For example;

* **Power:**   The movement from the main-frame to the desktop P.C. has devolved power from the central IT department to those with direct responsibility for operating and managing process .

* **Communications:**   From simple terminal, to complex networks, now enables information which was transmitted by paper to be transferred electronically.

* **Change:**   The PC network provides far greater flexibility in adapting to changes in strategy and organisation.

* **Work Pattern:**   Groupware technology is specifically about supporting the collaborative workgroup, across time and distance boundaries.

In many ways IT has put a filter between people and business. Information is now far less associated with the individual - it belongs more to the public domain. This tends to have a democratising influence. Authority becomes much less hierarchical, the boundaries more difficult to identify. Again, all about "empowerment", "collaboration", "information sharing", "teamwork". IT now really begins to offer a solution to the demands of operating a TQM culture.

The business process

A great deal of work has been done as has already been mentioned on the use of IT in automating the key processes. What seems often overlooked is whether the control mechanism (which must exist in some form or other) can cater for an increase in performance of its processes. Too often it results in the process getting out of control - only quicker. This is true the more so, as the change of performance is further increased to combat the competition, and indeed, the fight to survive.

When considering change, the first requirement is to gain control over the process in current use. Without knowledge of the current situation, it is all but impossible to define the steps required to implement the change, or to compare the performance before and after the change. Once the current process is under control and the output measured, it can be then established as to whether the control mechanism is adequate for the new process. The simple valve mechanism for the control of the steam that was the pride and joy of Stephenson's "Rocket" steam-engine, would have been woefully inadequate for the control of the "Flying Scotsman" many years later. In similar vane, the role of measurement and control is as vital as the design of the process itself, if the change is to be a success.

The Quality Management System - the lifeblood of business

There is currently a wide range of software which supports TQM techniques involved in the collection of output data, its use and interpretation; SPC in particular is well supported. But the Quality Management System requires information to be collected and processed before, as well as during and after the process has been completed, if management is to retain effective control.

Before:

Objectives	- What are the goals, targets of the business
Plans	- How these objectives are to be achieved
	- The processes involved
	- The inputs required. (skills, materials)
	- Designs, specifications
Procedures	- How the processes are to be operated.

During:

Feedback	- Checks on input materials
	- Checks throughout the process
	- Audits against procedure

After:

Feedback	- Customer complaints

To remain competitive, an organisation must ensure that a process of continuous improvement is sustained by the effective management of problems; taking preventive as well as corrective action, and monitoring any changes to ensure the future probability of the problem's reoccurrence is minimised, if not eradicated.

What does IT have to offer?

Only recently has the concept of workgroup computing come to the fore. This technology aims to provide much more than just a communications network;

*   To facilitate group communication and information sharing within the team, company-wide and globally

*   To provide effective management over the access to and security of information.

*   To streamlining the flow of information person to person, in line with the business process(es).

Although there are several smaller companies that specialise in specific areas of this technology, it is Lotus Development who are recognised as having conceived the concept of groupware technology, and Lotus Notes is regarded as the current industry standard by which all other products should be judged. This lead has been further consolidated as Lotus now is a subsidiary of IBM. Microsoft Exchange is competing hard for a share in this new and rapidly expanding market.

Exactly what role does this technology play?

The diagram below gives a pictorial representation of how the organisation (its managers and workers) can be linked to the processes, through access and ability to share information. (Information to the right person at the right time).

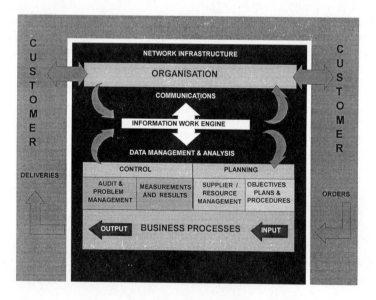

Figure 2.   *The "Information Engine".*

3.   CONCLUSION

It has often been claimed that ISO9000 is beaurocratic and involves a considerable amount of clerical effort. This makes the tacit assumption that the Quality System has to be paper-driven. This assumption is misplaced, and appears to have arisen from the general lack of IT expertise of many of the Quality consultants who have implemented Quality Systems.

IT has focused primarily on the automation of process. This focus needs now to be re-directed;

*   To provide the communications infrastructure that a TQM organisation demands.

*   To provide the QMS with adequate support for collecting, organising and presenting the feedback of information in a digestible and timely way. Document control, problem management, auditing and management review are the fundamental cornerstones within a QMS. Appropriate software could do much to augment their significance.

TQM has certainly benefited a number of very influential companies. Amongst its pioneers are such well known corporations as Xerox, IBM, Hewlett-Packard, General Motors, in addition to many other smaller organisations. But all is not sweetness and light. The high failure rate has not gone unnoticed. Perhaps it is not unreasonable to think that lack of consideration to the needs of the "information engine" (as shown in figure 2) might have been if not the sole cause, at least a contributory factor.. A Le Mans winner was never powered by an elastic band.

Groupware technology now offers a very real opportunity to drive the TQM culture towards the 21st century. Only if TQM takes on board the best that IT can offer, will its underlying management philosophy be awarded the true recognition it deserves.

4.   BIOGRAPHY

Anthony Pybus has considerable experience and knowledge of the IT industry, where he has spent much time as an internal consultant involved in systems design and implementation, and operations management. After a short spell as a Quality consultant he formed a company to supply computer solutions to companies seeking better ways of achieving Quality. He is an active member within the Institute of Quality Assurance.

38

TQM in financial services: an empirical study of best practice

Dr D. Longbottom
University of Derby
Derby
and
Professor M. Zairi
University of Bradford Management Centre
Emm Lane, Bradford, W. Yorkshire, tel. 01274 384317, fax 01274
384311, e-mail: M.Zairi@bradford.ac.uk

Abstract

This paper presents the results of research carried out at the University of Bradford's European Centre for Total Quality Management (TQM), investigating the status of TQM within the financial services industry in the UK.

The research finds that at the present time the financial services industry is in a state of considerable structural change, and competition is intense. This paper presents that the case for adoption of TQM as a generic strategy is now established and overwhelming. However it is apparent that financial services are lagging behind other sectors in this regard.

The research finds that TQM is not yet well established as an overall management philosophy. The leading group have two to three years experience of implementation, and are assessed as low to medium adopters when measured using the European Quality Award (EQA) model. There is strong evidence to show that the leading group have achieved marked improvement in performance. The research also shows, however, that some implementations have failed to deliver expected benefits, and in some instances costs have been extremely high and the consequences of failure significant.

The reasons for these differences are explored. Summary case studies are presented of five organisations from the leading group, and their approaches to implementation compared, and best practices identified.

Keywords

TQM Implementation, Financial Services, Self-Assessment, EQA Model, High Adopters, Business Performance

INTRODUCTION

The financial services industry in the UK is presently in a period of turmoil and major structural change. A number of factors demonstrate why this is so. Progressive de-regulation of the building societies in the last 10 years, Wrigglesworth (1994), Coles (1993), McKillop et al (1993). The maturing of the residential home loans market, McKillop et al (1993), Bootle (1993). Changes in the nature and structure of the traditional markets for personal savings, life assurance, and general insurance Morgan et al (1993), Bootle (1993), Coles (1993).

Others have argued that financial services are now becoming increasingly open to global competition Nellis (1994), Llewellyn (1995), Morgan (1992).

As a consequence the major institutions are seeking to consolidate their positions, with a number of substantial mergers announced in 1995 and other major building societies announcing their plans to seek conversion to limited company status.

Research by Altunbas et al (1995) supports the notion of consolidation finding that reasonable scale economies are achievable in particular for bank - building society mergers. McKillop (1994) also finds evidence to support economies of scale and scope. Aitken (1995), however, suggests that the main motivation for merger activity is largely defensive, to secure market share.

These extreme external environmental changes are in turn pressuring the major organisations to re-examine their organisation structures and business strategies with a need to seek structures, strategies, and systems, which are more suited with the new dynamic conditions. The pressures for better management of innovations, customer service, culture change, and process efficiencies are growing. The financial services industry has reached a major watershed in its history.

The case for TQM in financial services

Modern management theory supports the notion that TQM is becoming established as the new management paradigm. Grant et al (1994) argue that the only strategic generic option to TQM is what they describe as that of the Economic Model of the Firm, (as best described in modern times by Milgrom et al 1992). TQM they argue is more attuned with dynamic conditions, an orientation to the customer, and a balanced stakeholder perspective for measuring performance, whilst the economic model is essentially static, orientated to profit maximisation, and creating shareholder wealth.

Hill and Wilkinson (1995) argue that quality, and satisfying customers, is the guiding principle of the vast majority of organisations. They conclude that the principles of TQM are now well established and consider the work of the quality gurus (Deming, Juran, Crosby, Feigenbaum) is accepted as management common sense.

Their is supporting evidence from the field. Now long established in Japan, several studies have demonstrated the growth of TQM in the USA (Greene 1993 and 1995, Garvin 1991, Kano 1993, Easton 1993, Juran 1993) leading some to conclude that TQM is now the 'norm' Greene (1995), Grant et al (1994) Garvin (1993). This has undoubtedly been aided by the popularity of self assessment award schemes such as the Malcolm Baldrige National Quality Award from 1988, Garvin (1993). In Europe empirical studies have concluded that the movement to TQM is younger, but the momentum still strong Witcher (1994), Cruise O'Brien et al (1992), A T Kearney (1992).   The European Foundation for Quality Management (EFQM) now report over 500 members, EFQM (1994) of which notably, in the context of this paper, several are major banks and building societies. The challenge according to Hill and Wilkinson (1995) is not whether, but rather how to implement in the current harsh climate of economic conditions were many organisations are concerned with downsizing and delayering and are finding this difficult to reconcile.

Despite some seemingly mixed results from TQM so far in the UK (summarised in table 1), most of those starting appear to be still solidly committed to continuing, viewing the strategy as essentially long term and beneficial AT Kearney (1992), Witcher (1993), Economist Intelligence Unit (1992). Problems have tended to be more attributable to management and implementation factors rather than the underlying philosophy Zairi et al (1994), Hill and Wilkinson (1995).

On balance there is a strong case to argue that organisations in the financial services industry should be looking at TQM, and yet the evidence is that the industry may be lagging behind other sectors in this regard. The preliminary research for this study, which involved a survey of senior executives from the major organisations, would support this view. For example, 60% of respondents rated TQM vital to their organisation strategy, however, 75% said that expertise in their organisation was limited, and 70% were concerned that the top management were not sufficiently involved in quality improvement. One possible explanation for this relative lack of progress may be that, as Dean and Bowen (1994) observe, TQM derives from the principles of statistical process control and the early applications were in production management, and as a consequence services industries have tended to be slow in recognising the potential benefits. It is also evident from the exploratory research that many executives are hesitant, given the somewhat mixed results published so far (table 2) and reports circulating within the industry of unsuccessful and costly launches of 'quality' programs. The problem is not the principles themselves, but rather how to apply and implement them. The need to empirically examine best practices, and develop a set of recommendations or a model of implementation for financial services, is central to this study.

Table 1   TQM Implementations - findings from recent research

Research by / date	Method	Sample	Findings
A T Kearney (1992)	survey	100 UK organisations	80% of initiatives failed to deliver expected benefits
London Business School (1992)	MBNQA assessment	42 UK organisations	Points score between 100-400 low average out of possible 1000
Economist Intelligence Unit	case studies	50 European organisations	Problems with implementation, many initiatives failing.

(1992)

Durham University Business School (1992 and 1993)	survey	235 North of England / 650 Scotland	TQM still in its infancy and too early to judge - most organisations stay committed
Bradford University (1994)	measured financial performance	29 well established TQM companies	Better than average financial performance

Methodology

The review of the literature revealed an absence of empirical research into TQM applications in financial services in the UK. Other researchers have similarly found few empirical studies in this area and have commented that the industry is poorly served with empirically based research, Thwaites (1991), Birro (1991).

Exploratory research was therefore needed to determine the potential leaders in the field, and the overall extent of adoption and understanding. Two studies were undertaken in 1994. Firstly, an analysis of corporate reporting over a period of three years. Secondly, a survey of senior executives from the largest banks and building societies (achieving a response rate of 72%). From this analysis 20 organisations, with varying degrees of experience of TQM were chosen for further in depth case study.

Each case study involved measurement of TQM using an established model the EQA self assessment model. Within the EQA framework, critical factors for success, principles and techniques of TQM, were incorporated, utilising the available evidence from empirical studies of critical implementation success factors, Black (1994), Saraph et al (1989), Bossink et al (1992), Porter et al (1992), Ramirez (1993). Each organisation was scored against enabler factors (leadership, policy and strategy, people management, resources, and processes). The case study process involved interviews with a cross section of staff in each organisation to gain a range of opinion, and an iterative approach was taken to determine the evaluation. Feedback and discussion on the outcomes with participants was an essential step in the process, to assist with validation.

This process enabled a systematic and objective measurement of TQM to be taken, using an established model and methodology, but also, and critically, building on previous empirical studies by incorporating those critical elements and success factors.

The performance of each organisation was measured using traditional financial performance ratios. Thirteen ratios were taken and evaluated over a period of 5 years 1989 - 1993, covering capital strength, profitability, market growth, costs, and revenues. Outcomes were compared against industry averages taken from a performance index of the largest 20 building societies over the same period. The limitations of this approach to performance measurement are essentially that it becomes difficult to make comparisons with organisations that operate in different market sectors and have different operating structures. This however is largely avoided in the case of the building societies studied on the basis that there is reasonable similarity of   market mix and structure (and where differences do arise allowance in interpretation may be made reasonably). Similarly, it is possible to measure the changes in performance of the retail banks, however a greater amount of qualitative data needs to be introduced from the case study evidence to interpret the findings.

Findings/Discussion

The findings from this study enable some empirical conclusions to be drawn for the first time, regarding the status of TQM in financial services and also the impact on performance. The study also identifies best practices, and compares different approaches for strengths and weaknesses. From this analysis, a survey is conducted of quality managers in the industry (80 responses from 150), where respondents are asked to rate the relative importance of the emerging critical factors for success. The findings then taken together are used to develop a model for implementation of TQM within financial services.

Of the 20 organisations case studied 5 were identified as the highest overall adopters and scored in the range 200 to 250 points (out of 500). In comparison to EQA submissions the scores rank medium to low, EQA (1994). In comparison to MBNQA submissions the scores rank medium to low MBNQA (1994). Typically these organisations have two to three years experience of TQM implementation (which compares with five to ten years for past award winners).

The next five organisations scored between 150 to 200 points, and are judged low adopters with typically only one to two years experience of implementation.

The remaining organisations scored below 150 points. Within this group only limited programmes had been undertaken, and TQM was not considered to be an overall strategic driver for the organisation.

The remainder of this paper will present the key findings from the leading group, summarising the approaches to implementation.

Case one

Background :   Northern based national building society
                      over 300 building society branches
                      staff of c. 4000
                      assets £13 billion
                      market share for home loans 7% (new advances 1994)

Strengths :
Focus on quality with a definition and adoption of quality philosophy.
Focus on re-structuring organisation based around customer needs.
Adoption of process orientation, fundamental review of core business processes (including outsourcing / abandoning of non core activities).

Introduction of new competencies particularly BPR, Benchmarking, and Performance measurement (based on balanced scorecard approach), and the launch of personal development programs based on competency assessment.

Staff motivation for those adopting the new approach was said to be very high.

Weaknesses :
Fundamental change of culture not accepted by all.
Some staff alienated at senior levels.
Benefits of BPR review still largely to be realised 2 years into programme.
Redundancy programme in first year.
Performance :
The society improved its financial performance significantly increasing profitability, and market share, whilst maintaining its capital position and reducing costs. The society moved from 18th ranked to 9th ranked in the industry UBS ratings, UBS (1993).

Case two :

Background :   Midlands based, Regional society
                    120 building society branches
                    c. 1500 staff
                    assets £3.8 billion

Strengths :
Immediate focus on key strategic issues for survival.
Overcame traditional organisation inflexibility without major disruption.
New culture of quality introduced through focus on tangibles / activity not culture / values i.e. focus on 'hard' issues
Quality driven in hands on style from top.

Weaknesses :
Problems initially with large redundancy programme as society reorganised, divested.
Focus on short- medium term issues, longer term issues not tackled (e.g. process changes and technology investment, staff development and review of HR policies, corporate culture).
Some line managers / staff alienated in the new team structure.

Performance :
Rated as the most improved society in the UBS Rankings moving from 20 1991 to 6 UBS (1994) overall. Significant improvements in profitability, market share, capital strength, and cost reduction.

Case Three :

Background :   Midlands based, national retail bank
                    Assets £31 billion

Strengths :
Massive investment in training for launch of TQM
Moved on to self assessments from 1993.

Weaknesses :
Initial program seen as 'fanfare' and not successful
Top management not involved in early stages
Very high costs of training / consultancy in set up
Too much focus on culture and 'soft' elements.
Current self assessment approach more practical but seen by some as audit driven.
Large redundancy program has influenced staff moral throughout.

Performance :
Significant cost reductions bringing the bank closer to its main major retail bank rivals.
Profitability has improved but is marginally below that achieved by the major retail banks and
below that of the largest building societies.

Case 4 :

Background :   North West based, specialist bank in retail business cash services
                 Wholly owned subsidiary of national building society.
                 Staff c. 3000

Strengths :
Focus on process review / BS5750
External assessment / accreditation
Process improvements claimed in cost reductions, complaints down.
External accreditation believed to give marketing advantages.

Weaknesses :
Recognise a limited quality program only so far
Seen by some as an end rather than means to an end
Costs are high in early years - set up, consultants, training.

Performance :
Difficulties of strict comparison with other banks due to specialist nature of business, but
reported as star performer in Group by Parent building society. Marginal gain in market share.
Reduction in operating costs. Annual report for 1993 claims financial benefits from quality
improvements in excess of / 8 million, reduced keyboard errors of 52%, and customer
complaints down by 60%.

Case five :

Background :   Specialist retail bank, Credit Card, Personal, and Travel services.
                 South East UK and European Headquarters, subsidiary of USA
                 based world-wide corporation.

Strengths :
Following a trodden path e.g. by the parent
Following an established quality model
Major focus on processes.

Weaknesses :
Imposed by parent
Culture change - difficult to adjust.
Problems with integration of European network

Performance :
Comparisons with other banks difficult due to specialised nature of operations. The bank was under some pressure having lost market share to main competitors, however was now fighting back with a greater focus on resolving customer problems (from research feedback). The company had reduced its processing costs, and had other BPR projects in the pipeline.

Summary, Conclusions, and Recommendations

This paper has presented findings from recent research investigating the status of TQM within the financial services industry in the UK. The research finds that TQM is not yet well established in this sector with only a small number of organisations taking on TQM as an overall part of their corporate strategy.

From exploratory research which identified 20 organisations for case study, a leading group of five are identified and brief case summaries are presented.

The leading group have 2 to 3 years experience of implementation and are assessed as medium to low adopters using the EQA model.

There is evidence to show that each of these organisations has achieved performance improvements over the three year period, in the case of two building societies this is very significant improvement against their main rivals.

However, there is also evidence to show that other implementations have failed to deliver expected benefits, and in some instances at significant cost to the organisations involved.

Within the leading group of organisations each had taken a different approach to implementation. No one best method emerges: Overall those organisations which focused on the hard / tangible elements of TQM have achieved the greater progress with implementation and improved performance. Of the five leading group organisations, four are now moving to self assessment procedures, three adopting the EQA framework, one the MBNQA. There is also a strong emphasis on Business Process Re-engineering, Benchmarking , and Balanced Performance Measurement.

From this analysis a model for implementation based upon the best practices identified was developed. The model lays greater emphasis on diagnosis of internal organisation strengths and weaknesses, and supports the principle of self assessment models which are tailored to the organisation and incorporate the critical factors, principles and techniques emerging from this and other empirically based studies of implementations. Whilst a full discussion of the model is outside the scope of this paper the principal stages are outlined below and the model is illustrated in figure1.

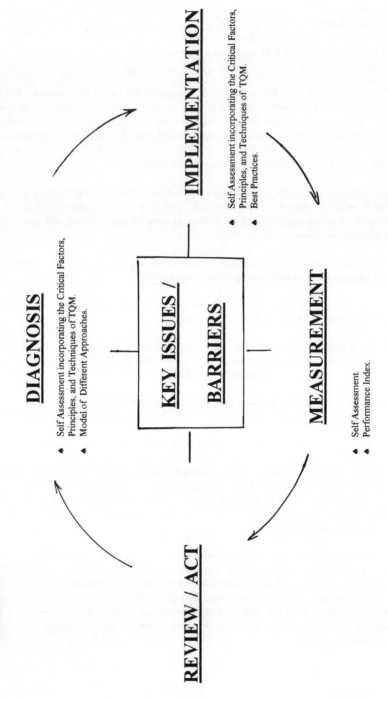

Fig. 1 A Framework for TQM Implementation in Financial Services

Diagnosis :

In common with other empirical studies this research finds that a high proportion of TQM implementations fail. In this study examples were found of very high cost attributable to failure. The reasons , however, support the argument that the problems lie in implementation and not with the underlying philosophy. Previous studies have tended to focus on lack of leadership skills as the principal cause. Whilst this may be an important factor in some cases, other causes are evident. Most fail simply because the organisation lacks the available skills, and as a result creates a strategic mismatch between desires and expectations and skills and attitudes to achieve them. Many of the early efforts were found to be too ambitious, short term focused, and lacking solid foundations.

The recommended approach from this study is that organisations conduct an internal diagnosis of skills and attitudes. A diagnostic approach is developed from this research which uses self assessment, the critical factors for success, and a methodology for matching different approaches to available skills and attitudes. In this way it is argued that organisations can tailor their approach s to implementation, and avoid the major pitfalls from strategic mismatches. A sensible launch and implementation strategy may then be devised which is realistic in objectives and in balance with the organisation.

Implementation :

The research findings support the use of self assessment processes as the principal means for implementation. This facilitates the appraisal of key organisation strengths and weaknesses, the determining of objectives, the determination of appropriate resources, and the aligning of these with overall strategy. This study finds that such frameworks are flexible. This enables organisations to tailor their approach. This will allow the findings from this research to be incorporated into the implementation process by building in the critical factors for success, and best practices which this study has identified.

Measurement and Review :

This study recommends that critical to implementation is the process of measurement and review. This study has used, and supports the use of self assessment procedures such as the EQA to provide a systematic method for measuring TQM. It also finds however that such measures need to be linked with overall performance. The research finds that the move towards a balanced stakeholder perspective is gaining momentum and methods such as the Kaplan and Norton balanced scorecard are consistent with self assessment.

Key issues / implementation barriers :

The research also identifies a number of specific issues for financial services which were considered to be adding to the difficulties of implementation.

REFERENCES

Aitken, J. (1995) Lloyds Bank : Black Horse wins Gold Cup. *UBS Global Research*

Altunbas, Y., and Maude, D., and Molyneux, P. (1995) Efficiency and Mergers in the UK (Retail) *Banking Market.*

Balmer, J. and Wilkinson, A. (1991) Building societies : change strategy and corporate identity. *SIMRU Conference papers,* April

Birro, K. (1991) The Evolution of Planning Systems. University of Bradford Ph.D. Thesis.

Black, S. (1994) Total Quality Management : The Critical Success Factors. University of Bradford Ph.D. Thesis.

Bootle, R. (1993) Analysing likely economic trends in the 1990's and their likely impact on retail financial services. IIR Publications - *Papers on customer competitiveness* May.

Bossink, B.A.G. and Geiskes, J.F.N. and Pas, T.N.M. (1992) Diagnosing Total Quality Management - part 1 and 2 *Total Quality Management Journal* Vol. 3 No. 3 pp 223-231 and Vol. 4 No. 1 pp 5-12

Camp, R. (1989) Benchmarking : *The Search for Industry Best Practices that lead to Superior Performance.* ASQC Quality Press.

Coles, A. (1994) The Director Generals Address. *Mortgage Finance Gazette.* Conference Issue. pp 10-14

Coles, A. (1993) *Recent developments in building societies and the savings and mortgage markets.* The Building Societies Association.

Crosby, P. B. (1979) *Quality is free.* McGraw Hill.

Cruise O'Brien, R. and Voss, C. (1992) In search of quality. London Business School working paper.

Dean, J. and Bowen, D. (1994) Management Theory and Total Quality : Improving Research and Practice through theory development. *Academy of Management Review* vol. 19 no. 3 pp 392-418.

Deming, W. E. (1986) *Out of the crises.* MIT Centre for Advanced Engineering.

Easton, G. S. (1993) The 1993 state of US TQM : A Baldrige examiners perspective. California *Management Review* Spring pp 32-55

Economist Intelligence Unit (1992) Making quality work - Lessons from Europe's leading companies. EIU / Ashridge Management School report.

EFQM (1994) Total Quality Management - The European Model for Self Appraisal

Feigenbaum, A. V. (1983) *Total Quality Control.* McGraw Hill.

Garvin, D. A. (1991) How the Baldrige award really works. *Harvard Business Review,* November / December pp 80-93.

Grant, R. M., Shani, R. and Krishnan R (1994) TQM's challenge to management theory and practice. *Sloan Management Review* Winter 1994 pp 25-35.

Greene, R. (1993) *Global Quality.* ASQC Quality Press.

Greene, R. (1995) *Competent Re-Engineering : advice, warnings, and recipes from eye witnesses.* Addison Wesley.

Hammer, M. and Champy, J. (1993) *Re-Engineering the Corporation.* Harper Collins.

Hill, S. and Wilkinson, A. (1995) In search of TQM. *Employee Relations Journal* - Special Issue on TQM Vol. 17, No. 3.

Juran, J. M. (1992) *Juran on quality by design.* The Free Press.

Juran, J. M. (1993) A renaissance with quality. *Harvard Business Review* July / August pp 42-53.

Kano, N. (1993) A perspective on quality activities in American firms. *California Management Review* Spring pp 12-31

Kaplan, R. S. and Norton ,D. P. (1992) The Balanced Business Scorecard - Measures that drive Performance. *Harvard Business Review.* January / February pp 71 - 79

Kearney, A.T. (1993) *Total Quality : Time to Take off the Rose Tinted Spectacles. A survey of a cross section of UK firms.* IFS Publications

Llewelyn, D. T. (1995) Market imperfections and the target - instrument approach to financial services regulation. *The Services Industry Journal* vol 15 no 2 pp 203-215

MBNQA (1994) The Malcolm Baldrige National Quality Award : 1994 Criteria. National Institute of Standards and Technology.

McKillop, D. G. and Glass, C. J. (1994) A cost model of building societies as producers of mortgages and other financial products. *Journal of Business, Finance and Accounting,* 21, 7, October pp 1031-1046.

McKillop, D. G. and Ferguson, C. (1993) *Building Societies : Structure Performance and Change.* Graham & Trotman.

Milgrom, P. and Roberts, J. (1992) *Economics, Organisation, and Management.* Prentice Hall.

Morgan, G. and Sturdy, A. (1993) Bancassurance : innovating strategies in financial services. Services Industry Management Research Unit Conference Papers, April.

Morgan, G. (1992) The globalisation of financial services : the European Community after 1992. *The Services Industry* Journal vol. 12 no. 2 pp 192-209

Nellis, J. (1994) Financial services in Europe. *Council of Mortgage Lenders Bulletin*, March.

Porter, L. J. and Oakland, J. S. (1993) Teamwork for Mission Achievement. ASQC Quality Congress 1993 pp 229 - 235.

Porter, L. J. and Parker, A. J. (1992) Total Quality Management - The Critical Success Factors. *Total Quality Management Journal* Vol 4 No 1 pp 13-22.

Ramirez, C. and Loney, Y. (1993) Baldrige Award Winners Identify the Essentials of a Successful Quality Process. *Quality Digest*, January pp 38 - 40.

Saraph, J. V., Benson, P. G. and Schroder, R. G. (1989) An Instrument for Measuring the Critical Factors of Quality Management. *Decision Sciences* pp 810 -829.

Sinclair, D. (1994) Performance Measurement : An Empirical Study of Best Practice. University of Bradford PhD Thesis 1994.

Snape, E. and Wilkinson, A. (1991) Human resource management in building societies : making the transformation. SIMRU Conference papers , April.

Thwaites, D. (1991) Innovation and Marketing Practices in UK Building Societies. University of Bradford Ph.D. Thesis.

Thwaites, D. and Edgett, S. (1991) Aspects of innovation in a turbulent market environment : empirical evidence from UK building societies. *The Services Industry Journal*, vol 11, no. 3 July pp 346 - 361.

UBS (1994) Building Societies Research : *The Major Players* . *Research Report* UBS Phillips and Drew.

Witcher, B. (1994) Clarifying Total Quality Management. Working paper Durham University Business School.

Witcher, B. (1993) The adoption of TQM in Scotland. Durham University Business School.

Wrigglesworth, J. (1994) Keynote Address - The Future of Building Societies. Euro Forum Conference Papers 1994

Wrigglesworth, J. (1994) The Mortgage and Savings Markets. *Mortgage Finance Gazette*. Conference Issue. pp 29 - 31

Zairi, M. (1992) *Competitive Benchmarking : An Executive Guide.* Technical Communications (Publishing) Ltd.

39

The implementation of Total Quality Management in small and medium enterprises

J.D. Lancaster M.Sc., D.M.S.
Sheffield Hallam University, Centre for Quality and Innovation
Hallamshire Business Park, Napier Street, Sheffield S11 8HD, U.K.
Telephone 0114 253 3163, Fax 0114 253 3161, e-mail John
Lancaster@shu.ac.uk

Abstract

This paper relates the use of the Organisational Development (OD) Process as a model (Figure 1) for the implementation Total Quality Management in small and medium enterprises.

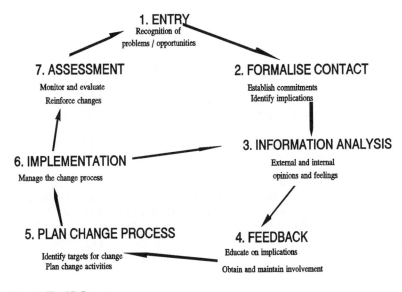

Figure 1 The OD Process.

The benefits and problems of using the "SWOT" analysis are discussed as a means of identifying the organisation's:

    a)   current "quality" orientation (Where are we now?)
    b)   desired "quality" orientation (Where are we going?)
    c)   strategy and actions required to be done to achieve b) (What have we to do?)

The benefits of many non-quantitative tools are discussed for use at appropriate stages of the change process. The objective is to use these tools to identify potential problems to prevent unintended outcomes.

Keywords
Organisational Development Process, OD Process, SWOT analysis, TOWS analysis, internal consultants, "brainstorming", mission, "influence" diagrams, "system" maps, "multiple cause diagrams", "rich pictures", "briefing" sessions, force field analysis, Gantt Chart.

1   INTRODUCTION

Of the various models for implementing change in organisations the Organisational Development (OD) Process (Figure 1) has been identified (Lancaster 1995) as the most appropriate for the implementation of Total Quality Management in small and medium enterprises.

The objective of this paper is to identify and discuss the relevant non-quantitative techniques that can be used at each stage of change to ensure ownership of the implementation process and thereby improve the likelihood of its success.

2   THE ORGANISATIONAL DEVELOPMENT PROCESS

Stage 1. Entry. The stimulus for change can come from many sources; a reduction in sales, a loss of customers, a reduction in profits or even the awareness that there may be a better way of running the business. These common stimuli usually prompt reactive, short term change whereas a well managed Total Quality Management programme will encourage the organisation to be proactive

Stage 2. Formalise Contact. It is essential to establish commitment to the programme. To achieve this the involvement, in each stage of the OD process, of those who will be required to implement or support the changes is prerequisite. The agents of change and the internal consultants (Phillips and Shaw 1989) of the organisation are identified.

The former are those who have the power to affect change, this would include those who constitute The Board and senior management. The internal consultants are those specialists who act as advisors to management, perhaps the quality specialist or particular process specialists. Together these are the individuals who can influence the remainder of the organisation to accept the intended changes. They all need to own the change process.

Failure to include a particular change agent will have an adverse effect on ownership of the change process and will reduce the likelihood of successful implementation.

Traditionally the opportunities are identified by use of the strengths, weaknesses, opportunities and threats **(SWOT) analysis.** This has proved very beneficial in identifying an organisations current "quality" orientation and then to identify the organisations desired "quality" orientation.

The process of doing the SWOT analysis in the traditional UK sequence of strengths, weaknesses, opportunities and threats is however flawed for two reasons:

The fact that weaknesses are identified after strengths leaves those involved in a state of relatively low morale for completing the analysis.

The fact that strengths and weaknesses are identified before opportunities and threats is likely to result in omissions in defining all the corresponding strengths and weaknesses.

It is therefore more logical to carry out the analysis in the sequence of TOWS. The results will be better because a more complete analysis will have been done and morale of those participating in the analysis will be more positive towards the results.

The relationship between the **TOWS analysis** and TQM is more apparent if the analysis uses, in turn; products, processes, customers, employees, quality and management as the subject.

Formal **"brainstorming"** can be used to identify and prioritise the threats and opportunities (TO), the external factors, that may influence the future of the organisation.

At the second stage "brainstorming" can be used to identify and prioritise the weaknesses (W) and finally the strengths (S), the internal factors, that can be brought to bear to overcome the previously identified threats, opportunities and weaknesses.

When the TOWS analysis has been completed it is appropriate to develop a **"Mission statement".** Its objective is to maintain in every employees mind the long term aims of the business and is usually related to products, processes, customers, employees, quality and management the same subjects as the TOWS analysis.

When the Mission statement is publicised internally it should assist in day to day decision making. Each decision that is made goes some way to ensure the Mission is met.

Stage 3. Information Analysis. External and internal opinions and feelings can be identified by corresponding with customers and employees in the form of suitably designed questionnaires.

Employees can give us feedback on their perceptions of our credibility regarding quality issues and their roles to meet the quality issues of the business.

Customers can advise us of their needs and how we fail to meet them, not only with reference to product quality, but their views on how well we handle enquiries, orders, complaints and other communications, which are all important in how the organisation is presented to the customer.

Stage 4. Feedback. The review of the analysis from Stage 2 and feedback from Stage 3 will help to identify the organisations shortcomings and failures.

Before the change agents begin to consider a strategy for improvement it is worth depicting the organisation and the factors which influence it, in the form of any combination of **"influence diagrams"** (McCalman and Paton 1992), **"system maps"** (Checkland and Scholes 1990), **"multiple cause diagrams"** and **"rich pictures"** (Checkland and Scholes 1990)

These pictorial representations are intended to give the change agents a vivid identification to and view of the influences acting on the business using an alternative visual medium to the written word. Thus by distilling the analysis and having involved the change agents in the process they will all be well qualified to mutually identify a strategy to improve the company and meet the mission.

Stage 5. Plan change process. This is the detailed planning of the strategy. The strategy will affect people, systems and structure of the organisation. (Clarke 1994) This may involve major reorganisation.

It consists of identifying what is to be done to meet the mission statement and overcome all the problems so far identified in stages 2, 3 and 4.

Secondly it will be necessary to identify and implement any metrics needed to monitor the improvement of critical processes, this may take the form of Statistical Process Control and or measurement of quality costs.

Thirdly it is a basic premise of TQM that success is most likely if a team approach is used. The organisation needs to decide what type of teams are most appropriate to its culture and available resources. The most common approach is to use either singly or in combination, operational teams or quality circles and / or project teams.

Fourthly it is necessary to carry out a training needs analysis for those who will be involved in and affected by the intended changes.

Part of the strategy will include some means of improving communication. The intentions of the organisation must be communicated to the entire organisation; nobody should feel that they have been left out. A good method of achieving this is to implement **"briefing"** sessions perhaps on a monthly basis, to inform everybody of what is happening in the organisation; its successes, failures, future prospects, customers, suppliers etc. These sessions begin at Board/senior manager level where an agreed, honest, credible briefing document is prepared that will be used to make a 15 - 20 minute presentation. Each manager then presents the brief to subordinates, allowing and answering questions, receiving feedback which may identify potential problems; the feedback can be included in later Force Field analyses.

This type of communication must start early in the implementation stage to add to the credibility of the organisation and to ensure that everybody is aware of how they will be affected by the intended changes.

When this is complete the detailed strategy can be finalised and documented. Because of the likely complexity of the strategy it is essential to break it down into a series of sub-projects and to create a plan for managing each one. The management of each sub-project will be given to the most appropriate change agent.

For each sub-project a **Force Field Analysis** is done. This, in conjunction with the pictorial representations from Stage 4, will serve to identify and weight those factors acting in favour of the intended change and those opposing the change. Knowledge of these forces and their weight will facilitate the prevention of unintended outcomes. Additional preventive actions will then be identified and added to the sub-project plan.

Each sub-project can be broken down into tasks, the responsibility for which, the start date and duration for each are defined and agreed and the project documented on a **Gantt Chart.**

All sub-projects should be reviewed regularly, probably weekly to ensure that the intended progress has been made. Where a task has not been completed, the change agents need to identify what delayed progress and what needs to be done to bring the project back on course.

Stage 6. Implementation. The implementation stage will take place as in the sequence of the sub-projects over a period of many months. Communication, organisational changes and training are likely to be the first of these. Feedback from employees and customers at these initial phases may lead to new opinions and feelings becoming apparent which were not initially comprehended at stage 3. Plans and sub-projects should be revised to accommodate this iteration.

This will be a very busy time for the organisation when the speed and quality of feedback is most important. Continuing management meetings on the progress of sub-projects is an ideal way of ensuring that the self-discipline of the change agents is maintained and that nothing is omitted from the implementation stage.

Stage 7. Assessment. There will be overlaps between stages 5, 6 and 7. As each sub-project is completed the results are monitored to observe that the intended changes have been fully achieved and that there are no unintended consequences. This evaluation is made by analysing the metrics identified in stage 5 and by repeating the employee and customer surveys initially carried out in stage 2.

Provided that the ideas presented in this paper are carried out wholeheartedly it is most probable that the changes intended will all be implemented successfully.

Successes should be publicised to employees and customers whenever possible using media which are part of the organisations normal culture, to celebrate the success and to improve company credibility and unity.

3   CONCLUSION

Organisations seeking excellence will continuously learn and further cycles of OD process are certain to follow.

4   REFERENCES

Lancaster, J.D. (1995) M.Sc. Dissertation, Sheffield Hallam University, *A critical review of the Implementation of Total Quality Management at Forged Rolls (UK).*
Phillips, K. and Shaw, P. *(1989) A consultancy Approach for Trainers.* Gower.
Clarke, L. *(1994) The Essence of Change,* Prentice Hall
McCalman, J and Paton, R *(1992) Change Management - a guide to effective implementation.* Paul Chapman.
Checkland P. & Scholes J. *(1990) Soft Systems Methodology in Action.*

5   BIOGRAPHY

John Lancaster is currently a Senior Lecturer and consultant in the Centre for Quality and Innovation at The Sheffield Hallam University. He is involved with national and International companies in implementing Total Quality and operations management. Formerly he was employed by General Motors with a variety of responsibilities including management of production, production engineering, new tooling projects and administration at IBC Vehicles, Bedford Commercial Vehicles and Vauxhall Motors Ltd.

PART EIGHT

Quality Measurement

40

Adapting the SERVQUAL scale and approach to meet the needs of local authority services

Donnelly, M.,   *Scottish Local Authorities Management Centre*
              Univ. of Strathclyde, Scotland. (0141 553 4143)
Shiu, E.   *Glasgow Caledonian University*
Dalrymple, J.F.   *Scottish Quality Management Centre*
Wisniewski, M.   *University of Stirling*

Abstract

This paper builds on the findings of research into the applicability and portability of the SERVQUAL Scale to Local Government service provision. It outlines criteria for judging the applicability of the method, suggests boundaries to the validity of the SERVQUAL approach, and recommends the development of a service taxonomy based on the extent of customisation needed for it to be used with confidence. Exploratory factor analysis of data from four case studies are presented which lead to a revised critique of the Gap 5 dimensions and the associated instrument items. Conclusions are drawn which will assist in the development of appropriate mechanisms to measure and monitor the quality of community services provided by local authorities either directly or through agency partnerships.

Keywords

Local Government, SERVQUAL, service quality

1   INTRODUCTION

Much has been written about the SERVQUAL approach since it was first introduced and developed in the mid-eighties (Parasuraman et al., 1985, 1988). Most of the applications of the method have been in the commercial sector with some in the public sector (e.g. Babakus et al., 1992, Soliman, 1992) and relatively few (e.g.Campbell et al., 1995, Dalrymple et al., 1995) in the local government service arena. A full description of the SERVQUAL model and associated instruments can be found in Zeithaml et al. (1990). Essentially the instrument used to measure Gap 5 - the gap between customers' expectations of the service and their perceptions of the service actually received - comprises 22 pairs of statements designed to capture customers' views across the five dimensions of Tangibles, Reliability, Responsiveness, Assurance, and Empathy which determine overall service quality. It is possible, indeed often necessary, to customise the basic instrument by adapting the wording of items; removing items completely; and inserting new items deemed important in the service context. Donnelly et al. (1995) raise issues about the applicability and portability of the approach into the public sector without resolving how the instrument might be adapted to meet the needs of local government. Indeed, the question of whether or not the SERVQUAL approach is valid in these environments is currently untested. Results of studies using suitably adapted Gap 5 survey instruments into Public Library service provision,

Domiciliary Home Help care, and a Food Safety Regulatory service are reported in Dalrymple et al. (1995). This confirmed the usefulness of the five dimensions underpinning the SERVQUAL method and of the 'gap' approach to assessing quality in these services. However, it omitted detailed analysis of the data to investigate the validity of the approach.

2   MODEL VALIDITY

The criteria by which the validity of the SERVQUAL approach to measure Gap 5 can be judged may be summarised as its Realism, Precision, Generality, and Resolution in the way it measures service quality in the chosen context.

By realism we mean the ability of the method to adequately reflect the general form of the situation being assessed. It is questionable if a single instrument can be sufficiently 'realistic' given the variety of service contexts within which local government operates. With the SERVQUAL instrument, extensive customisation is often required so that the instrument becomes unwieldy. An advance might be to categorise service contexts according to the degree of customisation required to satisfy the realism criterion. Additionally, the number of original SERVQUAL dimensions were arrived at following extensive primary research which has not yet been replicated in the public sector. Factors which distinguish the public sector such as common ownership, accountability, equity and others may be reflected in customers' mental report cards as important dimensions used to assess quality of service but are absent from the SERVQUAL instrument.

The precision of the method is, in a sense, the quantification of its realism. It is its ability to accurately estimate the levels of the important variables or dimensions involved. The precision required by a service organisation will be determined partly by the purposes to which it is put and partly by the dimensions being measured. Arguably the SERVQUAL dimensions are among the most difficult attributes of service performance to be measured and so any approach may be doomed to low precision. Certainly the experiences of our case study work is that the instrument can be very blunt. Perhaps repeated application and refinement of the instrument over time and service might result in achieving acceptable levels of precision.

An important claim made by many is that SERVQUAL is a 'generic' approach which can easily be customised for different service environments. The lack of realism and poor precision indicated above are perhaps consequences of this 'generality' of the method. It is debatable what trade-off in generality would be acceptable to improve the realism and precision of the approach to satisfactorily assess perhaps tightly defined or categorised service areas. Further, the driving force of the "bottom line" in commercial applications of SERVQUAL is less appropriate in a public sector environment where there may be many 'stakeholders' with competing objectives and views of what quality services are. Indeed some stakeholders do not directly receive (or might not want) the service under consideration whilst others make no financial contribution - either directly or indirectly - to the cost of service provision. In these circumstances the very concept of 'customer' is thrown into relief. Assessing the expressions of these different viewpoints of service quality, even when measurable, might be an extremely difficult task requiring quite different instrument items and dimensions. Balancing them might be even more problematic.

The property of resolution relates to the number of attributes or dimensions that the method tries to incorporate with clarity. Resolution is also affected by the time-scale over which the assessment is conducted. Thus, instruments with too few or too many overlapping dimensions being assessed over an inappropriate time horizon would have low resolution.

Underpinning all four criteria of realism, precision, generality, and resolution are the underlying dimensions used to measure service quality. Without a well-defined set of dimensions which allow customers in the chosen stakeholder group to fully and accurately express their assessment of service quality, none of these criteria can be tested. In an attempt to investigate the appropriateness of the SERVQUAL dimensions in different public service contexts the case data from Dalrymple et al. (1995) were analysed using Factor Analysis. The results of forcing a 5-factor solution on the case data-sets are shown in Tables 1 to 3 below.

We can see from Table 1 that there is a fairly good 'fit' of items around the *a priori* SERVQUAL factors in the Public Library service with the possible exception of the Empathy dimension. However, there is an apparent 'merging' of the Responsiveness and Assurance dimensions.

Table 1 Factor Analysis results for the first Public Library case study

	Public Library Service (Study A): *a priori* SERVQUAL Dimensions																									
	Tangibles						Reliability						Responsiveness					Assurance				Empathy				
Item	1	2	3	4	5	6	7	8	9	10	11	12	13	14	15	16	17	18	19	20	21	22	23	24	25	26
Factor 1													●	●	●	●	●	●	●	●	●	●		●		
Factor 2	●	●	●	●	●																					
Factor 3									●																	
Factor 4								●													●		●		●	●
Factor 5							●	●	●	●	●	●														

A repeat investigation of the same library service one year on revealed the same pattern of factors. The resulting four dimensions might be interpreted in this context as the service's Physical Environment (Tangibles), the Systems it deploys (Reliability), its Professionalism (Responsiveness and Assurance) and its People (Empathy). Factor Analysis of the Home Help data yielded the picture shown in Table 2. Here we see a less well defined, and perhaps different, grouping of factors although the Tangibles and (an inserted) Complaints factors are clearly identifiable.

Table 2 Factor Analysis results for the Domiciliary Home Help service case study

	Home Help Services: *a priori* SERVQUAL Dimensions																									
	Tangibles			Reliability					Resp.				Assurance				Empathy						Complaints			
Item	1	2	3	4	5	6	7	8	9	10	11	12	13	14	15	16	17	18	19	20	21	22	23	24	25	26
Factor 1							●		●	●			●	●		●		●		●		●				
Factor 2						●																	●	●	●	●
Factor 3												●		●	●	●				●	●					
Factor 4	●	●	●																							
Factor 5					●		●				●	●														

The lack of resolution in the other 4 factors in the Home Help service is even more emphatic in the Food Safety service results where no apparent grouping exists around the *a priori* SERVQUAL dimensions (Table 3). The ability of the SERVQUAL dimensions to adequately measure service quality in the Food Safety service, as represented by the data collected, is therefore very poor.

The defining features of the above services are that they range from those with close commercial sector analogues (libraries) through highly regulated and limited private provision (home helps) to statutory services which have no commercial sector comparators (food safety regulatory services).

Table 3 Factor Analysis results for the Food Safety service case study

	Food Safety Services: *a priori* SERVQUAL Dimensions				
	Tangibles	Reliability	Responsiveness	Assurance	Empathy
Item	1 2 3 4	5 6 7 8 9 10	11 12 13 14	15 16 17 18	19 20 21 22 23
Factor 1		● ● ●	● ●	●	● ● ●
Factor 2	● ●	● ●	● ●	●	
Factor 3	● ●	● ●	●	●	
Factor 4	●			●	● ●
Factor 5			● ●	●	●

3   CONCLUSIONS

The urgent need for valid means of measuring local government service performance extends to service quality across <u>all</u> of the services delivered by, or on behalf of, local authorities. If the SERVQUAL approach is to have credibility then it must have adequate realism and precision in capturing distinct customer groups' views of service quality. The tentative conclusion reached here is that, based on the studies made so far, a suitably customised Gap 5 SERVQUAL instrument seems adequate when the service under study has close commercial sector analogues and where there is a high degree of direct receipt of, and payment for, the service. The validity of the SERVQUAL dimensions appears to deteriorate as we move away from these service conditions. Applying SERVQUAL in these less applicable situations without replicating the primary research into the service quality dimensions will justifiably attract similar levels of professional criticism as the inadequacy of the government inspired, and defined, performance indicators used to assess other aspects of service performance. The results of the limited studies reported above indicate a need for caution when using even moderately customised versions of the SERVQUAL instrument to measure service quality in this arena. At its best, the inclusion of an appropriate group of well-focussed SERVQUAL instruments would be a valuable addition to the arsenal of local government service effectiveness measures.

4   REFERENCES

Babakus, E., and Mangold, W.G. (1992) Adapting the SERVQUAL Scale to hospital services: an empirical investigation. *Health Services Research,* **26(6)**, 767-786

Campbell, S.J., Donnelly, M., and Wisniewski, M. (1995) A Measurement of service. *Scottish Libraries* **50**, 10-11

Dalrymple,J.F.,Donnelly,M.,Wisniewski,M. and Curry,A.C.(1995) Measuring service quality in local government. *Total Quality Management: Proceedings of the first world congress*, 263-266

Donnelly, M.,Dalrymple, J.F.,Wisniewski, M. and Curry, A.C.(1995) The portability of the SERVQUAL scale to the public sector.*Total Quality Management: Proceedings of the first world congress*, 271-274

Parasuraman, A., Zeithaml, V.A., and Berry, L.L. (1985) A conceptual model of service quality and its implications for future research *Journal of Marketing*, **49**, 41-50

Parasuraman, A., Zeithaml, V.A., and Berry, L.L. (1988) SERVQUAL: a multiple-item scale measuring customer perceptions of service quality *Journal of Retailing*, **64**, 12-40

Soliman, A.A., (1992) Assessing the quality of health care: a consumerist approach *Health Marketing Quarterly*, **10(1/2)**, 121-141

Zeithaml, V.A., Parasuraman, A., and Berry, L.L., (1990), *Delivering Quality Service*, The Free Press, Maxwell Macmillan

41

Improving the dissemination of SERVQUAL by using magnitude scaling

M.C.Hart
Department of Public Policy and Managerial Studies
De Montfort University
Leicester
LE7 9SU

Tel: *+44 (0)116 257 7780*
Fax: *+44 (0)116 257 7795*
email: *mchart@dmu.ac.uk*

INTRODUCTION

The **SERVQUAL** survey instrument is one of the most widely utilised techniques for deriving a measure of the quality of service industries (Parasuraman, Zeithaml and Berry, 1985,1988; Zeithaml, Parasuraman and Berry, 1990). It has been extensively used, principally in the USA, for obtaining quantitative measures of consumer satisfaction. The instrument invites consumers to indicate the extent to which they agree with a series of statements which are designed to measure those elements of a service which consumers would expect as ideal (the Expectations score) and then those elements of a service that they have recently experienced (the Perceptions score) Satisfaction is then measured as the simple arithmetic 'gap' between Perceptions and Expectations (**S=P-E**). The scale is a composite of five dimensions (Tangibles, Reliability, Responsiveness, Assurance and Empathy). These dimensions will differ in salience as between different industries. In addition, consumers may place a higher value on some of these dimensions rather than others - for example, empathy might be more important in a hospital clinic but reliability in a bank. Respondents are also asked to indicate the importance of the relative weighting of the dimensions by allocating them a series of points which total to 100. In this way, it is possible for individual respondents to give much more weight to certain facets of the services under consideration than to others. A **SERVQUAL** score for each dimension can then be computed for each respondent by averaging the 'gap' scores for the questions relating to that dimension. It is then possible to produce a total weighted score for each customer by applying the weights that the customer attaches to each dimension. Finally, scores are averaged over the numbers of people sampled in any particular investigation. Typical results will tend to show a negative score as expectations of an ideal service tend to run ahead of evaluations of a service as actually experienced.

THE NATURE OF THE SCALE DEPLOYED IN **SERVQUAL**

As previously mentioned, respondents are asked to measure their levels of agreement or disagreement by circling a number in the range 1-7 where 1 represents complete disagreement with the statement in question whilst a 7 represents complete agreement. Although the authors of **SERVQUAL** do not explicitly discuss the point, it is evident that a scale deployed is essentially a Likert-type scale, which is ordinal in nature. However, conventional statistical orthodoxy would hold that arithmetic operations such as addition or subtraction are not legitimate (Siegel and Castellan, 1988). In the context of the **SERVQUAL** scale, a relevant question would be to ask whether the 'gap' between, for example, point 6 and point 7 on the scale is to be regarded in the same light as the difference between, say, point 1 and point 2 of the scale. If the **SERVQUAL** scale is regarded as an interval or ratio scale rather than an ordinal scale, then the 'gap' between the points in both of the instances mentioned above would be the same i.e. 1. However, it is not self-evident when respondents fill in rating scales that they deploy in their minds an essentially linear ratio scale. The authors of **SERVQUAL** have made the assumption that it not illegitimate to derive gap scores by a process of subtraction. Indeed, such a practice is common and one commentator has observed that many researchers have treated rating scales as interval data and failed to observe the minimal requirements for interval level measurement (Foddy,1993, pp.169-170). It is possible, therefore, that a scale such as **SERVQUAL** needs further refinement by exploring the meanings that respondents attach to indicating a point on a scale.

THE CONCEPT OF MAGNITUDE SCALING

Magnitude scaling is a term popularised principally by Lodge (1981) to indicate the process by which different points on a scale can be said to represent non-uniform weights or quantities. The process derives from the principles of psychophysics in which respondents are asked to assign magnitudes to such physical sensations as the intensity of sound, brightness of light, the heaviness of objects and so on (Goldstein, 1989). Drawing upon the principles of classical psychophysics, Lodge and his collaborators would take samples of respondents and instruct them in simple psychophysical tasks such as estimating the length of various lines, given the value associated with a given baseline (typically given a value of 50). If respondents can reliably estimate that a line of twice the length of the given baseline should have a value of 100, whilst one half the length should be given a value of 25, then the investigators could 'train' their subjects to think psychometrically by offering a series of lines of different lengths and asking respondents to estimate their lengths as fractions, or multiples, of the given baseline. The geometric mean of the responses, when plotted against actual line lengths, typically showed straight-line associations when displayed on a log-log graph.

Once it could be demonstrated that respondents have a reasonable competence in numeric line estimation, Lodge argue that through a process of 'cross-modality' it is possible to assign similar magnitudes to points on an adjectival scale. Thus respondents when faced with a list of words such as 'So-So' (representing neutrality) could assign magnitudes to such concepts such as 'Good', 'Very Good' and 'Excellent' (multiples of the baseline) or to 'Bad','Very Bad' and 'Atrocious' (fractions of the baseline). Lodge presents results (from a small sample of 48 respondents) indicating the following magnitudes associated with a commonly used 'adjectives' on a scale:

Table 1 Magnitude Weightings assigned to common adjectives - Lodge,1981   *(n=48)*

	Atrocious	Very Bad	Bad	So-So	Good	Very Good	Excellent
	4	12	15	(50)	107	141	233
Multiple/ fraction	0.1	0.2	0.3	0	2.1	2.8	4.7

The final row of this table (added by the present author) indicates the extent to which each column is a multiple, or a fraction, of the given reference figure for neutrality or 'So-So' of 50. This data confirms the suspicion previously expressed that respondents do not use a linear interval scale when making judgements concerning the magnitudes to be assigned to adjectival descriptors of the various points of a rating scale.

The instructions that Lodge gave to his subjects allowed them to think of any multiple (or of any fraction) that they wished when assigning numerical weightings to adjectives. It is evident that the geometric mean of 233 indicates that most respondents felt that 'Excellent' represented 4-5 times as much weight as the reference point of 50. However, given that the any numbers on the right-hand scale could be in excess of 50 whereas any number less than 50 was automatically confined to the range 1-50, an argument could be made that the absence of a constraint on the one hand but the presence of it on the other altered the behaviour of the respondents when assigning weighting numbers.

In order to replicate the Lodge results and also to overcome the potential problem identified above, the exercise was repeated with a larger sample but with one or two crucial differences. The reference figure was given as 100 (rather than 50) and respondents were asked to supply figures *greater than* 100 to represent the weightings that they would attach to adjectives with a similar exemplar (reactions to a TV programme). The following results were obtained:

Table 2   Replication and refinement of Lodge Magnitude Weightings *(n=85)*

	Atrocious	Very Bad	Bad	So-So	Good	Very Good	Excellent
	267	201	143	(100)	187	269	362
Multiple/ fraction	2.6	2.0	1.4	0	1.9	2.7	3.6

It can be seen immediately that there is a fair measure of agreement in the magnitudes to be assigned to the adjectives 'Good' and 'Very Good' (approx. 2.0 and 2.8 respectively) whilst the magnitude associated with the word 'Excellent' shows more divergence (4.7 compared with 3.6). However, when it comes to the weightings assigned to the left hand side of the scale, the discrepancies become more severe. At first glance, the Lodge data appears to show that respondents only assign 1/12 of the intensity of support to an adjective such as 'Atrocious' (4/50) whereas 'Excellent' represents 4-5 times as much support. Suspecting a scale effect, the data displayed in Table 2 probably represents a more accurate magnitude scaling of these common adjectives. It is very interesting in this case to observe that respondents are more inclined to be generous in expressing 'positive' support, whilst they are evidently less so when assigning magnitudes on the left hand side of the scale.

REFINEMENT OF **SERVQUAL** RATING SCALE

Table 3   Application of Magnitude Weightings to a **SERVQUAL** scale

	Strongly Disagree						Strongly Agree
Point on scale	1	2	3	4	5	6	7
Score of each point	-2.6	-2.0	-1.4	0	1.9	2.7	3.6

The **SERVQUAL** scale, as originally formulated in Zeithaml. et. al. (1990) only has the adjectival descriptors of 'Strongly Disagree' and 'Strongly Agree'. The data on magnitude scaling shown in Tables 1 and 2 above both suggest that rating scales cannot be regarded as interval scales and the subtraction of any two points on the scale would not give the results suggested by the framers of **SERVQUAL**. For example a movement from point 6 to 7 is 'worth' (3.6-2.7=0.9) whilst a corresponding movement from point 2 to point 1 is 'worth' (2.6-2.0=0.6) only two thirds of this. For this reason, it is suggested that when **SERVQUAL** type scales are administered, then the concepts of magnitude scaling be deployed in order to arrive at a series of putative magnitudes that can be assigned to different points on the scale, thus legitimating the original conception that satisfaction be conceptualised as the 'gap' between Perceptions of the service as delivered and Expectations of an ideal service.

REFERENCES

Foddy,W. (1993) *Constructing Questions for Interviews and Questionnaires*, Cambridge University Press,Cambridge.

Goldstein,B. (1989) *Sensation and Perception.* Wadsworth, Belmont,Ca.

Lodge,M. (1981) *Magnitude Scaling.* Sage University Paper series on Quantitative Applications in the Social Sciences, 07-025, Sage Publications, Beverly Hills and London

Parasuraman,A., Zeithaml,V. and Berry.L. (1985) A Conceptual Model of Service Quality and its implications for future Research, *Journal of Marketing.* **49** (Fall):41-50.

Parasuraman,A,. Zeithaml,V. and Berry,L. (1988) **SERVQUAL**: A Multiple-Item Scale for Measuring Perceptions of Service Quality, Journal of Retailing, 64: 12-40.

Siegel,S. and Castellan,N. (1988) Nonparametric Statistics for the Behavioural Sciences McGraw-Hill, New York

Zeithaml,V.,Parasuraman,A. and Berry,L. (1990) *Delivering Service Quality*, Free Press, New York

42

Business improvement programmes: measuring process in the Times top 500

J. M. Banks and C. L. Stone
The Total Quality & Innovation Management Centre,
Anglia Polytechnic University, Danbury, Essex, CM3 4AT, UK.
Telephone: 01245 225511; Fax: 01245 222143.
e-mail: mabanks@ford.anglia.ac.uk; cstone@ford.anglia.ac.uk

Abstract

Inadequacies in traditional measurement systems have led to a performance measurement 'revolution' (Eccles, 1991) which urges managers to encompass 'soft' measures, such as customer and employee satisfaction, in monitoring their business strategy. The paper exposes a significant gap between customer and employee based strategies and the use of corresponding measures of performance amongst the Times Top 500 companies. It concludes that there is still some way to go before management theory and management practice are reconciled.

Keywords

Quality, business performance measurement, customer satisfaction, employee satisfaction

1   INTRODUCTION

As a result of changes in the quality arena encompassing '... real customer focus ... and the unlocking of people potential ...' (Binney, 1992), conventional performance measures have become incapable of presenting a 'true' picture of corporate performance (Brown and Laverick, 1994). The search for a 'New Agenda' (Geanuracos *et al*, 1993) is therefore underway, encouraging managers to take account of the 'softer' nonfinancial issues in developing their performance measurement systems (Kaplan and Norton, 1996).

These 'revolutionary' changes led to the design of a survey entitled 'Improving Business Performance Through Customers and Employees' which set out to determine the level of progress made in the use of quality, customer, and employee related measures. The results were derived from respondents holding strategic positions in 45 companies, which were representative of industry type and size, and positioned throughout the whole Top 500.

2   STRATEGY FOR THE 1990s

Recent research (Redman *et al*, 1995) suggests that 'quality' is now an integral part of business. Responses from the Times Top 500 reflected this: 93% had involvement in at least one quality initiative, such as Total Quality, Business Process Re-engineering, or ISO 9000. In order to set these initiatives in context, strategic emphasis was weighted by respondents in percentage terms, revealing a bias towards profitability, followed at some distance by customers and employees (Figure 1). This highlights that whilst customers and employees have a place on the strategic agenda, the 'bottom-line' is still the main driver at this level. This bias was also found to be inherent in the basis of pay and reward schemes.

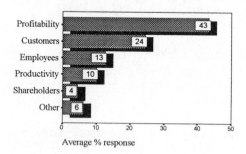 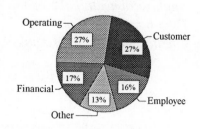

Figure 1 Board room strategic emphasis.   **Figure 2** The basis of quality measures.

2.1   Quality measures

However, quality measures were not reported to be as financially biased: of the 76% who have measures in place, the most popular usage is balanced between operational measures (such as cycle time reductions, reject/defect rates) and customer measures (such as complaints, delivery and customer satisfaction) with 27% of respondents claiming to use each. Figure 2 also reveals evidence that employee related measures, including employee surveys, labour turnover, and absenteeism, are filtering through for quality measurement purposes. On further analysis of the practical use of both customer and employee related measures, gaps can be identified.

2.2   Customer related measures

It was no surprise to find customer related measures ranking highly amongst quality measures used, since the literature is abundant with tales of how customer focused strategies can have a positive impact on bottom line results (Rust and Zahorik, 1992; Fornell, 1992; Heskett *et al* 1994). However, Heskett *et al* (1994) found that some of the weakest measures used concerned customer satisfaction. This was certainly found to be true in the Times Top 500.

A significant gap was exposed between the reported level of dependence for business on three of the 'common' theoretical customer based measures (retention repeat business and referrals), and their use in tracking performance: 78% were either 'largely' or 'completely' dependant on retaining customers, 75% as dependant on repeat business, with just 4% claiming to be either 'largely' or 'completely' dependant on referrals. However, only 9% recognise retention, 4% recognise repeat business and no one reported the use of referrals as a customer based measure in use to track performance. In addition, the ease at which managers appeared able to communicate the level of achievement in these three areas, seemingly without evidence, demonstrates that there is a gap between what managers believe to be important for their business and what they measure.

In line with current literature, the enthusiasm that economic value has been added as a result of efforts to improve customer satisfaction is high: 60% are either 'completely' or 'largely' confident, with just 4% in doubt. However, only 57% claim to have evidence in support of their beliefs, suggesting that the perceived value of customer focused activity is still difficult for managers to quantify.

2.3   Employee related measures

Employee-related measures constituted the smallest group of quality measures used (at 16% of the total), despite calls from professional bodies such as the Institute of Personnel and Development (1994) for a renewed focus on 'soft' cultural issues, and the reported virtues of strategic planning tools such as the 'Balanced Scorecard' which incorporates these measures (Kaplan and Norton, 1996).

In practice, the responding Top 500 companies reported that employee related measures were not used as extensively as the literature leads us to believe: only 9% revealed that they are used in determining business strategy on an integrated basis, with a further 16% reporting *ad hoc* use in plans for Total Quality initiatives, training and development, and pay and reward.

Concerns are being aired as to whether information generated is being used to anywhere near its full capacity (Walters, 1994). In this survey, 82% of respondents reported that the information derived from the surveys is acted upon either 'completely' or 'largely', however there is little correlation between this result and the degree of 'maturity' of use, which perhaps indicates a lack of knowledge and understanding of their full potential.

This group may be the least popular of the quality measures, as a positive linkage to the bottom line is not irrefutable. 44% of respondents believed to be at least 'largely' convinced that some economic value had been derived as a result their endeavours, however when asked if they had evidence to support their claims, only 35% responded positively. As with customer related measures, it still seems that managers are working on intuition and 'gut feeling' about the progress which consideration of 'soft' issues could help them make.

3   CONCLUSION

Despite the perceived benefits of using 'soft' measures, and the fact that '... quality measures are regarded as a fundamental element of quality management ...' (Preece and Wood, 1995), the degree of reported use was disappointing. However it does seem that frameworks such as the European Foundation for Quality Management and Baldrige Award (used by 43% of those who had a quality initiative in the Times Top 500) have a significant impact upon the measurement and use of 'soft' issues (Banks and Stone, 1996). The frameworks encourage the use of both customer and employee related measures, and it seems that they are being used to an increasing degree, at the expense of the use of the pure philosophies of the quality 'gurus'. It is reasonable to expect that improvements in the use of 'soft' measures will evolve, as the shift towards the use of these frameworks gathers momentum.

4   REFERENCES

Banks, J.M. and Stone, C.L. (1996) Improving business performance through customers and employees: the EFQM Model as a driver of new measurement practice. *EFQM Leading Edge Conference*, Paris, April.

Brown, D.M. and Laverick, S. (1994) Measuring corporate performance. *Long Range Planning*, Vol. 27, No. 4, pp. 89-98.

Binney, G. (1992) *Making quality work: lessons from Europe's leading companies*. The Economist Intelligence Unit, London 1992.

Eccles, R.G. (1991) The performance measurement manifesto. *Harvard Business Review*, January-February, pp. 131-137.

Fornell, C. (1992) A national customer satisfaction barometer: the Swedish experience. *Journal of Marketing*, Vol. 56, January, pp. 6-21.

Geanuracos, J. and Meiklejohn, I. (1993) *Performance measurement: the new agenda*. London: Business Intelligence.

Heskett, J.L., Jones, T.O., Loveman, G.W., Sasser, W.E., Schlesinger, L.A. (1994) Putting the Service-Profit chain to work. *Harvard Business Review*, March-April, pp.164-174.

Institute of Personnel and Development (1994) *People make the difference*. London: IPD.

Kaplan, R.S. and Norton, D.P. (1996) Using the Balanced Scorecard as a strategic management system. *Harvard Business Review*, January-February, pp. 75-85.

Preece, D. and Wood, M. (1995) Quality measurements: who is using the sums and for what purpose? *Human Resource Management Journal*, Vol. 5, No. 3, Spring, pp. 41-55.

Redman, T., Snape, E. and Wilkinson, A. (1995) Is quality management working in the UK? *Journal of General Management*, Vol. 20, No. 3, Spring, pp. 44-59.

Rust, R.T. and Zahorik, A.J. (1992) Modelling the impact of service quality on profitability: a review. *Advances in Service Marketing and Management*, Vol. 1, pp. 247-276.

Walters, M. (1994) *Building the responsive organisation: using employee surveys to manage change*. London: McGraw-Hill International (UK) Limited Book Company.

5   BIOGRAPHY

J. M. Banks BA (Hons) DipM is a graduate in Business Studies and Marketing. Having spent a number of years in the computing industry, she is now a PhD student, investigating the relevance of customer based measures of performance to strategy in service organisations. C. L. Stone BSc (Hons) is a graduate in Management and Systems. As a research assistant, she has been involved in industrial collaboration in the design and use of employee surveys, and her PhD investigates the extended use of employee related measures. Both have been involved in industrially led projects, in-depth case studies, and have had three papers published to date.

43
Cultural changes in functional deportment

K. A. Eaton

Finance Manager, Commercial - British Steel, Sections, Plates and

Commercial Steels, Redcar, Cleveland, TS10 5QW

1 BACKGROUND

Achieving 40% export sales has been vital to British Steel's well published turnaround. Export success demands success in securing payments for goods sold. For many markets, tradition, customer preference and/or insurance conditions dictate 'letter of credit' payment terms. A letter of credit is a written undertaking issued by a bank on behalf of the buyer to honour payment subject to the presentation of a set of documents which are exactly in compliance with stipulated requirements. This demands detailed supplier compliance to ensure prompt payment and to secure payment itself by protecting the credit insurance cover, as well as to minimise bank charges and to maintain customer satisfaction.

The unique nature of steel products, the specific handling and shipping, and the many variables associated with their manufacture, product description and selling had historically combined to produce an estimated 60% failure rate on presentations against letters of credit to UK and overseas customer banks. This high level of failure, associated with what is a complex product, needs to be considered in the context of a similar failure rate as the average UK performance on letter of credit presentations from all industry/commercial sectors.

The high level of failure was well known within the organisation but had not improved despite various previous attempts to solve 'the problem'. This problem was considered to be one of delayed payment caused by inaccuracies by staff within the sales invoicing/export documentation department; a function at the end of the process chain. This same department was under extreme pressure through the combination of British Steel's drive into exports and its parallel drive to reduce costs and manpower numbers; and the blame being attributed was, not surprisingly, negative to morale.

A senior manager was seconded to 'solve the problem', and his first task was to analyse historical failures. These confirmed for the period selected a failure rate of 61%, close to the national norm. On detailed analysis the major reasons for failure were found not to be documentation; but apparent lack of control over scheduling of orders to meet the tight disciplines laid down in the letters of credit, and late presentation of documentary packages as a result of late receipt of and/or inaccuracies in documents generated by other functions and only collated by the invoicing/documentation department. This is not to say there were no errors in the latter department. There were and they were quantified and analysed by detailed cause. These again included inaccuracies in documentation from upstream departments. Examples were found of similar mistakes being repeated on follow up shipments to the same customers and markets.

Whilst initially driven by a desire to improve payment performance and the associated concentration on 'cash as king' following privatisation, this initial exercise highlighted the fact that any discrepant presentation, no matter how minor the discrepancy, breached the credit insurance cover if the latter was subject to letter of credit terms. Indeed this fact replaced payment performance as the main driver behind subsequent action.

The exercise revealed also the historical difficulty of this department at the end of the chain to achieve necessary changes in upstream departments belonging to other functions over which it had no control. This was clear also in other areas of the department's working and many examples were found of skilled individuals having developed ways of managing round problems.

2 APPROACH

With the initial fact finding complete and the report issued there was pressure from senior management to establish a working party to address the issues raised, i.e. to follow the traditional approach. It was clear, however, that whilst there were some systems weaknesses for which there were quick fix permanent solutions, 'the problem' was not comprised of a small number of sub problems each of which had an easy solution. The range of contributing factors was significant and such that they would continue to arise and change as new customers, new markets and new banks all introduced their own peculiar letter of credit requirements in turn putting new pressures on and showing new deficiencies in the internal systems designed to address them..

Total Quality Management had been introduced into the Business some five years previously and indeed the Business has been widely regarded as a great success story of TQM implementation. Whilst this opinion was well founded, this reputation was built on progress achieved in manufacturing and engineering activities; and functional departments, although originally trained alongside manufacturing colleagues, had made little progress in adopting the TQM culture, lacking the high financial return drivers of the manufacturing projects. The decision to establish a TQM Group was therefore greeted with some scepticism, not least amongst those member of functional staff who had seen their expectations raised and dashed following TQM training some five years prior.

Nevertheless the problem issues seemed appropriate for a Total Quality approach and accordingly a team was established under the chairmanship of the Finance Manager, Commercial, and comprising representatives of the finance, commercial, shipping and technical functions. This representation crossed all status levels from junior clerical, through middle and departmental management to senior management. Those not represented directly through geographical impracticalities had nominee representation and feedback.

3 TQM METHODOLOGY

The letter of credit project provided the foundation for introducing routine performance measurement into the documentation process. Data began to be collected on a live basis by departmental staff, analysing failures both quantitatively and by reason for failure. Graphical interpretation of this data was provided by management, but the enthusiasm of two junior members of staff for home computing provided an opening to transfer the PC graphics skills directly to the staff at the earliest opportunity. The follow up provision to these staff of a dedicated PC enhanced the feeling of ownership of the data and of the seriousness with which management regarded maintenance of any improvements achieved. Overcoming the initial resistance to performance measurement has been critical to the success of this project, given that monitoring lies with the department historically blamed for the failure. After early success in reducing failures in external presentation to customer banks, there remained errors in internally generated documents. Although identified and corrected by internal checks ahead of external despatch, these were counterproductive to solving other issues. Monitoring was seen as looking for individuals to blame until responsibility for self monitoring was introduced with no requirement to forward individual results to management.

The TQM Group functioned by applying pareto analysis of the results of monitoring and applying brainstorming to uncover the underlying reasons. Where solutions could not be identified, then an owner closest to the problem was appointed to come up with a solution using other members of the group or additional staff as appropriate. Any problems that could not be solved were carried forward until a remedy could be found. When considered necessary, other personnel were drafted in and advice sought from 'experts', both internal and external. Feedback was promoted to geographically remote functional staff to include their ideas and include them in reporting of successes. Solutions required actions and commitment well beyond the immediate team and it was important to maintain a high profile for the project and for the successes achieved. Graphs of progress made have been displayed in 'process' departments and opportunities maximised for publicity in Company newsletters, etc.

4 IMPROVEMENTS SECURED

Amongst the many specific improvements made, the following may be of interest to the reader :

4.1 The introduction of a multifunctional team which meets for a few minutes each day to vet incoming letters of credit and agree actions, replacing the previous practice of some recipients only seeing the LC well through the process.

4.2 The staggering of export vessels to spread the load on document generation and presentation.

4.3 The prioritisation of tallying of vessels and document preparation for LC orders.

4.4 The modification of document format and computer systems to include some 'special' requirements within the 'standard'.

4.5 The achievement of high priority status for a major systems enhancement.

4.6 The use of new documentation to convey special requirements to external agencies.

4.7 The introduction of a two stage approval procedure with the external insurers for customer cover. Previously the delay in obtaining cover had caused the Commercial function to volunteer LC terms to secure an earlier decision and earlier acknowledgement of order. Finance were unaware of this until a TQM group discussion aimed at reducing the number of LC orders. This revelation generated a review of all the current insurance decisions, leading to a 90% reduction in previous LC conditional decisions, an ongoing reduction in the proportion of export sales for which insurance cover was dependent on successful LC presentation, and a major reduction in the risk to the Business of non payment from breaches of insurance cover.

4.8 The introduction of a formal system of risk management to strengthen control over release of order shipments in situations of known and unavoidable breaches of the terms of insurance cover.

5 PROJECT RESULTS

Against any traditional criteria the project can only be regarded as a major success with the previously regarded 60% failure turned into a much differently regarded 90% success.

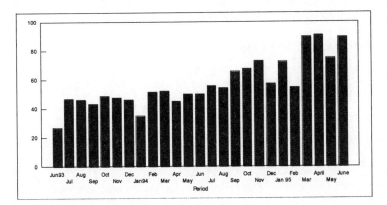

Figure 1. Overall success rate on letters of credit presentation before and after the adoption of TQM in April 1994.

The associated further restoration of control over financial risk is illustrated in Figure 2. showing
how non controlled failures are being squeezed out between the improvements in successful
presentation and 'risk managed' failures.

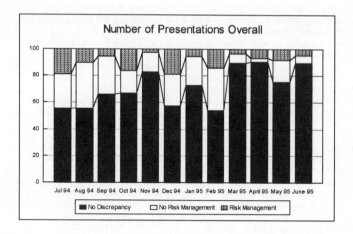

Figure 2. Analysis of letter of credit presentations showing the reduction in uncontrolled   failures.

The reduction in risk on letter of credit presentations is significant with the value of business
subject to these terms in 1994/95, already reduced by the actions detailed above, still a high £53
million.

Although driven in recent times by the need to reduce risk, progress on the 'original problem' of
delayed payments has also yielded an average 3 days earlier performance with an associated
working capital benefit in excess of £1/4 million.

6   CULTURAL ACHIEVEMENT

Whilst never initiated to drive cultural change, the successful Letter of Credit Project has proved a
milestone in the evolution of the Invoicing and Export Documentation departments. With wide
departmental involvement, all members of the team point to a 'feeling of pride cascading through
all functions involved'. The project turned what was very much a 'blame' attitude to the staff
concerned to a highly regarded 'success story' and there is a much wider and higher level
understanding of the issues involved.

Measurement and monitoring are now being introduced into other activities such as payment
performance and issue of credit notes in a drive towards 'best in class' standards. It would be wrong
to claim that the cultural change is complete, indeed much remains to be achieved. Further
manpower reductions have been announced in the invoicing and documentation area and it is not
surprising that the introduction of further measurement is still viewed with suspicion. The letter of
credit exercise did, however, involve a partnership of working between management and staff
which helped to break down barriers, which caused other concerns to be brought to the surface,
and which generally contributed to a new environment of openness in which issues such as the
manpower reduction are now discussed.

44

Customised interviewing: a research revolution

J.Kiernan
BT Customer Quality Centre
PP: 500A, 1 Portland Street, Manchester, M60 1HR UK
Tel: 0161 228 7746   Fax: 0161 228 7705

INTRODUCTION

This paper describes how BT has worked with FDS Research Group to develop a customer-driven satisfaction monitor. Each interview is unique, but the outputs provide quantifiable performance measures which drive staff rewards. Special software applications have been developed for reporting to senior client management and to create a multi-purpose survey management application.

1   BACKGROUND - THE CLIENT PERSPECTIVE

BT has been measuring customer satisfaction for some time, and is a leading player in the area of truly capturing customer perceptions and requirements through a number of comprehensive generic studies. This means traditional surveys where, essentially, all respondents answer the same questionnaire. Some people might be aware of previously reported surveys such as:

- Telcare;
- Event Driven Customer Satisfaction Measurement;
- The Major Customer Survey.

These studies have helped develop excellent processes for customer needs' identification and for the analysis within it of the key elements of satisfaction or dissatisfaction. More importantly each has provided a robust mechanism for BT actions to alleviate customers dissatisfaction and to improve the customers perception in time for the next interview. However, within the last 18 months, in the BT division dealing with its largest business customers, a radical new approach has been developed around the need to more accurately reflect the specific areas that each customer finds uniquely important. Also, the intention is to cover both what may be deemed as operational performance measures (such as the incidence of circuit faults) and those which can be used in survey perception measures.
The thinking behind this approach has a number of sources:

- An international business re-engineering project focused upon the need for a more "customer driven" approach;
- Benchmarking studies in the areas of customer service which showed that the best companies are always creative and radical in their approach to customer service, good examples include Virgin Atlantic and Walt Disney;

- An internal meeting between a customer and their BT service representative developing a far more customised approach; basically they both agreed to identify and regularly present performance measures the customer actually wanted.

What has developed, therefore, is more than just a survey with BT's Global Customers; it is a *Customer Satisfaction Programme*. The programme is based upon each BT service representative agreeing a list of measures of performance with their customer:

- Hard measures (operational statistics usually drawn from BT databases on the supply of services, fault repairs, billing times etc.);
- Soft measures (perceptual measures which could be developed in a set of questions through which the customers can rate BT on a regular basis).

This programme has been backed up by a number of crucial drivers:

- *Senior management sponsorship*;

One of BT's Directors' within the Global Communications Division has been personally involved and regularly updated as the project continued;

- *Target setting*;

All attributes of satisfaction recorded at the individual level are grouped into 5 broader dimensions of satisfaction which have stretching target in terms of the number of people who are very satisfied, and not just satisfied. In doing so, BT has tried to encourage, but have not insisted, that a semantic satisfaction scale is used by customers (very satisfied, satisfied, neutral, dissatisfied and very dissatisfied) rather than the more usual method of high/low numerical ratings out of 10. The use of more "concrete" expressions allows BT to understand more clearly what customers actually think than the rather more abstract interpretations that can be achieved from numeric scales.

- *The linking of employees rewards to levels of customer satisfaction.*

The reason BT started such a "customised" research programme was due to Service being increasingly perceived as a differentiation in these days of broadly similar product and service offerings. Research has repeatedly shown us that the people at the front end can make the difference. BT is investing in Service through dedicated people and service centres, and wants to develop better and closer relationships with its customers by truly understanding their businesses. If BT is to be successful at this, progress needs to be measured.

2   BACKGROUND - THE AGENCY PERSPECTIVE

FDS has had a long association with BT in the customer satisfaction research field. The company was awarded its first such contract in 1982 and during 1995 worked on continuous tracking studies with BT customers of all types, including:

- residential;
- small businesses without formal BT account managers;
- small to medium businesses with BT account managers;
- major national accounts; BT Global customers (BT's largest business customers both within the UK and outside).

Individual projects have varied in scale from over 100 000 interviews per year to less than 500. The focus of the interviewing also differs considerably. At the high volume end, in sample size terms, the research is usually concerned with tracking BT performance of handling specific individual "events" such as the installation of a product of the restoration of a faulty service. At the other extreme, surveys can be concerned with the monitoring of BT operations over a period of time, say three or six months, which for each respondent could involve numerous 'events' and repeated contact with BT.

Until the introduction of the BT Global Customers Satisfaction Survey, this work had at least one feature in common with the vast majority of all attitude measurement surveys. This is the use of a single questionnaire, administered to any given target audience, albeit incorporating filters and special modules to cater for the interests and behaviour of sub-groups. In February 1995, however, BT asked FDS for something radically different from the usual approach - the agency had already been operating in a more conventional mode for a year with BT's Global customers in Europe and Asia Pacific. This was to give each customer the opportunity to measure whatever attributes of BT performance were important to them, as they define it by most appropriate scoring methods. The objective was for around 2 000 interviews a year on this basis, with each one is likely to involve a unique questionnaire, agreed between BT and the customer. Each respondent was to be interviewed four times a year and BT wanted monthly, consolidated reporting in a consistent fashion in order to track performance, and also to use the results as a basis for calculating our staff bonuses. BT wanted to start a month following the request being made.

FDS knew that from a starting list of about 50 meetings between BT Global Customers and their Service Managers that they had to design 50 questionnaires as a pilot, carry out the interviews and analyse the results. FDS dismissed any attempt to use their Computer Assisted Telephone Interviewing (CATI) system because they could not guarantee that there would even be a common core set of questions. Each interview would require at least the generation of some questions peculiar to the individual respondent and even if there were a common core, the individual's routing through that question set would need to vary from interview, without any generic logical rules.

3   CLIENT PREPARATION FOR THE PROJECT

It would be fair to say that BT had a theory but needed to work on the practicality of starting the research programme very quickly.   The first step was to create a process and documentation for our internal "agents of delivery" - BT's Service Managers. The efforts of these managers were crucial in the survey process as BT wanted actionable research

Once performance measures had been agreed by the Service Manager and the representative of the customer, a basic set of questions could be created. The benefits to the customer were shown as producing measures of BT performance which are strictly relevant to their own criteria. Sometimes these criteria may already have been developed by the customer as a standard basis for assessing all of their suppliers. Conversely, it would also need the Service Managers to extract from the customer what is important as a set of measures.

In order to make this task manageable, a template or guide to typical service interface questions was created. Together with written process and flow-chart information, the template could be used to guide the customer and the Service Manager through the development of the question set. Key items include:

- reliability (ability to perform the promised service dependably and accurately);
- responsiveness (willingness to help customers and provide prompt service;
- tangibles (physical facilities, equipment, personnel, communications materials.

SERVQUAL has been constructed from empirical research which reduces almost 100 items affecting customer perceptions of service quality into the 5 critical dimensions described above. The creators of SERVQUAL argue that:

"The five SERVQUAL dimensions, by virtue of being derived from systematic analysis of customers' ratings from hundreds of interviews in several service sectors, are a concise representation of the core criteria that customers employ in evaluating service quality".[1]

Using this analysis BT can view itself against agreed critical service factors of any company. It did not lose sight of our more typical performance measures of Sales, Service, Value for Money and Billing but made sure we extended our narrow focus. In the survey each question that had been generated has been classified against one of the five SERVQUAL categories. The classification scheme also focuses people on checking whether there are areas where currently no questions or measures exist. It would be true to say that the question set for customers has evolved as time has progressed. Both the customers and the Service Manager review the questions for:

- specific focus;
- areas covered
- new products
- overall length
- actionability.

The final point was crucial to get all parties involved. Any measures agreed must be clear on the criteria for which any action can be seen as an improvement. In other words, what can BT in the person of the Service Manager agree to do that will show measurable improvements in the service provider. The customer's perception of change should be demonstrated in the review sessions by agreed factual measures. There were the "hard" measures of service which could provide the numerical benchmarks:

- availability;
- outages;
- agreed times of contract.

---

[1] Berry et al. Ibid

As a parallel development there was also a need to distribute and present research information more clearly to senior managers. Therefore an electronic data format was created as part of an Executive Information System for BT Service Managers. This was enabled by a user-friendly pictorial format with colours to show levels of satisfaction (e.g. red to denote extreme dissatisfaction and green to show where customers are delighted with BT).

4 PROJECT GOES LIVE - THE EARLY DAYS IN THE AGENCY

As the project moved from its pilot phase to roll-out, there were two key areas which needed to be addressed before BT could address the subject of data analysis - the development of appropriate data collection instruments and progress reporting tools.

4.1 Data Collection

Data collection instruments had to be refined in order to make the process of questionnaire design more efficient, more accurate and more consistent, in so far as it is possible to be consistent when the survey paradigm dictates that every respondent has the right to demand his or her own question set.

The first questionnaires were created, out of expediency, using a word processing package, but several drawbacks quickly became apparent and BT decided to re-create the questionnaire template in a spreadsheet package. This worked well for a short while but again limitations became visible, the most severe of these being the difficulty in maintaining the integrity and accuracy of the data set, requiring considerable effort which went beyond the resource allocations originally envisaged.

4.2 Progress Reporting

This became a major issue as the survey progressed. BT's Service Management organisation required an interviewing progress report published at the beginning of each week, reporting the interview outcomes from the previous week's work, divided into 8 business segments. These reports involved complex weekly distribution to 12 different addresses. In addition to the tracking of individual interview outcomes, it was important to BT to receive various statistical analyses of interviewing progress. There were also the added requirements for customised progress reports for certain BT departments.

As the second quarter approached it also become clear that BT Service Managers would expect to receive interview re-introduction schedule, so that each set of service attributes and contact details could be checked and revised with Customers, as appropriate. Creating such reports manually was another laborious and inefficient task and the need to automate the process became critical.

5   BEDDING DOWN THE PROCESS IN THE AGENCY

5.1 Making technology work for us

Before describing the next phase of development of the survey management process for this project, it is worthwhile reviewing the characteristics of this survey which distinguish it from more traditional ad hoc and continuous survey research.   Researchers are conventionally involved in projects which proceed as a series of discrete or batched tasks.   In an idealised world, each task is completed before the next begins.   The BT GCSS, however, involved FDS in a continuous design, production and reporting process.   They found themselves in a similar situation to manufacturers who have had to cope with the new techniques and working practices demanded by the movement towards Just In Time production.   To achieve this in the research context FDS needed to develop special production techniques and invest in new 'plant and machinery'.

FDS concluded, having taken a holistic view of the tasks we had undertaken and the information collected, distributed, analysed and reported, that the solution would lay in the development of a relational database project management application.   This system was designed to be implemented in several phases with each new module replacing part of the process and gradually building into a complete application which handles the various tasks.   It was necessary to proceed in an incremental fashion because the new tools had to be incorporated into a complex, live research project which it was not possible to stop in order to introduce and test a complete new system.   The phases of introduction were, in order:

- progress reporting module;
- questionnaire design and data entry module with individual record reports on papers
- electronic media
- results analysis and report module;
- results distribution module.

The system was developed and introduced over a 6 month period and was handling the complete survey management task by November 1995.   In the interim, of course, the project work had to continue and there were times when FDS had to work parts of the old and the new system in tandem.

The windows-based application has a very user friendly front end.   The questionnaire design module has brought enormous gains in efficiency and data entry is now far less error prone than before.   Now that the survey results are held on a single database rather than hundreds of individual Excel spreadsheets, BT is also much better able to manage the filing and retrieval of individual records.   Another benefit of the relational database approach is that BT is far better equipped to cope with requests to change or add analysis than before and without major re-engineering of the database design.   Several types of deliverable are now generated at the press of a button and can be supplied on demand or to a pre-arranged schedule.   These include interviewing progress reports, respondent re-introduction reports, individual interview summaries on paper or various electronic file formats and aggregated data tables.

Finally, the database contains all the information required to generate the daily distribution lists for each type of deliverable which, again, considerably simplifies what became a very labour intensive task. There are over 100 recipients of information from the survey and each deliverable has its own recipient list, delivery frequency, media specification (paper or electronic file) and transmission requirement (fax, mail, E-mail etc.).

5.2 Moving from 'abstract' performance targets to client-deliverable actions

BT has been determined to use the SERVQUAL paradigm to create internal performance targets for delivering quality service. All the agency's initial efforts were directed at delivering the mechanisms for capturing the information which would allow each customer to express their satisfaction with BT in each of the five key dimensions in terms which they, uniquely, recognised and in reporting to BT how it was performing at particular points in time and the direction of trends.

The next major challenge was to provide BT personnel who were being evaluated and targeted on this basis the means by which they could improve things. It is all very well telling someone that they need to show more customer empathy, for example, but they also need to understand how to do this and whether the actions that they should take as an individual are the same as for other colleagues in different functions or with different customers. Partly, BT was relying upon the operational performance targets agreed as part of each customer service plan.

However, the task of dealing with and changing customer perceptions required sensitive analysis and interpretation of the attitudes being expressed by the survey. This provided the agency with the opportunity to add value to the research. Each service attribute or question asked of the customer had been coded both for SERVQUAL and in terms of specific BT functions which its employees understood.

The system that we had set in place enabled the agency to measure, quantitatively, the functional implications of poor results in any of the SERVQUAL dimensions down to the levels of individual BT Global business segments.

By reporting these statistics and through careful analysis and reporting of the underpinning verbatim comments from customers, BT were able to provide customer facing personnel with the feedback that they needed from the survey in order to act in the most effective manner to enhance both individual and corporate performance.

Having got to grips with the unique logistical demands of the customised interview approach, FDS was able to use the traditional skills and expertise of the survey researcher, and the area in which they felt most comfortable, to provide the critical deliverable - the recommended actions needed to improve BT's situation.

6   THE BENEFITS

From BT's perspective, they are very much achieving the aims set at the outset. Many pitfalls and challenges were discovered but BT felt better for having progressed with the programme. It has attained a very distinct focus in the lives of many BT Service People in out Global Division.   The importance of an independent, regular source of customer-determined satisfaction data remains totally valid. BT has learned from its customers where the horror stories are and where BT also does things well.   BT has provided the basis for each of its Service Managers to work out exactly what they must do to drive their customers' satisfaction upwards in order to enhance their own rewards and status.

By the Graphical EIS system BT has also ensured that senior managers view market research data alongside financial performance and news.   Certainly this sight of the survey data and resultant actioning has helped to provide good sponsorship and credence for the project.   From the agency's standpoint, they take satisfaction from knowing that their client receives all the above benefits but also from the fact that their respondents, BT's customers, are witnessing how effective and beneficial research can be for them.   Indeed, both client and agency believe that the main winner in this process has been the customer.

The survey provides a vehicle for the customer to tell BT what drives their perceptions of quality performance from a major strategic supplier and business partner, in such a way that takes into account the unique requirements of their individual businesses.   The survey recognises the complete heterogeneity of service demands across large customer organisations who buy an extremely complex mix of products and services from BT.   Yet, the survey is able to categorise these demands into a set of homogeneous performance targets which motivate BT employees to strive continuously to increase customer satisfaction.   It also provides the details of specific operational actions needed for both individual customers and in terms of more general improvements in BT customer handling procedures.   The customers who have been exposed to this research programme feel that BT has achieved a far better understanding of the service levels they require and is better placed than ever before to deliver these demands.

The survey is also relatively painless for customers.   Interview content is seen to be relevant to all who take part, driven by what they deem to be uniquely important to the business objectives.   Also, interviews are typically short (less than 10 minutes each) and feedback from the research sponsor is both immediate and effective.   Response rates for the survey are high in consequence, with participation rates exceeding 90% of all effective contracts.

7   CONCLUSIONS

7.1 How much of a research revolution is customised interviewing?
From the agency's perspective, BT GSCC has required them to respond to the challenge of moving from batch production to a continuous cycle of design, data collection and reporting to a far more intense degree that other, so called 'continuous' research programmes with which they have been involved.   They have had to 'revolutionise' some of their working methods in order to do so.

The techniques described in this paper were also considered revolutionary within a client organisation which has made major investments in customer satisfaction research for many years. The programme unleashed a high level of debate and controversy among the various research buyers within the company, many of whom continue to find more traditional approaches to the measurement and tracking of customer satisfaction to be of value.

Arguments at the technical level concerned, for example, the pros and cons of using semantic differential ratings versus the numeric attitude scales which had become fairly entrenched in BT's customer satisfaction research. At the theoretical level, there were issues about the validity of SERVQUAL and how it can be most effectively operationalised.

As researchers, FDS might also have concerns about the single minded determination of BT to let each respondent set the agenda for the interview. If this rule were more widely applied, who knows where respondents might lead and how far that point will be from the objectives BT set itself for each project and are obliged to address in its reports? So, how far can this research revolution go? At this point, BT feels that customised, quantitative research (some might argue that qualitative research always operates, at least to a degree, in a manner driven by informants' attitudes and responses) has considerable potential in business to business research, particularly where the client-customer relationship is far more intense than that typically found in mass consumer or industrial markets. In such markets, each relationship often has a unique character which needs to be reflected in the tools which are used to measure the attitudes that determine its health. BT feels that the approach to customised interviewing described in this paper provides a genuinely innovative way of dealing with the complexities of conducting research under these conditions.

In total, therefore, BT GSCC believes that the methodological characteristics of this research project and the ways in which it has applied modern technology make it a worthy case study of presentation at the Sheffield Conference.

8 BIOGRAPHY

John Kiernan has been heavily involved in customer satisfaction management with BT for the past 6 years. He is presently the Project Manager of the Global Customer Satisfaction Survey within BT's Customer Quality Centre. As well as research projects he works as a consultant on Customer Service process projects. He is now involved in extending the research to customers based overseas.

INDEX OF CONTRIBUTORS